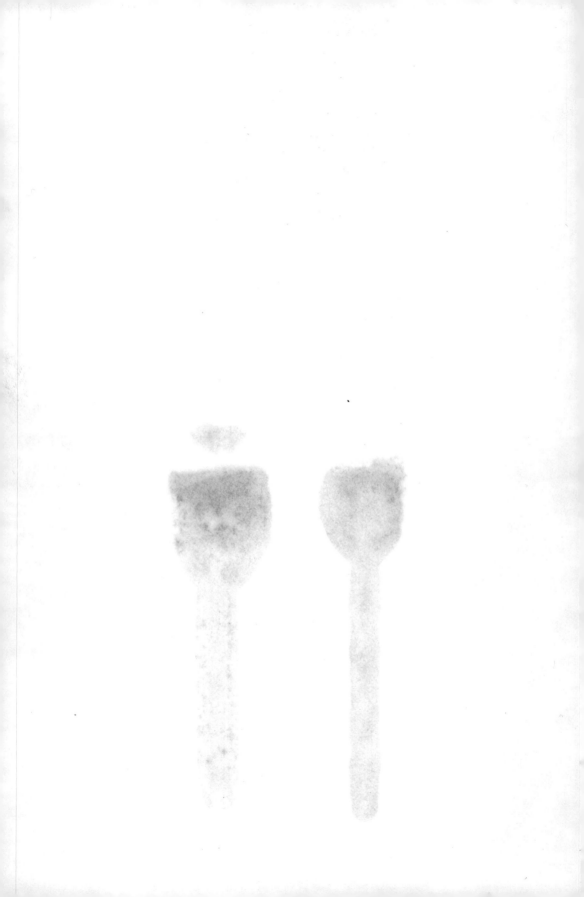

The
American
Opportunity

Also by Edwin Hartrich

THE FOURTH AND RICHEST REICH

THE AMERICAN OPPORTUNITY

Edwin Hartrich

3783

MACMILLAN PUBLISHING CO., INC.
NEW YORK

COLLIER MACMILLAN PUBLISHERS
LONDON

Macmillan Publishing Co., Inc.
866 Third Avenue, New York, N.Y. 10022
Collier Macmillan Canada, Inc.

Library of Congress Cataloging in Publication Data
Hartrich, Edwin.
The American opportunity.
Includes bibliographical references and index.
1. United States—Economic conditions—1945–
2. United States—Economic policy.
3. Economic history—1945–
I. Title.
HC106.8.H367   1983   330.973′0927   82-24880
ISBN 0-02-548510-5

10   9   8   7   6   5   4   3   2   1

Printed in the United States of America

This book is for Tim, Peter, Mike and Tony
and for that other woman in my life,
Maria Theresia.

Contents

———

Foreword

IN 1971 a seminar of internationally minded economists and sociologists was held in Budapest to survey the world scene and assess the probable future. Addressing this group, U.S. Senator Abraham Ribicoff offered a thought-provoking observation: "I am convinced that in the last quarter of this century, ecopolitics will replace geopolitics as the prime mover in the affairs of nations."

That concept has been imprinted on my consciousness ever since I first read it, and it ultimately led me to write this book, for what Senator Ribicoff predicted is slowly but inexorably coming to pass.

In the period immediately following the second world war, colonial empires collapsed and new states proliferated from their ruins. Each new nation became increasingly assertive and demanding as it progressed from infancy to puberty without quite reaching maturity. Geopolitics—increasing international power through the use or threat of military force—was in the ascendant as these nations were pulled into spheres of influence aligned either with Moscow or Washington, although many sought to remain unaligned. The "cold war" between the superpowers followed its spasmodic course, occasionally intensifying into shooting wars in Korea, Africa, the Middle East and Southeast Asia, and culminating in America's disastrous intervention and defeat in Vietnam.

Almost unnoticed in those early and chaotic decades, two separate but related developments were under way that were to herald the dawning era of ecopolitics. Postwar Japan and West Germany, two totally defeated and war-devastated ex-enemy nations, were swiftly and unexpectedly transforming themselves into modern industrial powerhouses. In a surprisingly short period of time they emerged from the wrack and ruin of World War II to rank third and fourth economically in the world, just behind the United States and the Soviet Union.

Before their defeat, Japan and Nazi Germany had been the prototypes of a geopolitical state. Their leaders were obsessed with the conviction that only through conquest of neighboring lands could their own national destinies be fulfilled; only with superior military force could they achieve their goals of unchallengeable political security and the prosperity of the robber baron. They followed the Clausewitzian *Diktat* that "war is the continuation of policy by other means."

Defeat and massive wartime destruction caused the postwar leaders of Japan and West Germany to execute an abrupt about face in reappraising their standards and values—social, political, economic, both domestic and international. They abandoned geopolitics in favor of a new and as yet undefined ecopolitical outlook and policy line, seeking to accomplish national goals by exploiting their economic capabilities and resources, that is, by expanding their industrial productivity and technology. And it is a great paradox that these two nations, formerly enemies, emerged from the traumatic passage of being conquered and ruled by the victors' armies to reap through ecopolitical practices the rewards that had been denied them when they adhered to a geopolitical line.

For example, by means of wars of conquest to seize and subjugate territory, Japan tried to build what it styled a "Greater East Asia Co-Prosperity Sphere." This comprised a group of satellite nations in Southeast Asia and the greater part of China itself under the political and economic dominance of the Japanese government. Today, an ecopolitical Japan is the economic leader of a bustling constellation of newly industrialized far eastern states that has become, in fact if not in name, a greater East Asia co-prosperity sphere. Hitler's Nazi Germany began its wars of aggression in search of *Lebensraum* (living space). Today, West Germany has all the *Lebensraum* it can handle in its expanding global markets for its goods and services. Ecopolitics has transformed West Germany into the number two trading nation in the world, after the United States. Today these two "reformed" nations have become more affluent and more secure, politically as well as economically, than their former geopolitical leaders ever dreamed possible.

The metamorphosis of Japan and West Germany is one of the significant benchmarks of the postwar era. These two nations have demonstrated conclusively that mankind's search for security and stability—by superpowers and small countries alike—does not necessarily depend on military strength or on a political ideology. Ecopolitics has shown that it can succeed where geopolitics cannot accomplish its objectives; that a free market economic system is a more effective tool than the sword or socialism in promoting the growth, prosperity and stability of a nation. And this lesson is being studied with ever-increasing interest throughout the Third World. It is the logical and practical approach to the greatest of postwar global problems: how to bring even a modicum of economic growth to those "have-not" nations, whose submarginal existences contribute to the political instability of a crisis-ridden world. It is not altruism to seek such an objective; it can also produce profit-making business opportunities for all those who pick up this challenge.

Ecopolitics can only function in a free market system. The basic ingredient is freedom for the private business sector—in other words, the industrialists and entrepreneurs—to operate with a minimum of government interference and control, except that measure necessary for public welfare. Essentially that is the secret of the postwar emergence of Japan and Germany as the major economic powers in Asia and in Europe. The Japanese and the West Germans concentrated all their resources, their talents and their energies on the reconstruction and *modernization*—above all else—of their industrial, commercial and financial establishments. Their respective governments provided support in the form of lavish tax incentives and subsidies, enabling their industries to be more productive and more competitive on the world markets for their goods and services. Finally, postwar Japan and Germany from the start rejected any political panacea or ideology as a blueprint for their economic renascence. Instead the governments in Tokyo and Bonn enlisted one of the most powerful and enduring stimulants available to pull themselves out of the abyss of defeat and to make themselves rich and strong in the family of nations: they gave free rein to mankind's unquenchable appetite for material gain. That was the high octane fuel which enabled the Japanese and West German industries to surge ahead of their competitors on the world markets. Prof. Ludwig Erhard, the first postwar economics minister and architect of the West German *Wirtschaftswunder* (the economic miracle) cut to the heart of the matter with his injunction, "Turn the money and the people loose and they will make the nation strong." And they did, with breathtaking speed and magnitude.

From the early 1930s until the mid-1950s—except for military service in World War II—I had been a working journalist, mainly concerned with political reporting in Washington, London, Paris, and in wartime Berlin and postwar Germany. My professional focus shifted in 1952 from politics to economics when I became the correspondent for the *Wall Street Journal* in West Germany. That was the beginning of my education in global *Realpolitik* as I began my serious study of international economic affairs. In 1955, I started my own firm, serving as an international consultant for American and Japanese firms operating in Europe and West German firms in the United States and Great Britain. Thus I managed to learn more about the foreign policies and practices of big business corporations, as carried on behind closed doors.

I had become a student of the amazing postwar comeback of West Germany and its reappearance on the world scene as the premier industrial nation of Western Europe. This led to the writing of my book *The Fourth and Richest Reich* (New York: Macmillan Publishing Co., Inc., 1980). But my research led me further afield. What had happened in West Germany was also happening in Japan. Through my consulting work for leading Japanese firms (Mitsui, Fuji Bank, Nippon Kokan, among others) and for the Japanese embassy in Bonn, I became aware of the scope and force of the Japanese economic revival and its impact in Europe and elsewhere.

The passage of years and my continuing study of international economic affairs led me back to the United States. In its two centuries of existence, America became the number one superpower largely because of its economic—industrial and financial—capabilities and technology. From its formative years until today, largely governed by its geographical isolation from Europe and Asia, America has been essentially ecopolitical and not geopolitical in its outlook and in its actions.

As we enter upon the last two decades of the twentieth century, the United States appears threatened as never before in its history. Our frightened allies are wavering in their support. The Soviet imperium has more nuclear missiles in place on their launching pads, aimed at the United States and its allies, than the Pentagon can muster. The U.S. economy is in the doldrums. Pundits of all credos are preaching that Doomsday is at hand. Is the vaunted "American century" to come to an early and premature end?

And yet . . . the distant roll of a different set of drums can be dimly heard, gradually becoming louder. A new order is at hand. The age of ecopolitics is dawning; geopolitics is found wanting and its days are numbered. The United States of America may be entering upon the truly productive days of its full maturity in the decades ahead. As the archetype of an ecopolitical nation, America has the opportunity to become the prime mover in the affairs of nations.

The purpose of this book is to explore this impending turning point in contemporary history.

E.H.

Orland Park, Ill.
August 1982

Ecopolitics:
A Decisive Weapon

Military strength today is not merely military power, but it is economic and industrial strength. It is also fiscal. It is technological resourcefulness and it touches every field of knowledge . . . and whatever else contributes to our being able to retain all these elements, including our financial strength, keeps us fit and competent to wage war. Above all modern war is economic and it is worldwide.

> —JAMES V. FORRESTAL, Secretary of the Navy,
> to a U.S. Senate committee, March 1947

The intellectuals of the West are at liberty to vituperate technology and its monstrous development; but for four-fifths of mankind, technology means the application of scientific knowledge, the promise not of abundance but of a decent life, or one of less fearful poverty. The West, far more than the Soviet Union, has the means of translating this promise into a reality.

> —RAYMOND ARON, *The Century of Total War*
> (Boston: Beacon Press, 1955)

T "*Political power grows out of the barrel of a gun.*"[1]

THIS hard-line principle has been responsible for the worldwide expansion of Communist power ever since Lenin overthrew the Russian government in the Bolshevik revolution of 1917. The frontiers of Communism in postwar Europe, Africa, and Asia have been extended by Red Armies. Guns and not ideological doctrines have "converted" nations to totalitarian rule in the name of Marxist-Leninism. Raw military power was and still is the principal instrument of Soviet foreign policy, as Russia continues its expansionist course at the expense of free nations of the world.

However, a new truth is emerging and finding growing acceptance by peoples and governments outside the Communist bloc. Today, political power also grows out of the smoking chimneys of a modern industrial economy. It is generated twenty-four hours a day, and its influence is felt continuously. As we move into the turbulent 1980s, the prime factor in the affairs of nations will be their economic capabilities and resources. Each nation's power and influence on the world scene will be measured in terms of its productive capacities of consumer and industrial goods and services, its supplies of fuel and energy as well as vital raw materials, its agricultural output and technology, and its transportation and communications systems. These and other components of economic strength and resources also contribute to a country's security. For they are the vitamins to energize the military muscle, as well as to sustain and improve the civilian way of life.

So the struggle between the Communist bloc and the free world is taking on a new dimension. Economic power will play a greater role in

[1]This quotation is taken from a series of essays on how to conduct guerrilla warfare, written by Chairman Mao Zedong in his cave headquarters in Yennan in 1938. Years later, Mao's guerrilla strategy and tactics were successfully implemented by Ho Chi Minh, enabling North Vietnam's ill-equipped armies to defeat the French colonial as well as U.S. forces in the postwar struggle for Indochina.

world affairs, because it will be involved with a universal problem—
the living standards of all human beings. Economic power and its
influences cannot be blocked by iron curtains. It is as pervasive and as
hard to control as a militant religion, because it has a direct appeal to
human aspirations and needs. Yet, as we shall see, this development
today, and also for the immediate future, rekindles the cold war between the superpowers. At the moment the Soviet Union enjoys military superiority over the United States, as it will for the next few years.
But the United States is the strongest economic power in the world
today, and it is mobilizing its resources to restore equality with Russia
in the field of military power. Once that objective is accomplished,
together with the employment of all of its industrial and technological
capacities, the United States can regain the security and stability
which it enjoyed in the first decades after World War II. America's role
in an increasingly hostile and turbulent world is dependent on first
recognizing this stark new development in international relations and
then acting intelligently to adjust to it. *Ecopolitics* is gradually replacing *geopolitics* as the prime mover in the affairs of nations. In short,
world events are being formed and shaped more by economic than by
political or military considerations. That is why the 1980s will be the
most crucial decade in America's history.

The habitable world, from the affluent industrial nations to the
undeveloped countries of the Third World, is in a state of transition. It
is a slow, almost imperceptible process. Though hardly recognizable
when viewed against today's headlines, a major trend is setting in
which in the years ahead will result in profound changes—evolution-
ary and not revolutionary—in the economic structure and operations
of the non-Communist world. The main thrust of this trend will be a
shift in power and influence away from those nations which depend on
military force to maintain or to advance their position on the international scene to those nations with the greatest industrial and technological potentials.

There is a new word in the language of international affairs:
ecopolitics. Though somewhat imprecise, in general it is the antithesis
of *geopolitics*. The latter involves the employment of military force and
geography to serve the national interests of a country. In contrast,
ecopolitics concerns itself with the mobilization and direction of a
nation's economic capacities and resources, so as to protect and promote the country's basic self-interests. In the contest between the
smoking gun and the smoking chimney, the latter is beginning to take
the lead. In other words, economic strength is real power. A modern
industrial infrastructure, high-quality technology, a work force of

skilled labor, agricultural surpluses, competitive exports on the world markets, and substantial gold and dollar reserves can be transformed into political instruments to give an ecopolitically strong country greater leverage and flexibility of maneuver in its international affairs. That is why governments intervene with increasing frequency in international economic affairs, once largely dominated by multinational private companies. As the *Wall Street Journal* pointed out at the end of the 1970s, "The world has been changing. U.S. hegemony has been weakening, and more and more of the world's commerce is controlled, one way or the other, by governments rather than by private corporations."[2]

The rise of the United States to superpower status in the twentieth century has largely been the result of its unceasing economic growth and capabilities—and not of its military power or its political influence. America developed the industrial capacity to manufacture the whole range of capital and consumer goods, more than any other nation could produce. Yet it was its own best customer. It was only marginally dependent on foreign trade for its economic survival.

America also had the industrial and scientific skills and equipment, as well as the compulsion to make continual advances in all fields of technology, including development of the nuclear weapon. U.S. industry better exploited the inventions of others, principally the Europeans, than their countries could. The Europeans, for example, invented the motor car. It became the vehicle for the rich, until Henry Ford's assembly-line production of the Model T provided a car for the masses. The subsequent phenomenal growth of the American automotive industry made it one of the pillars of the U.S. economy.

The great prairie states of the American Midwest, covered with rich black soil, became the most productive agricultural area in the world. Between the Appalachian and the Rocky Mountain ranges, the output of beef cattle, wheat, and corn was a veritable cornucopia of proteins and carbohydrates, unmatched anywhere in Europe or Asia. What made this possible was the U.S. inventions of modern agricultural machinery, beginning with the McCormick reaper of the 1830s, which opened up thousands of square miles of fertile land, from horizon to horizon, without interruption. No horse-drawn equipment could have handled the agricultural development of the Midwest; there were not enough horses or farmers available. But American agricultural machinery transformed the Midwest into the greatest "bread basket" in the world, thereby also making the United

[2]*Wall Street Journal*, Dec. 26, 1979.

States invulnerable on the food front. It is an asset very few nations possess, a guaranteed food supply through fat and lean years of production. And all this surging industrial, agricultural, and commercial activity created wealth, so much wealth that Wall Street became the banker of the world by the 1920s and has remained so ever since.

An examination of America's turbulent past will disclose that U.S. foreign policy has, in general, been influenced or governed by *ecopolitical* considerations ever since the earliest days of the Republic. The United States has been the first true *ecopolitical* nation of contemporary history. America has evolved its own unique and durable character and formula of governance. It has created a rich and powerful nation through its economic growth and technological development, at the same time remaining a stable democracy. That in itself seems to be an anachronism, judged against the pattern of history. In the past, nations acquired wealth and power by geopolitical methods—if not by war, then by war's first cousin, colonial exploitation.

It is true that the Atlantic and Pacific oceans gave America's development a peculiar insularity, which has affected Americans' thinking and actions on the international scene. This isolation from Europe's geopolitical wars and crises enabled the United States to concentrate on its internal development and expansion across the continent to the distant Pacific Coast. But when the basic self-interests of the United States were threatened by outside events or forces which seemed to impinge on its economic domain, the Americans mustered their forces in a successful defense. The Monroe Doctrine of 1823, which was the basis of U.S. foreign policy until World War II, declared the Western Hemisphere off limits to predatory European powers. At the same time, it was implicit that the United States would not intervene in Europe's affairs. This isolationary outlook stimulated America's concentration on its own economic growth and expansion, laying the foundations for its ecopolitical development.

In the costly and destructive conflict between the Northern states and the Southern Confederacy, the ecopolitical power of the North was decisive in defeating the South. For instance, Washington's threat to cut off the vital grain shipments to Great Britain during the Civil War deterred the British from openly and actively providing military and naval support to the Confederacy in return for the South's shipments of cotton to the expanding English textile industry. Bread won over cotton in the policymaking decisions at 10 Downing Street, because the British needed food more than fibers. Britain's traditional sources of wheat from Russia had been drastically curtailed. Of course, it is true that the Northern states' far superior industrial capacity also decisively affected the outcome of the Civil War.

At crucial periods in its history, when the U.S. government has utilized its economic muscle to achieve political objectives in the international arena, it has been remarkably successful. A prime example of America's reaping rewards for doing what comes naturally was the imaginative and immensely practical Marshall Plan, which provided a lesson many of us seem to have forgotten. World War II had barely ended when the "cold war" between the erstwhile Allies, Russia and the United States, broke out. The Kremlin was displaying its "ruthless opportunism"—Henry Kissinger's apt description of the underlying motivation of Soviet Russia's foreign policy—in seeking to extend its political sway over the European continent as far as possible. At that point, the Western European countries were recovering from their defeat and the long, hard years of Nazi occupation. They had been stripped of their wealth, and their peoples had been made the helots of their Nazi overlords. When at long last they emerged from the darkness of occupation into the sunshine of liberation and peace, they came empty-handed. They were virtually powerless, politically, economically, and militarily. Western Europe was ripe for plucking—or so reasoned the men in the Kremlin at this favorable turn of events.

The Russian strategy to dominate Europe was simple and seemed attainable. As Ambassador George Kennan, who actually drafted the Marshall Plan, relates in his *Memoirs: 1925–1950*, the Kremlin's blueprint for the political takeover of Europe was based on the following wrong assumptions:

First, after its colossal expenditures of money and matériel in World War II, the United States would suffer a severe economic crisis[3] and hence could do nothing to halt the further economic deterioration of the European nations. Also the Russians thought it probable that the Americans "would not be able to muster, as a nation, the leadership, the imagination, the political skill, the material resources, and above all the national self-discipline necessary to bring material stability, confidence and hope for the future to those areas of Western Europe which had been brought low by the effects of the war."

Second, the Kremlin was certain that the postwar economic prob-

---

[3]Prof. Eugene Varga, a leading Russian economist, took a contrary view. He advised the Kremlin that the United States would not undergo an economic depression after World War II. However, his estimate ran counter to Stalin's expectations, and Varga was demoted for his heretical opinions. Several years later he was reinstated after publicly confessing to "errors" in his economic forecasting.

lem which wracked the liberated nations of Western Europe could not be solved if the Russians cut off the transport of food and other vital supplies from Eastern Europe, the traditional "bread basket" of the Continent, then under the military control of the Red Armies. As George Kennan later relates, the Russians believed that they had "only to deny these resources for a little while longer so as to put themselves in a position where they will be able to practically name the political price on which to make them available."[4]

However, the men in the Kremlin, whose vision of the non-Communist world is conditioned by Marxian dialectic, formulated in the mid-nineteenth century, grossly miscalculated in their postwar assessments. Their first assumption collapsed. The United States did not go into an economic tailspin when the war ended. On the contrary, when the wartime controls and regulations were lifted, the U.S. economy took off like a bird released from a cage. America entered into the most affluent and productive years of its two centuries of existence. The gross national product was $284 billion in 1950, rising to $503 billion in 1960, then to $977 billion in 1970, and $1.4 trillion by 1974.[5] Nor did the U.S. government lack the skills, imagination, leadership, and resources to directly challenge and overcome the threatening Soviet takeover of Europe. The Marshall Plan was the instrument, providing loans and grants totaling over $16 billion, to finance the economic reconstruction of war-battered Western Europe. It supplied the food and other vital necessities which the Russians had been withholding from the Europeans. The Marshall Plan effectively blocked the westward expansion of Russian power and influence by restoring Western Europe to economic health and giving it hope for a future. The U.S. ecopolitical formula was also simple and proved superior to Russian blackmail: Marshall Plan dollars neutralized the geopolitical threat of the Soviet armies poised on the other side of the Iron Curtain, allegedly ready to march to the Rhine River. Instead of collapsing into chaos, Western Europe was restored to economic health and vitality by the transfusion of U.S. Marshall Plan funds. Out of this came the military alliance of the transatlantic community of nations, NATO.

But the United States committed an almost fatal mistake in the 1960s and '70s. The government in Washington lost touch with reality. It seemed to forget the basic self-interests that made this nation great and strong. It traded substance for illusion. America thought it could be the "world's policeman," a sort of benign and avuncular global dictator, by virtue of its superior wealth and weaponry. It imagined

[4]George Kennan, *Memoirs: 1925–1950* (Boston: Little, Brown and Company, 1967).
[5]In March 1982, the GNP passed the $3 trillion mark.

that it had the formula for setting everything to rights, including man's unceasing inhumanity to his fellow man.

We must first set the stage so as to give a proper perspective to this costly error in policymaking. Not since Caesar Augustus in 31 B.C. took control of the burgeoning Roman Empire has any nation been so dominant as was the United States at the end of World War II. It had waged and won its wars in Europe and the Pacific. Its industrial and technological capabilities had expanded on a massive scale. It could manufacture without strain fleets of bombers and merchant ships and all the other matériel of war, as well as support its own domestic economy and put together the first atomic bomb. Its mechanized farmlands could harvest sufficient food to feed not only its own forty-eight states and its armies in the European and Pacific areas of war but also its allies. Cans of South Dakota–produced Spam nourished the Red Army soldiers fighting at Stalingrad, as well as the British Tommies in the desert wastes of North Africa. After the shooting stopped, the United States provided the food and other necessities for the millions of victims of the war, not only in the liberated countries but also in the ex-enemy states. This explosion of American industrial and agricultural activities reached levels hitherto thought impossible of achievement. World War II transformed the United States into the first modern superpower of the twentieth century. Alone of all the participating countries in this global conflict, the United States emerged from the struggle richer, stronger, and more productive than it was at the outset of the war.

Until America's involvement in Vietnam—its subsequent defeat was euphemistically described as a "withdrawal of U.S. forces"—the United States engaged itself only in wars in which the odds (and this includes World Wars I and II) were in its favor. In each of these earlier wars, the United States was victorious. It also came out of each struggle with a modernized and expanded industry and improved technology, as well as greater and more efficient production of food. The United States is essentially not a militaristic country. For each of these past wars, it has had virtually to recreate from scratch its armed forces. But this handicap has always been swiftly overcome by the nation's industrial and agricultural productivity, which could be readily expanded. These assets proved decisive in the winning of these wars for America and her allies.

Field Marshal Paul von Hindenburg, who commanded Kaiser Wilhelm's armies in World War I, put his finger on America's unique contribution to the art of successfully fighting wars. In his memoirs, *Aus Meinem Leben*, von Hindenburg grudgingly stated that the key factor in Germany's defeat was the "brilliant, if pitiless, war industry of America which entered into the patriotic struggle and did not fail it."[6] The same can be said to explain how the industrialized Northern states overcame the Confederacy in the Civil War, as well as how America's "arsenal of democracy" provided the sinews of war to defeat the Germans in Europe and the Japanese in the Pacific in World War II. According to the postwar memoirs of his naval colleagues, Admiral Isoroku Yamamoto, commander in chief of the Imperial Japanese Navy, predicted after his successful attack on Pearl Harbor that America's superior industrial capacity would eventually defeat the Japanese, unless they could obtain an early and favorable peace settlement with the United States.

In any event, America's apparently unique ability to emerge from all its wars—until the disaster in Vietnam—stronger and more prosperous has been a puzzling phenomenon, especially to Marxist theoreticians in the Kremlin. It is contradictory to the dogma laid down by Karl Marx and reaffirmed by Lenin. This tenet holds that every war in which a capitalist nation involves itself brings it that much closer to economic and political collapse. But the United States appeared to invalidate that bit of Marxian dialectic. The Soviet theoreticians described this inexplicable situation as "the American Exceptionalism." Yet, in reality, the United States seemed to have a deep-seated pragmatic sense that kept it out of all wars that posed a serious threat to its ultimate economic security and survival. That is, until the war in Vietnam.

The major mistake the United States committed in the 1960s and 1970s was to abandon this pragmatic sense in its foreign relations. It shifted from its basic *ecopolitical* outlook—that is, from a policymaking largely governed by the basic economic self-interests of the United States. Instead it gradually began to think and act more in *geopolitical* terms. In short, military and political rather than economic considerations were the dominant factors in foreign policy.

After the war in North Korea, which ended in a military stale-

---

[6]Hindenburg and the German High Command received somewhat of a shock in their initial military encounter with U.S. forces in France. In their first combat offensive against the Germans in World War I, on Sept. 26th, 1918, the Americans opened the attack on the Meuse-Argonne sector with a three hour long artillery barrage by 3,800 guns. In this relatively short period, the Americans fired off a greater tonnage of shells than had been used by both the Union and Confederate armies in the four years of the U.S. Civil War. The Meuse-Argonne barrage was an explosive demonstration of the industrial resources that backed the Allied forces and guaranteed their victory in World War I and would repeat that feat in World War II. Hindenburg's memoirs were published in Berlin in 1920 by Fertig Verlag.

mate, Washington began to seek geopolitical solutions to its foreign-affairs problems. For example, the United States would seek to "contain" the Soviet Union and its satellites within a ring of military alliances in Europe, Asia, the Middle East, etc. An acute case of political short-sightedness afflicted the successive administrations of Eisenhower, Kennedy, and Johnson. There was the growing conviction that because the United States was the strongest military power in the world, it was also capable of operating effectively in this relatively new, though arcane, field of geopolitics. However, the leading advisers of the presidents in this period—the Dulles brothers, Dean Rusk, Bundy, and so on—never had the background or experience of a Metternich, a Castlereagh, or a Talleyrand of the Congress of Vienna school of geopolitics. The Americans rushed in where angels would fear to tread.

The apotheosis of this magnificent self-delusion is to be found in John F. Kennedy's inauguration speech of Jan. 20, 1960. From the podium before the U.S. Capitol, in words that captured the rich, evangelical flavor of America's newfound, self-imposed mandate as keeper of the world's peace and order, the youthful president messianically proclaimed to the cheering throngs and the world at large:

Let the word go forth from this time and place, to friend and foe alike, that the torch has been passed to a new generation of Americans. . . . Let every nation know, whether it wishes us well or ill, that *we shall pay any price, bear any burden, support any friend, oppose any foe, to assure the survival and success of liberty. . . . This much we pledge and more. . . .*

Kennedy's inaugural address was eloquent speechmaking, but geopolitical nonsense nonetheless. It was the antithesis of the essentially hardheaded, clear-sighted *Realpolitik* which the U.S. government had employed in the past. This crusading appeal to Americans was certainly not the basis for a successful foreign policy for a nation wishing to survive and prosper in a hostile and competitive world.

President John F. Kennedy was the pied piper who led us out of the land of prosperity and stability and into the quagmire of a geopolitical war in Indochina in a vain effort to halt the spread of Communism to Southeast Asia. Following JFK's assassination, President Lyndon B. Johnson continued and expanded on Kennedy's geopolitical crusade to wipe out the spread of Asiatic Communism in the forbidding jungles of Vietnam. Johnson also decided the nation could afford both "guns and butter," a feat of political and financial legerdemain which we will be paying for for many decades to come.

He initiated a new multibillion-dollar "Great Society" social-welfare program to meet the demands of the blacks and other minorities, in addition to financing the multibillion-dollar outlay for supporting the U.S. armed forces in distant Vietnam.

The results of this double-entry bookkeeping proved beyond a shadow of a doubt that a nation—even a rich country like the United States—cannot maintain a guns *and* butter economy. You can have one or the other; but you can't have both, if you want to maintain a healthy economy and the highest living standard in the world. The geopolitical adventure in Southeast Asia tipped the scales decisively against the economic stability of the United States. It was the point of origin of the sagging dollar, American inflation, and the host of other economic problems that plague the nation today. We can trace the beginnings of America's surprising decline on the international scene to the war in Vietnam. It was set in motion by President Kennedy's pledge that the United States would "pay any price, bear any burden . . . to assure the survival and the success of liberty," especially in those Third World areas, such as Indochina, which have never known political freedom for their peoples in all the years of their existence.

The cold war, which has been waged intermittently since 1945, is now building up to a crisis in the 1980s. The Soviet Union's massive expansion of its nuclear and conventional armed forces in the last two decades is the paramount factor in international affairs. Until almost the end of this decade, the Russians will probably enjoy military superiority over the United States. But logic dictates that the Russian leadership will avoid a direct military showdown with the United States. There is the definite possibility that it can achieve its long-range objectives without triggering a war, involving the risk of atomic devastation of U.S.S.R.

What Russia will do in the next few years obviously is unknown. Winston Churchill once described the Soviet Union as "a riddle wrapped in a mystery, inside of an enigma, but perhaps there is a key. The key is *Russian self-interest.*"

The basic objectives of Russian foreign policy have a common denominator: to weaken and/or to eliminate wherever possible the power and influence of the United States in Europe, Africa, and Asia. More specifically, Russia's observable goals appear to be:

1. To detach Western Europe from its alliance with the United States, to render it politically neutral as Finland is, and to exploit Europe's superior industrial capabilities and technology for the imme-

diate benefit of the Soviet Union.[7] This would *not* involve the transformation of West Germany, France, etc. into Communist satellites under the direct police control and supervision by the Russians. That would be a step backward, for Western Europe would then become as disorganized and unproductive as the Soviet Union itself.

2. To politically dominate the Middle East oil-producing states. For the Russians, their "road to Paris" runs through the Strait of Hormuz. Western Europe is largely dependent for its fuel and energy on crude oil imported from the Middle East. With its own oil supplies assured—Russia is still the largest oil producer in the world today—the Soviet Union is in a position to disrupt oil production in the Persian Gulf areas without going to war or damaging its own economy. The Russians always work through surrogates whenever possible to avoid direct and overt involvement. The Middle East is a veritable stewpot of ethnic, religious, and racial mixtures and conflicts. It does not need much more heat to boil over in a fierce spasm of killing. As the overthrow of the shah of Iran has demonstrated, it is easy to "rent a riot" for short-term use in the volatile Middle East. The KGB has a solid background and experience in this field of guerrilla geopolitics.

On Christmas Eve 1979, Russian troops crossed the Oxus River, which marks the boundary between the Soviet Union and Afghanistan. With this act of armed aggression, did the Russians "cross the Rubicon"?[8] There are those who think that the Russians have moved the cold war to a turning point, committing the Kremlin to a course of action from which it cannot retreat, except at great political cost to itself and its control of the Red empire. As the *Economist* (Dec. 26, 1981) pointed out: "The Rubicon (in Afghanistan's case, the Oxus) had been crossed. Russia had shown that it was prepared to wield its military might outside the post-Yalta boundaries. If this was in legitimate self-defense to secure Russia's borders, well,

[7]Confirmation of this Soviet goal comes from Eugen Löbl, a former director of the Communist State Bank of Czechoslovakia, who stated in an article for *Business Week* (Feb. 22, 1982): "The goal of Stalinist imperialism is to benefit from the highly efficient economies of West Europe, thus enabling it to run its own inefficient planning system. For the time being the Soviet bloc has the advantage of remarkable credits and technological help from the West, which makes it possible to increase its military power, while maintaining a mere subsistence level for the overwhelming majority of the nations within its empire. The strategic goal of the Soviet Union, then, is the domination of Europe and Japan through intimidation. There is one great obstacle to that goal: the United States."

[8]In 49 B.C., Julius Caesar and his legions crossed the small Rubicon River, marking the frontier between Cisalpine Gaul and Italy. This was an irrevocable first step in Caesar's civil war to seize full power in the Roman Republic. His action changed the course of world history by laying the foundations for the Roman Empire that was to last almost six hundred years.

maybe Soviet self-defense was something the world needed protection against."

The invasion of Afghanistan demonstrated to the world that when the Soviet Union feels it will suffer no serious challenge or damage, it is prepared to undertake military action, violate treaties, and do whatever else is necessary to serve its own national interests. The weakness and indecisiveness of the Carter administration convinced the Kremlin that the time was ripe to take a giant step closer to dominance of the Persian Gulf states.

Russia is in a race against time. It has only a few years in which to extract the maximum geopolitical advantages out of the present military imbalance now in its favor. Since the 1962 Cuban missile crisis, the Soviet Union has been engaged in an all-out effort to catch up with and then surpass the United States in sheer military strength and resources. It has paid and will continue to pay a high price to achieve and hold this objective. Its civilian economy has been denied the fruits of its labor, which have been absorbed by the massive armaments program. Industrial development, except that involved in arms production, is in reverse. Agriculture is a chronic invalid. Czarist Russia was a food-exporting country. Soviet Russia has become a food importer. Harvests have progressively declined to a point where the annual grain-production figures are no longer published. Inclement weather is the excuse given for reduced food supplies. As one Moscow observer put it: "It seems that the Soviet Union has endured sixty-three years of successive 'bad weather,' a meteorological record unsurpassed by any other country in the world."

Shortly before the end of the 1980s, America's new and superior Trident and MX nuclear missiles will be in place on their launch pads. The "window of vulnerability," which now limits America's freedom of maneuver, can be slammed shut with a world-resounding bang. The United States will have regained its military credibility; the Russian threats and pressure tactics will begin to lose theirs.

However, a restoration of military parity between the two superpowers won't end the cold war. Something newer and more innovative is required. The Soviet Union will never cease trying to extend its power and influence unless it is confronted with a development that threatens its very existence and that cannot be eliminated or neutralized by Russia's armed forces. Lacking such a development, the cold war will continue and its constant escalation of weaponry and political crises will increase the chances of igniting World War III. The United States must meet this challenge with something more than superior military power. The battle for the future will acquire a new dimension: economic power and resources. The battle will be decided not by the sheer weight of armaments but by industrial and technological capacities of the free world against the Warsaw bloc.

This is the opportunity for the United States to exercise its superior economic strength; in short, to do what comes naturally. America is the leading economic power on the world stage. This asset, which has been utilized so successfully in the past, must again be mobilized as a force to halt the geopolitical aggression of the Soviet Union. The great weakness of the new Red empire is that behind its impressive and threatening military facade lies a vast economic swamp. To be sure, there are untapped reserves of oil and gas, coal, minerals, and other raw materials needed by any industrial nation. But Russia lacks the trained manpower and the technology to exploit these domestic riches fully.

The smoldering cold war can be brought under control in the forseeable future through the introduction of an ecopolitical program. It is the only effective firefighting equipment that is available.

In the following chapters, we will survey the global scene as it relates to major new economic and political developments that are becoming apparent. I have concentrated on certain countries and areas because their postwar histories best illustrate the principal trends of our times, both positive and negative. The purpose of this *tour d'horizon* is to provide a fresh and informative perspective on the decline of geopolitics and the rise of ecopolitics and how this affects the United States of America.

CHAPTER ONE

Russia Walks on One Leg

. . . the Soviet state may have the head and shoulders of a superpower but its feet are made of numbly incompetent clay.
—The London *Economist*,
August 23, 1980

I do not think we can look forward to a tranquil world so long as the Soviet Union operates in its present form. The only hope, and this is a fairly thin one, is that at some point, the Soviet Union will begin to act like a country instead of a cause.
—CHARLES E. BOHLEN, U.S. Ambassador
in Moscow, 1956–60, in *Witness to Power*
(New York: W.W. Norton, 1973)

PRINCE Grigori Aleksandrovich Potemkin (1739–91), the lover of Russia's great Empress Catherine II, was also an eminent soldier, a statesman, and, for a time, the most powerful man in Russia. Potemkin expanded Catherine's domains across the Ukrainian steppes to the shores of the Black Sea. In 1787 he arranged for Catherine to make a grand tour of her newly acquired territories. As Potemkin had unlimited access to state funds, he dressed up the towns and villages through which the empress would pass, so as to give the impression that these backward and poverty-stricken areas were busily occupied and populated by prosperous and contented peasants. His ability to camouflage the areas of distress in Catherine's inspection visit has given us the expression "Potemkin village."

The Soviet Union today is a Potemkin village on a massive scale. It presents to the world a picture of monolithic omnipotence, centered in the Kremlin in Moscow, with tentacles reaching throughout the world. It is a gruff authoritarian state that permits no challenge of its actions, ready and quick to punish those who stand in its way. It is armed with nuclear missiles carrying megatons of explosive force, sufficient to erase cities from the face of the earth. It is a geographical colossus, spanning the great Eurasian landmass from the Pacific to Europe. The Trans-Siberian Express from Moscow to Vladivostok traverses 5,600 miles of track in a seven-day trip, the longest railroad journey in the world today. But the limits of Russia's domain stretch even farther, to Central Europe, where Red Army garrisons mark the western frontiers of Soviet rule. The Soviet navy's fighting ships are cruising the sea lanes of the world, from the Caribbean to the northern Pacific, from the warm waters of the Indian Ocean to the ice-cluttered Arctic seas. The Soviet Union is a powerful and truculent bully. It claims to be the "wave of the future," the precursor of the "workers' paradise," as promised by Karl Marx and Vladimir Lenin. Yet today, more than six decades after the Bolshevik coup d'état in St. Petersburg, we have reached a definite "bottom-line" critique of the progress made to date by the "dictatorship of the proletariat":

Since about 1959, the Soviet Union's 215 million Europeans have grown more educated, more alcoholic, more bloody-minded, more prone to massive absenteeism from work and less willing to breed children. While the Soviet Union's 45 million Asians know they are richer than the Asians living across their borders (in China, Afghanistan, Iran and maybe Asiatic Turkey), the Soviet Europeans are beginning to realize that, if you measure their standard of living at black market prices, *they are just about the poorest white people on earth in relation to their rather high level of education.*[1]

If it were possible to strip away the government-imposed screen that covers up the reality inside the Soviet Union, we would see a superpower unable to cope with an internal crisis that threatens its very existence. This conglomerate of a nation, covering one-sixth of the earth's land area, is facing an economic crisis steadily growing in intensity because of the Kremlin's single-minded concentration on surpassing the United States as a military power. The Russians appear to have achieved this objective, at least in conventional armed forces for the immediate present, in the opinion of most experts. But they have gained this advantage at the expense of seriously weakening the already jerry-built economic structure of the Soviet Union. This chronic and inflamed crisis, brought about by the all-out drive to be the world's dominant military power, is an illness that "could be terminal"[2] for the Soviet Union and its satellites.

To employ a medical metaphor, the Soviet Union is suffering from hardening of the arteries. Unless this worsening condition is soon remedied, a paralyzing stroke is inevitable. As seen by the outside world, Soviet Russia presents an impressive front, radiating military power and purpose. Russia's industrial capabilities, its technology, and its economic and financial resources have been mobilized to maintain this Potemkin-village facade of power and strength, regardless of the damage and dislocation inflicted on the domestic economy and on the living standards of the Russian people. For the last decade,

[1]*Economist*, Aug. 23, 1980; italics added.
[2]Ibid.

the masters in the Kremlin have been allocating an estimated 15–30%[3] of the gross national product to the buildup and modernization of their armed forces, from the ranging fleets of nuclear submarines to space satellites, constantly circling the globe, which possess incalculable power to threaten world communications and the security of the western powers.

The basic weakness of the Soviet Union is simply this: Despite its size, its wealth of natural resources, and its other attributes, it cannot function as a modern industrial power. Russia is cut from a different bolt of cloth; its social structure is radically different from that of other nations which have to depend on their God-given wits and abilities, rather than on an ideology, to support them in the world marketplaces of ideas and goods. Before the revolution in 1917, Russia was an autocracy ruled by a czar whose word was the law of the land. There was no political freedom; a secret police force operated freely to imprison any dissenters, to quell any incipient rebellion. It was known as the *Okhranki*, anglicized into Okhrana. However, there was little interference in the relatively free market economy functioning at that time. After the revolution, Russia was ruled by a "dictatorship of the proletariat," led by a small band of ruthless Bolsheviks, whose numbers did not exceed ten thousand, according to reliable observers at that time. However, under Lenin and his colleagues, including Stalin, there was neither political nor economic freedom in this new "workers' paradise." The Bolsheviks implicitly believed that they had in their hands the blueprint for a new Utopia, based on the Communist ideology. They believed that all political, economic, and social problems could be solved through Marxist socialism. They created an ideology that had a worldwide impact, but was forcibly imposed on the hapless and prostrate Russian people.

It is ironic that Russia had only one free election following the overthrow of Czar Nicholas II. On Nov. 25, 1917, shortly after the Bolshevik seizure of power on October 17, an election was held to create an assembly to draft a constitution for the new Russian democracy. It had been scheduled for some months previously and could not be called off despite Lenin's attempts to sabotage it in advance. In the final tally, the Bolsheviks got only 168 out of the 703 contested seats.

---

[3]Eugen Löbl, former director of the State Bank of Czechoslovakia, during the brief administration of Premier Dubcek, wrote the following in *Business Week* (Oct. 29, 1979): "When I headed the State Bank, using the Eastern bloc's accounting procedures and methods, we estimated that as much as 30% of the Soviet Union's GNP was actually devoted to military activities." By comparison the United States has been spending 5% and less annually, while other NATO nations have been spending an average of 3.5%.

The opposition Social Revolutionaries won an overwhelming majority of 418 seats, but that was their high point. The Bolsheviks ignored the results of the election, as if it had never occurred. The attempts of the assembly to write a constitution collapsed; its members were dispersed and rendered powerless by Lenin's new terrorist police force, the Cheka. Vladimir Ilyich Lenin, leader of the Bolsheviks, preached a simple if frightening dogma to justify this and other acts of political rape. In his constant exhortations to his circle of lieutenants and followers, so as not to lose their revolutionary fervor and momentum, he spoke forcefully and bluntly, announcing that "the dictatorship of the proletariat is power, based directly on force and unrestricted by any laws."[4] In effect, the ability to seize power and to hold it against all challenges, legal or otherwise, is considered, in itself, a proof of its legitimacy. Other revolutionaries, dictators, and despots, have never been so brutally frank and honest in justifying that "might makes right."

The Magna Carta and the Declaration of Independence form the cores of the political philosophies which have been the guidelines for the two greatest democracies, Great Britain and the United States. Similarly, these words of Lenin's have been the animating principle governing the world's greatest totalitarian state, the Soviet Union, ever since its violent beginning on Oct. 17, 1917.

In the intervening years, the successive Communist regimes of Stalin through Malenkov, Khrushchev, and Brezhnev have outlawed organized religion. Yet they have enshrined a god of their very own making, the embalmed corpse of Vladimir Ilyich Lenin—or a very convincing facsimile thereof—exposed to view under glass in the giant marble mausoleum in Moscow's Red Square. It is all very symbolic. On the great days of the Soviet political calendar, the members of the Politburo and leading military personalities gather in an unsmiling phalanx on top of Lenin's tomb to review the parades passing below, which honor the glories and greatness of the Communist state. The political and military leaders are lined up on top of this hallowed building as if they were the living archangels of the new god of Marxist socialism, who lies immured a few feet below their polished Russian boots. After such an event, nobody leaves the spectacle in any doubt that the Soviet leaders draw their unchallenged authority to rule the masses from the name and ideology of the late sanctified Bolshevik

[4]V.I. Lenin, quoted in *The Proletarian Revolution and the Renegade Kautsky* (New York: International Publishers, 1934).

leader. And the embalmed corpse of the god of a materialistic, atheistic philosophy lies, pickled under glass, unable to know of the giant hoax being perpetrated on the Russian people.

The guidelines of the totalitarian state were laid down by Lenin. After this death in 1924, his successor, Josef Stalin, transformed the dictatorship into a harsh reality by his elimination of all opposition, by killing or imprisoning millions, from stubborn kulaks to marshals of the Red Army. Anyone who might oppose his dictatorial rule was taken away in the night by the agents of NKVD secret police. It has been reliably estimated that over 20 million Russians perished in the twenty-three years of the "Great Terror" imposed on the hapless Soviet Union by Stalin and his NKVD.[5]

The "dictatorship of the proletariat" of necessity required the complete control of the administration of the Soviet Union by the Communist Party's leadership in Moscow, reinforced by the state security police (first known as the Cheka, or Extraordinary Commission, then as the OGPU or the GPU, later as the NKVD, and today as the KGB). There was no freedom of action to revise or to change any of the Kremlin's plans or operations given to the lower echelons in carrying out the actual governing process. The structure of the government was inflexible and monolithic, both politically and economically. "Follow the plan" was the guiding principle of administration. And with the passing years this unquestioning acceptance of Moscow's orders and directives hardened into rigidity.

Undoubtedly, this Soviet system of overcentralized control and planning was necessary in the formative years of the Soviet Union. The Politburo had to marshal large amounts of capital and labor so as to begin to industrialize this undeveloped giant of a country that was essentially agricultural in character.[6] But what contributed to its progress in the early years—the exclusivity and the self-perpetuation of the Communist Party's ruling elite—has become its cancer by 1980, the sixty-fourth year of the existence of the Union of Soviet Socialist Republics.

The Soviet Union has no open or flexible political system, such as the democracies possess. There are no free elections. Therefore, there is no outside political road to travel for an ambitious Russian who wishes to advance into the upper levels of the Soviet government,

---

[5]Cited by Robert Conquest in his *Great Terror* (New York: Macmillan, 1968).
[6]At the time of the Revolution in 1917, there were hardly 3 million industrial workers in Russia, out of a total population of 143 million.

armed with a mandate from the people. Instead he must work his way upward within the party system, espousing the party line with enthusiasm, accepting the party discipline with unquestioning obedience. For example, Nikita Khrushchev maneuvered his way into the Kremlin by being Stalin's lackey, his most diligent "yes man." The rewards are great for the intelligently sycophantic in the Soviet power structure. For Stalin created an administration ruled by fear and terror. This provided a tight, cohesive structure of government, but one with little initiative or imagination. Stalin reckoned correctly that men would pay a high price in service and loyalty to his regime in return for some assurance of personal security against death or imprisonment.

One of the threadbare clichés of Marxist-Leninist ideology is that the capitalist nations, and particularly the United States, are "materialistic." These non-Communist nations have no true "social values," such as the Soviet Union preaches from its political pulpits but does not practice in its daily life. For instance, Communist propagandists claim with pride that the Soviet system provides every man with a job. Unemployment, the prime cause of poverty and social instability, has been wiped out in Russia, in theory at least. However, in reality, the Soviet rulers have fashioned a social system that is every bit as "materialistic" as a $500-a-night Park Avenue call girl.

The whole of Russian society is divided into two groups, best and accurately termed the haves and the have-nots. There is an elite ruling class, which shares one common status emblem, membership in the Communist Party. The Party itself comprises some 16 million Russians over eighteen years of age, or about 9% of the total Russian population of 193 million. Every responsible official in the Soviet government must be a party member. In addition to the officials and leading bureaucrats, the top-ranking officers of the armed forces and of the state security police (KGB), the leading industrial managers, scientists, and technicians (with a few exceptions), and even the outstanding members of the artistic, literary, and entertainment worlds must of necessity be true-blue Communists. The government, as well as the control of the assets and resources of the Soviet Union, is firmly in the hands of this elite group. They jealously guard their privileged status in life. Membership in the party is open only to those candidates whose talents and loyalties demonstrate clearly that they will serve to perpetuate the "dictatorship of the proletariat" in its present oligarchic form and character.

The have-nots are the great masses of Russians outside the charmed circle of the Communist Party, whom Karl Marx himself so aptly called *das Lumpenproletariat*, "the ragged proletariat."[7] They are the traditional humble figures of the human tableau—the drawers of water, the hewers of wood, the toiling peasants, the grimy industrial workers—whose collective efforts somehow keep the country functioning in its own piecemeal fashion.

What sharply separates the two groups of Russian society is a simple economic fact of life. A ruble earned by a member of the *Lumpenproletariat* has not the same purchasing power as the same ruble in the hands of a member of the elite ruling class. This situation is a matter of supreme importance in a country where there is always a chronic shortage of food and other necessities, not to mention the occasional luxury expenditure. In short, though the Russian worker has guaranteed employment and a steady income, he can't buy what he wants for himself and his family. Consumer goods, even the most elemental, such as pots and pans and simple household appliances, as well as food, are always in short supply. In contrast to the plight of the *Lumpenproletariat*, a Communist bureaucrat earns a ruble salary that has substantial purchasing power. He buys what he needs in special stores, which provide him with unrationed food and consumer goods. The general public is barred from these shopping centers for the privileged classes. In the Soviet Union one's own personal living standard is governed not by the money in one's pocket, but by one's position in the social hierarchy.

Each level and sector of the ruling elite has its own network of shops. These outlets, hidden behind nameless doorways, have greater and more varied supplies of food, household appliances, and foreign-made articles the higher one progresses up the bureaucratic ladder. Promotion always opens up new vistas of a better, more comfortable way of life. A bigger apartment in the city, a *dacha* or summer house in the countryside, the opportunity to travel abroad, good education for the children, the best of medical care in special clinics reserved for the party members, a car with chauffeur, and other "perks" are reserved for those in the upper reaches of the party bureaucracy. All this exists in a Communist Russia, ostensibly dedicated to the principle of social equality. So quite obviously this privileged class has a vested interest in preserving its way of life at all costs. Its members are the new middle class, dedicated to the maintenance of the status quo.

The masses have some consolations. There is a thriving black

---

[7] *Lumpenproletariat* was the literary creation of Karl Marx, who first used it in his *Communist Manifesto*, written in German and published in 1848. The expression suggests little love or respect for the great unwashed masses.

market in all the populated areas, where scarce food and consumer goods, from screwdrivers and light bulbs to blue jeans, are available if the price is right. In fact, this extralegal market economy has grown to such proportions that it is now estimated to equal about 10% of the gross national product, worth about $75 billion annually.[8] A large percentage of the goods sold on the black market are stolen by workers from their factories. The government officially admitted fifteen years ago that one quarter of all crimes committed involved thefts from the state.[9]

Another solace for the *Lumpenproletariat* is vodka, unrationed but expensive ($5 for a pint bottle). It is the escape route to ease the tensions and frustrations of the lower classes in Russia. Drunkenness is endemic and has been a major social problem for centuries. Today it is the prime cause of absenteeism in industry. Heavy drinking is a major factor in all crimes—in 90% of all murders, 50% of all traffic accidents, 40% of all divorces, 63% of all drownings—and in 33% of all ambulance calls.[10] The government's attitude toward this national vice is decidedly ambivalent. Occasionally campaigns are launched to reduce drinking, but the rate of consumption keeps on rising. The Soviet government enjoys a state monopoly on the production and sale of vodka. So this nullifies any serious temperance movement, occasionally suggested by the authorities.

When Stalin died on March 5, 1953, from a brain stroke in the Kremlin conference room of the Politburo, his reign of terror came to an abrupt halt, temporarily at least. Nikita Khrushchev soon grasped the reins of power as the successor to the tyrant. As an ambitious and energetic leader, he was aware that some drastic reforms were necessary if the "dictatorship of the proletariat"—that is, the control of the country by the Communist Party—was to be saved from disintegration. The situation was somewhat reminiscent of Lenin's famed "strategic retreat" of 1921, forced on him by the breakdown of the postwar-

---

[8]The *Economist* of London (Aug. 23, 1980) explored a prime factor of this development in a long editorial, as follows: "The most self-important bureaucrats in Russia are the local planners, who handle the requests by local factories and shops for allocations of raw materials, comfy shoes, etc. These bureaucrats used to get special job satisfaction from saying 'no' to those without political influence, while crawling obsequiously to those with it. But the gradual de-politicization during the 62-year-old revolution means that *more goods are allocated now in Russia through straight corruption.* An open market advance to freer price competition would rob lots of these important bureaucrats in the local Communist parties of their job satisfactions, their influence, their most lucrative source of income—and uncover scandals that would send some of them to prison." (Italics added.)

[9]*New York Times*, Nov. 22, 1980.

[10]Figures from Hedrick Smith, *The Russians* (New York: New York Times Book Co., 1976).

revolutionary economy in the early days of the Communist regime. Lenin introduced the New Economic Policy, a return to a modified free market system, to revive the production of food and other necessities, then virtually unobtainable either from the government or in the market place. But in reality, this short-lived period of ideological apostasy from the doctrines of Karl Marx was necessary to save the minority Communist government from being overthrown by an angry and rebellious civilian population. After Lenin's death in 1924, Stalin was able to assume full control of the instruments of power in the Kremlin. He killed off the NEP and restored full state control of the national economy in 1927. All industry was nationalized; all farms, great or small, were collectivized. Those opposing these rude changes were executed or shipped off by the millions to the new concentration camps in Siberia. In 1928, the first of a succession of five-year plans was introduced, which set up the production quotas for every category of industry. The basic idea behind it all was to avoid the ups and downs of the capitalistic system by requiring all industry and agriculture to be subject to a master planning blueprint drawn up by the Communist bureaucrats in Moscow. Every factory and every farm in the Soviet Union was to be monitored and controlled from the top down. On paper, this would avoid mass unemployment and guarantee every Russian the necessities of life, or so they theorized in their Marxian dialectics. In short, "the plan" prevailed over experience and history.

Khrushchev realized that if his economic and political reforms were to have any chance of being accepted, the Byzantine despotism of Stalin would first have to be discredited in the eyes of the top echelons of the Communist Party. In his famous "secret speech" to the 20th Party Congress of Feb. 24–25, 1956—he talked for more than six hours over a two-day session—Khrushchev detailed the crimes and the mistakes of Stalin and his government to a rapt but uneasy audience of fourteen hundred top party bureaucrats.[11]

But the ebullient and earthy Ukrainian, a former coal miner who rose through the party ranks to catch Stalin's attention, embarked on a series of reforms that can best be called erratic. He ordered a crash program to increase food supplies in the markets by opening up new farmlands in the wind-blown steppes of Kazakhstan. To stimulate industrial output, he tried to decentralize the planning and controls of the economy from Moscow to regional councils. He even loosened

---

[11]We know of the full contents of the speech because the CIA obtained a copy of it, which was then widely distributed throughout Western European governmental circles and the press.

Moscow's iron-fisted dominance of its satellite bloc. Freedom of expression and publication was partially restored to the intellectual world. Solzhenitsyn was allowed to publish *One Day in the Life of Ivan Denisovich*, a revelation of the true dimensions of Stalin's reign of terror. But in the end Khrushchev's reforms came to naught.

In October 1956, Hungary staged a political rebellion, ousting Communist boss Erno Gero and replacing him with Imre Nagy, an advocate of liberal policies, contrary to the "master plan" laid down by Moscow. The Russians quickly put down the insurrection with the Red Army, at a cost of thousands of Hungarian dead. Gosplan, the central planning agency in Moscow, regained control of the management of Russia's economy from the short-lived regional councils. The attempt to make agriculture more efficient and productive by opening up new farmlands in the east led to one disastrous harvest after another. And the brief spell of freedom enjoyed by the writers and intellectuals was ended by the resumption of national censorship. Though having been briefly subject to questioning, the Stalinist power structure was never actually dismantled under Khrushchev's program of reform. As the *Economist* of London (March 4, 1978) pointed out:

> . . . the main reason for Khrushchev's failure was more fundamental.
> . . . He was trying to overhaul the system from above, with the help of an apparatus which needed to preserve the system in order to preserve itself. To get rid of Stalinism, it would have been necessary to attack the power and privileges of the huge bureaucracy, the party secretaries from Moscow on down to the smallest district; the host of functionaries at all levels in the machinery of administration, the police and the armed forces. Not all these *apparatchiks* enjoyed the life of the men at the very top, with their dachas, their chauffeur-driven limousines and their exclusive shops. But all owed their status and their creature comforts, such as they were, to the hierarchical structure established by Stalin. After Stalin's death they wanted only one reassurance: that, for them at least, the five o'clock knock would be the milkman's. From Stalin's successors they demanded security of tenure, the chance after years of bloody purges, to enjoy their positions in peace and quiet.

Nikita Khrushchev was too radical and unpredictable for the predominant old-guard conservative faction in the Kremlin. He was booted from his post as secretary-general of the Party into the netherlands of civilian life in October 1964. His replacement was Leonid Brezhnev, while Alexei Kosygin took over as premier.

The industrial growth rate had been steadily declining under Khrushchev's administration. So Kosygin was authorized to carry out another program of economic reforms, which allegedly involved permitting a profit system to revive the sagging economy. The state-owned industrial enterprises would be allowed more authority to initiate their own plans, to make their own direct-sales contracts and price arrangements with their customers, and to retain a larger percentage of their profits for investment purposes.

The inspiration for this program was Prof. Yevsei Liberman, an economist from Kharkhov University who wanted to eliminate state controls as far as possible. The program attracted widespread attention in the foreign press. *Fortune* magazine (August 1966) headlined an article on the Liberman program: RUSSIA: THE ECONOMIC REVOLUTION.

Certainly, wide-ranging changes were required to make such a program produce more capital and consumer goods. For example, Soviet economists at that time estimated that between 25% and 50% of Russia's potential output was lost because of faulty planning. Every one of the nation's 200,000 industrial enterprises had been saddled with its own "plan" and quota. Each factory manager had not only the masterminds in Moscow closely checking on his performance, but also the local Communist Party bosses, who were constantly looking over his shoulder and quite free with their own special demands and criticism. The "quota system" fastened onto industry was faulty because it was solely based on quantity production, not on quality or, more important, on what was needed by the consuming public as a whole. The inherent weakness of this system was compounded by the incentives which it offered the managers and workers in each factory. If they met their monthly production quota, they were eligible for a bonus. Hence, any interruption in the factory's operations, such as would be caused by the installation of new and more efficient machinery or a new manufacturing process, was resisted. Such interruptions would reduce the factory's chances of meeting its production target, even though in the long run it might manufacture better and more needed capital and consumer goods. As a result, there has been little incentive to modernize a factory, or to take advantage of new inventions. For instance, it takes about one year for the Americans or the West Germans to put more than 50% of their new inventions into actual operation. In the Soviet Union, the same innovation process takes on the average of three years.

This is clearly demonstrated in the utilization of machine tools. The Soviet Union has about 2 million machine tools, or about two-thirds as many as are in operation in the United States. But in Russia only half the machine tools are in daily use; the other half are idle or being repaired. A survey showed that 80% of the decisions made to replace machinery in the factories were because the machines in question were so worn out as to be beyond repair; the other 20% were because the machines were too obsolete. As the *Economist* of London (Dec. 29, 1979) further expands on this crucial problem of Russian industry:

The penalty of hanging onto the assets until they become worn out comes in the form of huge repair bills. Capital repairs in the Soviet industry add up to *one-quarter of all gross investment and occupy one-tenth of the entire industrial work force.* . . . It has always been the proud claim of Soviet leaders that socialism helps modernisation while capitalism represses it. Experience suggests the opposite. [Italics added.]

There is abundant information available in the West to confirm the backward state of Soviet industry. What is clearly apparent is that the quota-plus-bonus system is, in the final analysis, self-defeating. It serves to reduce, rather than to increase, Soviet productivity of light and heavy industry.

Furthermore, political developments effectively sabotaged Kosygin's highly publicized economic reforms even before the program was put into operation. To achieve the profits and quality production set forth as goals, the factory manager had to have the power to fix his own wage scales and get rid of unproductive or redundant workers. This practice, however, might encourage the workers to organize, as did the Polish shipyard workers in September 1980, forcing the Communist government to accede to their demands. And an independent trade-union movement was the last thing the Kremlin wanted to see develop in the U.S.S.R. So the reform program began to collapse, hastened by events in neighboring Czechoslovakia.

As it had earlier in Hungary, in January 1968 a liberalization movement exploded in Czechoslovakia. Antonin Novotny, the Stalinist boss, was deposed as party chief and succeeded by Alexander Dubcek. Dubcek announced that henceforth "Communism would be made democratic." Frightened by this breakaway, Moscow ordered the Red Army, plus forces from the Warsaw Pact nations, to invade Czechoslovakia and to snuff out this flickering revolt. What had happened in Prague shocked the men in the Kremlin. They were given a demonstration of how swiftly any loosening of economic and political controls in a Communist society could develop into a serious challenge to their own bureaucratic "dictatorship of the proletariat." And so quickly, under Brezhnev, the old order was restored and reinforced. Prof. Liberman disappeared from the scene and little more was heard of his "reforms." And the industrial decline was allowed to continue inexorably downward. The growth rate of the Russian national income has dropped from 10.8% for the 1951–55 plan period down to 3% for the 1976–80 period. In the same time span, Russian capital investment, which had been steadily growing, reached a high of 12.3% in the early 1950s then dropped to 3.6% for the 1976–80 plan period. These figures show the steady deterioration of the domestic economy, despite the growing military strength of the Soviet Union.

Despite his failure to carry out any basic economic reforms that would free the Soviet economy from the stranglehold of the party bureaucrats, Alexei Kosygin scored one triumph. He was the author of the policy of détente. It was probably the most successful foreign-policy innovation in the postwar history of Russia, in terms of what it obtained for the Soviet Union from the western industrial nations.

Kosygin began agitating for closer East-West economic relations in the 1960s. He persuaded Party Chairman Leonid Brezhnev to endorse détente as a substitute for economic reform on the home front, which had been constantly undermined or sabotaged by the government officials and party bureaucrats. Détente allowed for the import of badly needed industrial goods and technology from the western nations without, at the same time, opening up the country to dangerous and subversive political ideas from the western democracies. Besides, the Soviet Union was able to buy western capital goods and equipment on easy lines of credit.[12] Today, Russia is approximately $19 billion in debt for this influx of goods.

Considering the lack of discipline and the technological inexperience of the Russian workmen, it was decided to import and install complete industrial or technological units from the West, as far as circumstances permitted. A prime example of this was the Togliatti automobile plant on the Volga River. It was named after the late Italian Communist leader Palmiro Togliatti, because Italy's Fiat automobile company was both the prime contractor and the supplier of all the basic equipment. All the planning was also done by the Italians. The Togliatti plant can produce about 600,000 small passenger vehicles a year, a portion of which are exported under the trade name Lada.

In 1974, President Richard M. Nixon made his well-publicized visit to Moscow to make détente official, as the two superpowers publicly announced they were friends and not enemies. Nixon stayed within the walls of the Kremlin during this visit, exemplifying his trust in Brezhnev and his Politburo colleagues. However, shortly

---

[12]"Almost all the advanced instrumentation in Soviet laboratories is imported," *Time* magazine reported in its special issue "Inside the U.S.S.R.," June 23, 1980.

thereafter Brezhnev addressed a secret session of the top level of the party hierarchy, stating: "For a while, we will cooperate with the capitalists so as to benefit from the modernization of our technology and agriculture." Brezhnev then went on to state that a massive rearmament program was under way and that by about 1985, the American military advantages would have been canceled out. From that point on the Soviet Union would have the upper hand in its relations with Western Europe.[13]

The question arises: If the economy of the Soviet Union is in such perilous shape, how is it possible for the Russians to produce atomic-powered submarines and bombers that equal or surpass America's, put spaceships into the outer atmosphere, and field armed forces that possess the greatest concentration of conventional and nuclear weaponry in the hands of any nation today? The answer is to be found in the fact that there is an "industrial-military complex" functioning in the Soviet Union, somewhat similar to one which exists in the United States to service the needs of the Pentagon. The industrial production of Russia operates on three levels. Top priority is to equip and maintain the army, navy, and air force; second priority is to supply the limited export market, mainly to the Communist-bloc countries; and what is left of industrial and consumer goods is for the domestic economy.

The armed forces can directly handle their own planning and supervise the production of weapons and ancillary equipment, including the aerospace program and communications. These are top-priority fields. They command the best of technology, materials, and machinery available, as well as skilled workers. They have their own manufacturing plants and their production is rigidly governed by quality; they reject the "quantity-quota" system that applies to the civilian economy. This explains why 10–15%, or perhaps much more, of the gross national product is allocated to the armed forces at the expense of the civilian needs. The workers serving these privileged sectors of the economy are more skilled and get higher pay than those employed in producing goods for civilian consumption. Because exports have to compete with foreign goods as to price and quality, this second sector of industry also enjoys greater freedom and flexibility from the planners in Moscow in setting its own standards. The civilian sector is at the bottom of the list of industrial priorities, which ex-

[13]Sources for this information were twofold: a speech by U.S. Admiral Harry Train given to a NATO Defense Ministers' executive session in Brussels in December 1980, and a long and factual report about Brezhnev's speech published in the Oct. 15, 1980, edition of *Die Welt*, a national daily newspaper in West Germany.

plains in large part the erratic and shoddy production of domestic goods.

George W. Ball, financier and former undersecretary of state in the Kennedy and Johnson administrations, points out that ". . . the Soviets' most widely heralded production achievement is military hardware, primarily because the military constitute the only consumers with the powers to reject or return inferior merchandise—or, in other words, the only effective market force in the whole Soviet system."[14]

The Soviet Union is already paying a stiff price for the massive buildup of its armed forces in recent years. This toll on the debilitated Russian economy will continue to rise, unless there is a drastic change in the nation's order of priorities. Russia is plagued with a severe manpower crisis, but before exploring this aspect some pertinent background must be considered. Squandering of human life has been profligate in Communist Russia, particularly during the years when Josef Stalin was the unchallenged despot in the Kremlin. His government is estimated to have been responsible for between 43 million and 56 million unnatural deaths for the period 1927–58, covering the years of Stalin's government by terror.[15] These figures include deaths caused by political repressions and by the casualties of World War II, which, by themselves, totaled a staggering 30 million men, women, and children. Then, in addition, some 13 to 22 million people died before and after the war as a result of the forced collectivization of farms, the elimination of anti-Soviet minorities, famine, and blood purges, including the genocidal death rates exacted by the Siberian prison labor camps.

As a result, there was no "baby boom" in the Soviet Union after World War II, as there was in many other countries, particularly in the United States. So today there is a large gap in the population structure between the young and the old, which should be filled by the normal component of middle-aged people. But the bodies are not there be-

[14]From George W. Ball, *The Past Has Another Pattern* (New York: W.W. Norton, 1982).

[15]The source for this amazing report is Iosif Dyadkin, a geophysicist from Kalininsk on the Volga, who sought to make a compilation based on official governmental statistics of just how many Russians died unnatural deaths during Stalin's bloody regime of terror and oppression. He has since been arrested by the KGB and has disappeared. However, a copy of his report reached the West and Aleksandr Solzhenitsyn, author of *The Gulag Archipelago.* He has endorsed it as accurate. Murray Feshbach, an internationally recognized expert of the U.S. Census Bureau who specializes in Soviet demographics, has also stated that the Dyadkin report "looked like a very serious evaluation."

cause they perished in World War II and in Stalin's political purges. Their absence shows up in the falling birthrate.

Coupled with the manpower shortage, there is an alarming rise in infant mortality in the Soviet Union, to an estimated 35 to 40 per 1,000 births, compared to 12.7 per 1,000 in the United States. In the mid-1970s the Russian government stopped publishing these and other vital statistics, but information contained in various technical and medical journals has enabled western demographic experts to discover what has been happening in Russia. In June 1980 the U.S. Census Bureau published a detailed report on the current population changes in the U.S.S.R. It found that a prime cause for rising infant mortality was "fetal alcohol syndrome"—that is, hard-drinking pregnant women give birth to babies less able to survive their first rude contacts with the world outside the sheltering womb. Inadequate feeding and poor-quality baby foods also contribute to rising infant mortality. Coincident with this development is the fact that Soviet women, at least in populated centers, have an average of six abortions during their childbearing years.

Meanwhile the Soviet adult, who in the 1950s enjoyed a longer life expectancy than his American counterpart, is now dying off at an earlier age. In the last decade the life expectancy of the Russian male has declined from sixty-six to sixty-three years while that of the American male has risen to over seventy years.

The significance of these reports about dying babies and declining life cycles, encapsuled in the dull statistics of demographics, indicates that the Soviet Union is going through a general and widespread—at least in all urban areas where 60% of the population now live—deterioration of public-health care. It also means that money that should be spent for public health and welfare is being siphoned off to finance the military-industrial complex. The Russian civilian population suffers as a direct result.

This alarming development is bringing about a change in the once puritanical attitude of the Russian Communists about sexuality and its place in modern society. Lenin had warned his colleagues in the early days of the Bolshevik regime that "dissoluteness in sexual life is bourgeois." That was the ultimate in pejorative dismissal of what in other countries is regarded as one of the pleasures that never palls, never loses its appeal to all members of the human race. Now a number of sex clinics are opening their doors in the Soviet Union. However, their main objective is not primarily to educate young men and women about the joys and pleasures of sex, but rather to stimulate the falling birthrate. Dr. Tanghiz Meshki, director of Zhordania Institute, a sex clinic in Tbilisi, explained to an American journalist: "Our basic task is to make marriages more fertile; to help people produce more children."[16] Because there is not so much warm romance in the cold climate of the Soviet Union, Dr. Meshki and his fellow sexologists have their work cut out for them for years ahead.

Before his death, Premier Kosygin publicly admitted that the Soviet Union would experience a serious shortage of 8 million workers for the next five years. He also said he could foresee no increase in the labor force for the next ten to fifteen years. The Soviet Union does not have the money, or the lines of credit, to purchase the necessary technology and modern industrial equipment from the West—even provided it could do so—to bring its industrial level up to western standards. Automation and robot production are many years away, at least on a broad-scale basis. Hence, most of the big Soviet industrial projects on the drawing boards will be labor-intensive. One reason for their delay is the dwindling supply of workers.

To partially alleviate the worker shortage, the Soviet Union has been importing several hundred thousand workers from Vietnam. Reportedly this involves forcible exportation by the Communist government in Hanoi of thousands of political dissidents. Western diplomats are quoted as saying that Hanoi's main incentive in exporting this labor to Russia is its $3 billion foreign debt, including $1.6 billion to the Soviet Union for the massive assistance Vietnam received in its wars in Indochina.[17]

Industrial production is dependent on having skilled foremen, technicians, maintenance workers, and others who are adept with machinery. And these categories are in the shortest supply in the Soviet Union. The truly skilled "middlemen" of industry such as one finds in Ruhr steel plants, on Detroit automobile assembly lines, and in Japanese shipyards are not to be found in comparable numbers in the Soviet Union.

Another factor in the labor shortage is the yearly conscription of about a million eighteen-year-old Russian males into the armed forces. They must serve a minimum of two years in the army or air force or three years in the navy. The Soviet Union has 3.6 million men in uniform, compared to 4 million in Red China (an estimated figure which is hard to document) and about 1.5 million in the United States.

Nowhere is the labor shortage more apparent or so damaging as it

[16]Quoted by Moscow correspondent Jim Gallagher, in the *Chicago Tribune*, Oct. 29, 1980.
[17]This information has been reported by the *Wall Street Journal* (March 24, 1982); by the United Press International (Nov. 4, 1981); and the London *Economist* (Sept. 17, 1981); and by a number of French newspapers in December 1981.

is in agriculture. Soviet food production is declining because the collective farm system is affected with a terminal illness: It provides no stake in the future for the individual worker. The root of the problem goes back to the brutal and ultimately successful campaigns of Josef Stalin in the 1930s to break the back of the stubborn political resistance of the millions of kulaks, the property-owning peasants, to the expropriation of all their farmlands. Those who opposed were driven off in slavery to the labor camps of distant Siberia; others died by the millions in defending their right to own their own farms. But in the ensuing years the yoke of state control on agriculture has always chaffed this great beast of burden.

Russia has two-thirds more land under cultivation than the United States, yet its net output is only about four-fifths of what America produces in food and grains. In Russia about 20% of the nation's work force is employed on the collectivized farms compared to 4% in America, but every year the Communist Party has to literally dragoon hundreds of thousands of students, old-age pensioners, and industrial workers to help gather in the harvest. The best and the brightest of the men and boys born on the farms have migrated to big cities. They have left behind a work force that is 65% female. The collectivized farms are short of tractors, drivers and mechanics, crop sprayers, and bookkeepers—in fact, most of the skilled help needed to operate an agribusiness, which is what, in theory at least, a collective farm should be. For example, in the northern, western, and central sections of European Russia, where the labor shortage has been acute, in the last four years (1976–80) almost half a million young men were trained to operate combines and tractors. As of today, only about fifty thousand have *remained* on the farms to handle these machines.

The Soviet government has been fully aware of the deficiencies of food and grain production, but the corrective measures never seemed to have any beneficial results. Then in 1977 the so-called Soviet Constitution was changed, by a Kremlin decree, to permit every farmer to own and cultivate a small plot of ground. He can sell whatever he grows or raises on it on the open market for his own profit. The individual plot could be no larger than a half-hectare (1.25 acres) and the amount of livestock was also limited to a few animals. However, a new decree of Jan. 17, 1981, makes additional land available for private farming and the number of animals (cows, pigs, and chickens) can be increased.

These tiny private plots are only 1.4% of the total land under cultivation in the Soviet Union. Yet, incredible as it may seem, they produce nearly one-third of all the meat and milk consumed in Russia, a third of all vegetables, almost a third of all eggs, and almost a fifth of all wool.[18] This development is a startling example of what the profit incentive can add to the GNP. Now the upper echelons are encouraging private production of food by the peasants as an immediate means to alleviate the food shortage. This new post-Stalin breed of kulaks is certainly much more efficient than the collective farmer. For example, these private plots average about 4 kilograms (9 pounds) of grain to produce 1 kilogram (2 pounds) of meat, while a collective farm requires almost 13 kilograms (30 pounds) of feed to produce the same amount of meat.

But the managers and other key employees of the kolkhozes have been strongly opposing this development, fearing that government support and encouragement of "private" food production may divert investments, as well as equipment, from their state enterprises. Their means of fighting private farming are simple and effective. They can withhold pasturage, as well as seed, from the owners of small plots for their livestock or for their planting of vegetables. Moreover, sale of the privately-produced food, meat, and dairy products can also be prohibited in the local kolkhoz's own market, and private farmers can be denied use of transport or the opportunity to buy young livestock from the herds of the kolkhoz. These measures effectively thwart government plans to encourage private production of food.

However, in the final analysis there are definite physical limitations on the output of these private plots: (1) their small acreage, and (2) the amount of time that the farmer or the farm woman—who also has to work on the kolkhoz—can devote to their own private farming. At the same time, farming implements for private use are very difficult to acquire. Mechanization of private plots could substantially increase their output if small motor-driven tractors or even tools, such as are commonplace in the United States, were available in Russia. A plant in Sverdlovsk wanted to manufacture hoes for small private farms, but the plan had to be abandoned when it was discovered that no approved Soviet standard for small hoes existed—and nobody was about to take the initiative to propose such a blueprint. And when a small machine plant in Pskov wanted to produce a small tractor for private farms, it was denied permission because it was not licensed as a manufacturer of agricultural machinery.

Collectivized farming—"nationalized agriculture" is, I think, a more accurate definition—has always been the Achilles heel of the Soviet Union. And so it is for other countries which have adopted the

---

[18]*New York Times*, May 24, 1982.

Marxist way of life. After the Russian Revolution of 1917, when the whole country was thrust into sustained chaos, even Lenin recognized that to get through this crucial gestation period for the embryonic new Soviet state, sufficient food had to be made available for the masses. He decreed the New Economic Policy (NEP), which among other concessions, reinstated private ownership by the peasants of their farms. Food came back into the public marketplaces. However, after Lenin's death in 1923, Stalin ordered the collectivization of all arable land. As Peter Drucker aptly put it: ". . . the collective farm [was] imposed on Russia just at a time when it had become technologically and economically the wrong agricultural system. . . . To abolish the collective farm altogether and to switch to large family farms producing for the market—the only truly efficient form of agriculture in Russia under modern technological conditions—is politically impossible and would require an overthrow of the regime."[19]

That is the dilemma facing the Kremlin leaders today, a dilemma that can be solved only by a second revolution, which is highly unlikely at this writing.

The Soviet Union covers 8,647,000 square miles; the United States covers 3,615,000 square miles. Obviously, for the economic health and progress of the Soviet Union, a functioning transport system is a priority. That goes double in spades for the armed forces, whose defense perimeters stretch from Central Europe in the west to the Pacific Ocean 7,000 miles to the east. Unlike western industrial nations, the Soviet Union is almost wholly dependent on its railway system for internal transport. It hauls 70% of all the freight shipments, an amount equal to approximately one-half of all the goods moved on all the world's railways. And the Soviet system has only about one-ninth of the world's railway trackage, which indicates the high degree of congestion and pressure on this transportation system.[20]

The Soviet Union has 82,828 miles of railroad track in operation, compared to 210,500 miles in the United States. The Russian railway network is completely inadequate for the volume of traffic it must handle and the obsolete rolling stock it utilizes. Quite surprisingly, Josef Stalin realized that an efficient railway system was vital to the

---

[19]Peter F. Drucker, *Management in Turbulent Times* (New York: Harper & Row, 1980).
[20]Figures from *New York Times*, Jan. 9, 1980.

economic survival of the U.S.S.R. During his tenure in office, in each five-year plan he allocated one-fifth of all capital investment to improve transport, including development of commercial aviation. However, his successors, Nikita Khrushchev and Leonid Brezhnev, slashed this transportation allotment to one-tenth in their subsequent five-year plans. Hence, after almost a quarter century of poor maintenance, the Soviet railway system—except for the prestige trains, such as the Trans-Siberian Express—finds it increasingly difficult to cope with the growing freight and passenger traffic. By the late 1970s the volume of rail traffic began to decline. This development had wide repercussions throughout industry and agriculture; goods piled up, raw materials did not reach the factories, and manufacturing in all categories has suffered.

Correspondent George Feifer reported in the London Sunday *Times* (July 20, 1980) on the growing disruption caused by the reduction in railroad operations. Feifer wrote that the shortage of transportation is so acute that even trains and rolling stock are "kidnapped" by those agencies, factories, or officials who cannot get transport of their goods or products from factory to consumer:

Commandeered locomotives are secretly worked in one district desperate to fulfill its plan—while trainloads of fruit rot in neighboring sidings. Other trains are driven empty up and down remote lines to attain bonus-producing mileage norms, while nearby bottlenecks explode for lack of wagons. Whole trains disappear, as did one recently from Kishinev for Odessa, 120 miles southeast. . . . It was officially confirmed that a second train sent to find the first also disappeared, as did three locomotives dispatched directly from the factory.

The Soviet Union transport system is further complicated by a wholly inadequate network of roads. In 1978 only half of the 1,423,500 kilometers (834,100 miles) were hard-surfaced and capable of handling trucks. By comparison the United States has over 3,100,000 miles of surfaced roads, which are heavily traveled by the nation's 130 million private and transport vehicles. And, as any German soldier who fought in Russia during World War II can testify, the dirt roads during the autumnal rains and springtime thaws become quagmires of mud, bringing heavy traffic to a virtual stop.

Russia's two largest cities, Moscow and Leningrad, are connected with a bumpy two-lane highway system, without lights or a center line. Other intercity roads are also of secondary quality. In Communist

Russia, the auto is a utilitarian transport, not a pleasure vehicle, except for the privileged few of the party elite.[21]

Far and away, the blue-chip economic asset of the Soviet Union is its abundance of energy resources—that is, if they can be fully exploited on a scale comparable to that in the Persian Gulf area. Today the U.S.S.R. is the world's largest oil producer, pumping out 11.9 million barrels a day, compared to Saudi Arabia's 9.5 million barrels. The vast landmass of the Soviet Union holds an estimated 60 billion barrels of oil reserves still untapped, compared to Saudi Arabia's 166 billion barrels of reserves and America's 26 billion.

On the Yamal Peninsula, a desolate finger of frozen wasteland that protrudes 150 miles north of the Arctic Circle, Soviet geologists have discovered what is reported to be the greatest untapped reserve of natural gas in the world—26 trillion cubic meters. At present, negotiations are underway to finance and build a $10–15 billion pipeline, stretching some 3,000 miles from this Arctic treasure trove to Waidhaus in West Germany. If all goes well, the Yamal Peninsula field will furnish 40 billion cbm of gas yearly to European consumers, supplying about 30% of the consumption in France and Germany. These two countries are expected to furnish the billions of dollars required to complete this massive pioneering project, and to be repaid in deliveries of natural gas.

If it comes on stream—1986 is target date to begin operations— the Yamal field should be a potent earner of hard currency for the Soviet Union. At present, exports of crude oil and natural gas account for about 50% of its hard-currency income, producing an annual revenue of $6–8 billion.

But this roseate picture of Soviet energy potentials is blurred by several major economic and technical factors—problems which can be solved only with a greater hard-currency income to pay for needed technology and drilling equipment, and with skilled manpower. And such income and manpower are currently in short supply.

The Soviet Union exports 3 million barrels of oil per day, of which 2 million go to its satellite states and 1 million are sold to Western European consumers. The production of oil is steadily falling. The original five-year plan covering the 1980 period shows a

---

[21]Party Chairman Leonid Brezhnev had no personal transportation problems to impinge on his daily life. In addition to official limousines, he had a garage full of luxury autos, including a Rolls-Royce (a gift from the British government), a Cadillac Eldorado (given to him by President Nixon), and a Mercedes-Benz (donated by the Bonn government). Communist Russia is analogous to George Orwell's *Animal Farm*, where "everybody is equal but some are more equal than the others."

decline in output from 620 million metric tons, as scheduled, to only 606 million tons. The production of other key products, such as electricity, coal, steel, timber, and concrete, have also dropped below the previous year's figures.

Early in 1981 it was disclosed that the Soviet Union had been reducing its oil exports to Western Europe by between 20% and 25%, while at the same time guaranteeing to supply the oil needs of the Warsaw Pact nations. This amounts to roughly 2 million barrels per day. These Eastern European nations receive about 80% of their oil from the Soviet Union, and any cut in their oil imports could swiftly impair their industrial and commercial operations and have dangerous political repercussions, such as its current situation in Poland.

Based on the general decline that has already set in, the CIA has reported that Russia's oil production will continue to drop, predicting a total output of only 8 million barrels per day by 1985. If this occurs, that means the satellite nations, which are mainly dependent on the U.S.S.R., will also be adversely affected by the reduction in fuel and energy. In the Soviet Union there are already large-scale energy-conservation campaigns under way. Construction of a second large automobile and truck manufacturing complex have been dropped. Plans to expand car production beyond the present million units yearly have been postponed. The reasons for the industrial slowdown are not hard to locate, they are tied up with the declining production of fuel and energy.

Modern technology is a major problem for Russia—one that is needed to overcome the severe energy obstacles posed by Mother Nature. The large oil and gas reserves are located mainly in the northern latitudes of distant Siberia, the icebox of the world for nine months of the year. They are found in the depths of Siberia's forested lands and tundra, hitherto largely inaccessible to man. To survey and to drill these oil and gas fields, entire new transportation systems have to be built to bring in the necessary equipment and infrastructure. Moreover, the Russians have learned that they cannot produce the high-quality steel necessary for use in pipelines from the Siberian wellheads. In the depths of the Arctic winter, ordinary steel becomes brittle, shattering like glass if put under heavy pressure. So the Soviet engineers have had to import their steel pipe from Germany; Mannesmann of Düsseldorf, one of the world's leading pipe and tube producers, has finally developed a quality steel that can successfully resist the Siberian "frostbite," which can drop down to 60 degrees below zero Fahrenheit—and stay there for weeks at a time.

A second technical problem which has yet to be solved is the obsolescence of Soviet equipment. Russian engineers take fourteen months to drill down to 10,000 feet, while American teams can reach the same depth in thirty-four days. Russian seismic equipment is also far behind American standards. So while there are major oil and gas reserves buried below the frozen Siberian tundra, as well as other mineral riches, the Russians are not yet able to extract them from the earth at a rate commensurate with the rising energy consumption in the Soviet Union and the member countries of the Communist bloc. It has been estimated that Russia needs $35 billion in capital investment to "open up Siberia with its vast wealth of mineral resources."[22]

The litany of Russia's economic woes and problems is virtually endless. The country's tragedy is that despite its resources and its disciplined society, it simply cannot function as a modern industrial power—at least not one able to compete against the western industrial nations. The Soviet Union operates on the basic principle that economic growth and development on the civilian front must be subordinated to the international political and economic objectives laid down by the Politburo in the Kremlin. In other words, politics controls economics. What this means in practice is that the Russians have committed their economic potential and resources to the strengthening and modernization of their armed forces. The principal instrument of Soviet foreign policy is its raw military power.

Russia today is like a giant porcupine. The front it presents to an adversary is bristling with weapons. But if rolled over on its back, it exposes its soft underbelly—its weak and faltering economy. The ruling Communist Party has failed to keep its promises and obligations to the Russian people. The promised "workers' paradise" is still a political mirage. Instead, the "dictatorship of the proletariat" has sought world dominance. It has squandered the nation's wealth and resources, to the fullest extent they could be mobilized, to transform the Union of Soviet Socialist Republics into the world's strongest military power.

It is probable that the cause of this serious threat to Russia's economic health and progress can be traced back to the Cuban missile crisis of October 1962. By a swift mobilization of U.S. naval and air forces, President John F. Kennedy forced Chairman Nikita Khrushchev to withdraw Soviet nuclear missiles from Cuba, when they had been surreptitiously installed with the approval of Fidel Castro. For

[22]*Economist*, Dec. 29, 1979. That is the sum necessary to buy the technology to make this vast project economically feasible and viable. However, the Soviet Union has *already* incurred debts of about $19 billion to western nations for imports of their industrial goods and technology. Western bankers are worrying whether the eastern bloc can settle these accounts as they come due.

Khrushchev and the members of the Politburo, as well as the generals and admirals of the Soviet armed forces, it was a humiliation that was to have some profound repercussions in the years to come.

Confirmation of this top-level Soviet reaction to the retreat from Cuba is to be found in the following episode. Vassily V. Kuznetzsov, a senior Russian diplomat, was assigned to negotiate the final details of the Soviet withdrawal from Cuba with lawyer-ambassador John J. McCloy, then on special assignment to the U.S. State Department. At the conclusion of their collaboration, Kuznetsov turned to McCloy to make a final bitter rejoinder: "This is the last time you Americans will ever be able to do *this* to us."

From that point on, the Russians began the full-scale buildup of their army, navy, and air forces. Never again would there be a second "retreat from Cuba." To coordinate this program Brezhnev appointed the head of the armed forces, Marshal Dimitri Ustinov, as well as Yuri Andropov, chief of the KGB, to membership on the Politburo. It was also a form of political life insurance for Brezhnev and his colleagues at the top of the party bureaucracy. It was better to have the leaders of the armed forces and the security police inside the tent than on the outside, as a precaution against possible coups d'état.

What can be expected in the foreseeable future, judging from the past performance of the Russians? By 1980 it was widely recognized in Washington, as well as in European capitals, that the military balance of power was definitely tilting in favor of the Soviet Union. Recognizing the widening gap between the American and Russian armed forces, the U.S. Congress and the White House embarked on a multi-billion-dollar program to restore the military imbalance between the two superpowers. This will take time; it probably will not be accomplished before 1985, under the best of circumstances.

But the Russians are not expected to sit idly by and let the Americans regain a state of parity, thus wiping out Russia's temporary military advantage. They want to maintain their credibility as the more dynamic of the two superpowers: Russia is in the ascendancy, getting stronger and more powerful with every passing day, while the United States is in a state of political and economic decline, the "ultimate fate of all capitalist states." That is the scenario written by the Kremlin as its version of the present state of affairs in this changing and turbulent world. However, the members of the Soviet Politburo are not wild-eyed, irresponsible jingoists—their average age is seventy at this writing. They are not likely to risk a shooting war with the United States. The military balance of power has not tilted *that* far against the Americans at this stage.

CHAPTER TWO

The Third World Deception

In the 21st century population structure and population may well again be stable. But in the last decades of the 20th century, population structures will be the least stable and the most drastically changing element in economics, society and world politics, and probably the single most important cause of turbulence.
—PETER F. DRUCKER, *Managing in Turbulent Times*
(New York: Harper & Row, 1980)

Socialism has been nothing but capitalism of the lower classes.
—OSWALD SPENGLER, *Jahr der Entscheidung*
(The Year of Decision), 1933

THE most successful mass deception of modern times has been perpetrated by the Third World, a collective term to cover the backward, as well as developing, nations of Africa, Asia, and Latin America. In reality, there is no Third World as a distinct political, economic, or geographical entity. Instead there is a conglomerate of some hundred extremely varied states which share only one thing in common: They live off foreign aid supplied to them by the affluent and industrial (developed) nations of the free world. Prof. P.T. Bauer of the London School of Economics put it neatly: "The Third World and foreign aid are inseparable. Without foreign aid there is no Third World. The latter is, in effect, the collection of countries, whose governments, with the odd exception, demand and receive foreign aid."[1]

In other words, the Third World is an instrument to extract as much wealth and technology from the rich and industrially developed nations as the traffic will bear. It is a grandiose and unabashed international "share-the-wealth" program. It is motivated by envy and resentment, which in turn nourish some of the most pervasive myths that have ever gripped the imagination of man. Primary among them is a hardy perennial: All men are created equal. Therefore, all men are entitled to share equally in the fortunes of the world we live in, as well as in the opportunities for individual advancement and enrichment. The second myth which finds wide acceptance around the world is an accusation that has become dogma with constant repetition: The Third World countries are poor, backward and undeveloped because

[1]P.T. Bauer, "The Harm That Foreign Aid Does," *Wall Street Journal*, June 9, 1980.

of the "pillage" of their raw materials and "conspiracies" to depress world prices covering these vital commodities by the affluent industrial nations.

A typical example of this rhetoric about colonial exploitation came from Kwame Nkrumah when he was president of Ghana. In his book *Africa Must Unite*, Nkrumah traduced the white European colonial administrations as follows:

> They were all rapacious; they subserved the needs of the subject lands to their own demands; they circumscribed all human rights and liberties; they all repressed and despoiled, degraded and oppressed. They took our lands, our lives, our resources and our dignity. Without exception they left us nothing but our resentment. . . . It was when they had gone and we were faced with the stark realities, as in Ghana on the morrow of our independence, that the destitution of the land after long years of colonial rule was brought sharply home to us.[2]

However, Kwame Nkrumah neglected to mention other important aspects of British colonial rule of his country, once known as the Gold Coast. For example, in the early 1900s there were only three thousand children being educated; by the 1950s about half a million boys and girls were learning their "three R's." By the 1930s the colony had a network of roads and a railway system which opened up its agriculture to world markets. When the Gold Coast became independent the sum of $240 million was on deposit in London banks to the credit of the Cocoa Marketing Board, established and operated by the colonial administration. This very substantial fund was turned over to President Nkrumah of the newly independent Ghana to finance its start in life as a sovereign nation. That seems to be a new form of reverse "pillage."

Then there is a never-ending stream of complaints from Julius Nyerere, president of Tanzania. Though his country has received more foreign aid on a per capita basis than any other nation of black Africa, Nyerere repeats and repeats the accusation that the rich nations are getting richer and richer at the expense of the poor countries of the world.

Robert Mugabe and Kenneth Kaunda, respectively presidents of Zimbabwe and Zambia, the two major copper-producing countries in Africa, have constantly charged that the western industrial nations have conspired to depress world copper prices, at the same time giving the impression that these two countries are the major sources of supply for this metal. They probably are unaware that "the mines of

---

[2] Kwame Nkrumah, *Africa Must Unite* (London: Heineman, 1963).

Butte, Montana, had produced by the second half of the 20th century more copper than any other single area in the world."[3] It is highly unlikely that the Anaconda Copper Co., which has developed the rich Butte copper lodes, was or is engaged in any conspiracy to depress world copper prices and thus harm its own major investment in U.S. copper production. In fact, the continued operation of copper mining at Butte, Montana, was and still is an assurance that Zambia and Zimbabwe got a "fair" price—that is, the going world price—for their own copper output.

The world is in a state of transition, no longer dividing along old ideological lines: the Communist bloc versus the NATO powers. The cold war is giving way to a new struggle between the rich industrial nations headed by the United States, on one side, and the Third World developing countries hugging the equatorial latitudes of Africa, Asia, and Latin America on the other side. The latter bloc is supported by their powerful allies, the Soviet Union and its satellites, Red China, and oil-producing states of the OPEC cartel. Hence the political compass reading shifts from the familiar "East-West" to the new "North-South" confrontation.

The central theme of this international conflict is basically economic: the abrasive clash between liberal-capitalistic societies (the affluent industrial nations) and those societies of varying political structures—Marxist, socialist, and unadulterated military dictatorship (the last group especially prevailing in black Africa)—which are poor, backward, or both, and are opposed to liberal capitalism in principle. That is why these less-developed countries are always attacking the United States. They are never critical of Soviet Russia. And as Prof. Irving Kristol has pointed out: "Indeed the very definition of the Third World entails hostility towards liberal capitalism. Otherwise, how can one explain why Saudi Arabia, Cuba and Algeria are fully accredited members of the Club, whereas Israel, Taiwan, South Korea and Turkey are not?"[4]

It is somewhat ironic that the United States government, long before the Marxist ideologues in the Kremlin, foresaw the inevitability of the emergence of the Third World as one of the results of World War II. President Franklin Delano Roosevelt, in the closing months of his life, made it abundantly clear that U.S. military power would not be used to restore to Great Britain, France, and the Netherlands the

[3]*Encyclopaedia Britannica*, 1971 edition.
[4]Irving Kristol in the *Wall Street Journal*, July 17, 1978.

colonies they had lost to the conquering Japanese armies. After the surrender of Japan, FDR was determined that the governance of these former colonies would be handed over to their native leaders. As the acknowledged leader of the Allied powers, postwar America was in a position to ring down the curtain on the colonial era of modern history.

Thus began the dissolution of the once great colonial empires in the Far East, Asia, and Africa. Reluctantly the governments in London, Paris, The Hague, and Brussels came to the realization that their rich colonial domains could not be restored to their prewar status. With as much dignity and prestige as they could muster, they lowered their flags in Hanoi, Batavia (now Jakarta), Singapore, New Delhi, and other former colonial capitals.

However, these events in Asia and Africa were largely overshadowed by postwar developments in Europe: the beginning of the cold war and the Russian challenge to the Americans for the postwar dominance of Europe. The prize in the struggle was defeated Germany, which straddles Central Europe. As recent history has amply demonstrated, whichever power is in control of this chunk of Middle Europe can be the decisive force on the Continent.

After the war, the Russians had full military and political control of East Germany (population 17 million). They also wanted to take over what is now West Germany (population about 55 million, including 10 million refugees from East Prussia, Poland, Czechoslovakia, etc.), so as to extend the political frontiers of the Soviet Union to the Rhine River. At the end of World War II, when the Nazi armies were finally driven to surrender, Europe was a looted and devastated continent. Europe itself was incapable of resurrection to a viable political and economic existence without outside help and assistance. It was ripe for political takeover by the stronger of the victorious powers.

At this point in the delicate and crucial competition over postwar spheres of influence on the stricken European continent, the United States played its ace card. It offered the Marshall Plan to restore economic life and hope to a moribund Europe, including defeated Germany. A $15 billion program of grants of food, raw materials for industrial production, machinery, and other necessities was provided to revive economic life in Western Europe, with no strings attached. Defeated Germany, the western half occupied by the American, British, and French armies, was to receive almost $4 billion from the Marshall Plan funds. This stroke of enlightened foreign policy was decisive. It immunized Western Europe against the further spread of the virus of Communism. It laid the foundations for the secure rebuilding of postwar Western Europe. It accomplished these objectives not with military force, or even the threat to use it. Rather it employed *ecopolitical* power, the employment of economic resources to achieve a political objective, i.e., halting the westward push of the Soviet sphere of influence.

The importance of the Marshall Plan lay in the fact that it quickly taught U.S. officials—and the postwar governments of Truman and Eisenhower included some of the brightest and most sophisticated, internationally minded men ever to serve the government in Washington—that economic measures could be as effective a foreign-policy tool as sheer military strength. It was truly a watershed in the development of the United States as a world power. This was the genesis of the U.S. "foreign aid," which has become an integral part of American foreign policy ever since. In fact, by Jan. 1, 1975, the United States had poured out a total of "loans"—a great part of which will never be collectible—as well as outright monetary grants totaling $172 billion.[5]

Extending financial help, either to buy friends or to fend off or disarm potential enemy countries, was not invented in Washington. For years France, Britain, Germany, and other European powers have used financial handouts as an integral part of foreign policy. Before World War II, French "loans" to Balkan countries were effective instruments to implement the Quai d'Orsay's prewar foreign policy in this trouble spot of Europe. However, never in history has any nation equaled the financial scope of the U.S. "foreign aid" program, either in total volume or on a proportionate basis.

President Truman's Point IV program followed on the heels of the Marshall Plan to provide economic and technical assistance to the emerging new countries in Asia and Africa that were shedding their former colonial status. The objective was simple: to help these new nations to acquire an economic viability that would enable them to stand on their own feet and resist any subversions offered by Moscow.

But at this point American foreign policy, so to speak, went off the rails. In Europe, Americans had been dealing with governments and societies that had operated along political and economic patterns familiar to the United States. In short, the Western Europeans had a society and body politic that was fully comprehensible to us. Different though these individual countries were from the United States, in helping to revive postwar Europe we were familiar with the building blocks; we knew where most of them fitted into the general mosaic of the European social structure. That is why the Marshall Plan program

[5]Figures from the Agency for International Development, U.S. State Department, 1975.

could be closed down after four years. It had accomplished its objectives. In fact, it was so successful that defeated and devastated West Germany was shortly to become an exporter of capital and to finance its own foreign aid program.

However, when the United States expanded its foreign aid program to the "new" countries in Africa, Asia, and the Far East, it got into an entirely different ball game. Washington had to deal with native governments that were so new to politics and administration that they literally did not know how to govern. It was like expecting a primary-school pupil to undertake a university education far beyond his comprehension and capabilities.

The underlying thesis of U.S. foreign aid after World War II was simplistic to an extreme. Washington believed that giving financial assistance to any underdeveloped country would enable it to establish a sound economic foundation. Out of this would grow a "democratic" country—one anti-Communist and pro-American in its political outlook. It has been the most expensive delusion of contemporary political history.

Perhaps American naiveté reached its peak with the formation of the Peace Corps in 1961 under the aegis of President John F. Kennedy. It was an appeal to idealistic American youth to go to the developing countries and work side by side with the natives in order to improve the lot of the indigenous population. However, these zealots in blue denims left no noticeable mark on LDCs in the twenty years of the existence of the Peace Corps. Cruel but largely true was the caustic comment of the *Wall Street Journal* about the practical political value of the Peace Corps: "What person . . . can really believe that Africa aflame with violence will have its fires quenched because some Harvard boy or Vassar girl lives in a mud hut and speaks Swahili?"

When the Third World was in the process of its postwar formation, the primary concern of the leaders of these "liberated" ex-colonies was to grab onto political and military power and hold it by every artifice at their command. For gaining control of a government meant control of its treasury and its revenues—the quickest way to consolidate one's power, gain the support of the military forces, acquire wealth, and begin piling up millions in a numbered Swiss bank account. The revival or the rebuilding of the economies of these new nations was of secondary importance. Nor were the leaders of these "new" nations converts to "democracy" as a political way of life. As Henry Kissinger astutely pointed out: "Democracy has less appeal because the leaders of the developing countries did not undergo the risks of the anti-colonial struggle in order to make themselves dispensable."[6] The new rulers of the liberated colonies had little appetite for democracy and its elections, which posed a constant threat to their remaining in office.

Postwar Washington with its new and unsophisticated global approach was dealing not with nations with mature economies, but with societies that were taking their first and faltering steps toward modernization. The first priority of nation-building was to acquire political power, not the plans for its economic development. The new and tough-minded leaders of these new Third World nations had not undergone the long and bitter struggle to obtain independence from their former European masters to risk losing their mastery in a popular election. In short, the name of the game is to acquire power and to hold on to it by all means at the one's disposal. The gun and not the ballot box has been the instrument for political change in black Africa.

Raul Prebisch, an Argentinian banker, economist, and intellectual, is the man who gave form and movement to the Third World and has directed its assaults on the financial bastions of the affluent industrial nations. He was one of the first to grasp the postwar realities of the decisive economic power and wealth of the United States and its relationship to the newly liberated countries arising out of the breakup of European colonial empires. He foresaw then that the outpouring of billions through America's Marshall Plan and the Point IV programs, and subsequent annual foreign aid handouts, was a way to redistribute some of the world's wealth and to help bridge the gap between the rich and the poor nations.

Prebisch was something of an anomaly in the esoteric field of international economics. He was a founder and former head of Argentina's Central Bank, and his unorthodox policies created waves of criticism in the conservative business community of Buenos Aires. He was a convert to the monetary doctrines of John Maynard Keynes, but then later became convinced that laissez-faire economics did not apply to the new and developing countries in Africa, Asia, and Latin America. He was appointed head of the United Nations Economic Commission for Latin America (ECLA) in 1948, and that was the debut of his new career as economic leader and organizer of the embryonic Third World. He was also the chief foreign adviser to the U.S. government on its Alliance for Progress to strengthen the bonds between Latin America and its often forgetful neighbor north of the Rio Grande. In 1960 he was chosen to be the secretary general of a new United Nations Conference on Trade and Development (UNCTAD). That was

---

[6]Henry Kissinger, *The White House Years* (Boston: Little, Brown and Company, 1979).

the beginning of the Third World as a political force on the world stage. What power and influence UNCTAD enjoys today is largely due to Raul Prebisch, a silver-haired aristocrat who likes to drive his Mercedes-Benz at breakneck speed. And he gave swift impetus and force to the demands of the poor and backward nations—which he picturesquely described as the "Third World"—for a bigger share of the world's wealth and goods.

UNCTAD's first appearance was in Geneva, Switzerland, in March 1964, when eighteen hundred delegates from 122 nations gathered. It was a forum of conflicting opinions that produced no concrete results; nor did subsequent UNCTAD conferences since then, also masterminded by Prebisch. The poor and backward countries were loud and demanding; they called for a massive international sharing of the world's wealth at the expense of the industrial democracies, headed by the United States. However, the rich nations have dug in their heels against surrendering any substantial portion of their wealth, technology, and goods to the Third World bloc.

In the years since the first UNCTAD meeting, the Third World has found an ideal forum for its moralizing, its constant clamoring for money, and its propaganda and political activity. For all practical purposes, the Third World has taken over control of the United Nations in midtown Manhattan, New York. It commands a solid voting bloc of 90 to 100 out of the 157 members of the UN. When he headed the U.S. delegation to the UN, Daniel P. Moynihan told them to their faces that the Third World delegates represented a "tyranny of the majority . . . that votes the politics of resentment and economics of envy."

The eternal socioeconomic conflict between the rich and the poor of this world—in olden times it was always considered to be a local welfare problem to be handled separately by each community—has now expanded to global proportions. Under Prebisch's initial prodding the Third World countries banded together at the UN to demand large-scale transfusions of financial aid, technology, and other assistance, largely financed by the affluent industrial and capitalistic nations of the free world. While they have not effected any major transfer of the world's wealth from the haves to the have-nots, the Third World countries have been able to borrow over $500 billion, as of January 1, 1981, from the governments and the banks of the industrial nations. Hence, in an oblique fashion, they have made considerable progress in redistributing the wealth of the family of nations, because a very large percentage of the $500 billion in loans will never be repaid. In addition, the Third World countries have achieved a major objective: to make foreign aid assistance from the affluent industrial nations a permanent annual commitment to the Third World. It is the sacred cow of international affairs, never to be questioned or challenged as to its validity or intrinsic worth.

However, after two decades some hard and uncomfortable facts about continuing foreign aid have emerged which can no longer be ignored or denied. In general, foreign aid does not really impinge on the lives of the millions of poor and hungry Africans and Asiatics. The world press publishes pictures of those starving children with their matchstick legs and arms and distended bellies, of their mothers whose sagging breasts are empty of life-giving milk. But foreign aid does not remove hunger, disease, and hopelessness from their lives. Rather the foreign aid grants and loans are diverted by the governments of Third World countries for other much less humanitarian purposes, which, in the main, serve only the personal and political interests of their rulers. As Professor Bauer, a veteran observer of the contemporary Asian and African scenes, has pointed out: "Foreign aid only increases the money, patronage and power of the recipient governments and thereby their grip over the rest of society. It only increases the disastrous politicization of life in the Third World and intensifies the struggle for power."[7]

As we shall explain in greater detail in subsequent chapters, the diversion of foreign aid breaks down into several categories that are in conflict with the original objectives of this program:

1. The leaders of recipient countries use foreign aid to strengthen their own political power bases; they reward their followers with high-paying government jobs and lavish expense accounts. Their police and security forces are expanded to harass or intimidate any political opposition.

2. Foreign aid is used to keep afloat the inefficient and deficit-ridden socialistic "planned economies," as well as to subsidize the equally unprofitable industrialization programs which are usually beyond the capacity of a Third World country to handle.

3. "Prestige projects," such as a national airline, skyscrapers, football stadiums, presidential palaces, four-lane highways that end at the jungle's edge, and a host of ego-gratifying expenditures absorb large sums of foreign aid money.

4. Expensive consumer and capital goods are imported, which drain away slim reserves of hard currencies.

5. Lavish purchases of high-cost advanced weaponry are made. This last category is the most flagrant and dangerous misuse of

---

[7]Bauer, "The Harm That Foreign Aid Does."

foreign aid funds by Third World countries. For example, in 1980, the developing nations spent a total of $18.5 billion for planes, tanks, guns, and other assorted armaments. By contrast, foreign aid funds to the Third World in 1981 were about $20 billion. Since 1977 the Soviet Union has sold the Third World countries about $15 billion worth of modern arms. In the past decade, the United States has supplied about 45% of all the weaponry purchased by the Third World bloc.[8]

India, which has been a foreign aid breastfeeder since the end of World War II and stubbornly refuses to be weaned, spends lavishly to buy arms. In 1974, it was revealed that Indira Gandhi's government was allocating some of its foreign aid funds for the research and development of an atomic bomb. When critics in the United States called for a close-off of foreign aid to India, the *New York Times* rushed to its defense, stating (editorially) that "though this development may dismay many in this country, there is no excuse for ignoring the legitimate agricultural and monetary needs of the Indian government." Quite apart from the lack of probity in diverting funds from the hungry and needy to building an atomic bomb, one can also raise the question: Does India or any other Third World nation have any "legitimate" right to foreign aid, especially for military purposes?

The question has arisen again. In autumn 1981, India contracted to buy $3.3 billion worth of Mirage fighter-bombers from France. India also applied for and was granted a $5.8 billion loan from the International Monetary Fund to "strengthen its balance of payment position," among its other financial needs. Obviously the IMF loan will help to pay for the purchase of the Mirage fighter-bombers, generally at the expense of those countries which have invested in the IMF. The American share of the loan is 20%, though Washington tried unsuccessfully to block it.

In addition to the $5.8 billion loan, India has been receiving regular foreign aid assistance. In 1980 the total was $1.4 billion. Yet in the last few years, thousands of Indian laborers now at work in Persian Gulf oil-producing states have been sending home between $1 and $2 billion in hard-currency remittances annually. This is a new source of revenue for India, which could be an adequate substitute for its present yearly foreign aid allotment.

Neither India nor any other Third World country is prepared to relinquish foreign aid. They all are aware of the corollary: The moment foreign aid ceases, the Third World will disintegrate. Nothing will remain of a myth that has become a reality; not even a skeleton.

[8]Figures from a *Time* magazine cover story, "Arming the World," Oct. 26, 1981.

Foreign aid has created the Third World. In turn it has become the instrument by which its adherents extract billions of dollars from the affluent industrial countries, all in the name of international humanitarianism. It has also become essential to them because it gives them a larger measure of political independence from the western industrial nations and the Communist bloc—the First and Second Worlds respectively—than they would otherwise enjoy.

Finally, perhaps the greatest value of the Third World myth or concept is its propaganda value. Working through the United Nations, its leaders, skillful and experienced in this art, continually project an image of a world dominated by the rich and powerful industrial nations oppressing and exploiting the poor and undeveloped countries of Asia, Africa, and Latin America. There is a constant rehashing of distorted history of colonial times. There is a never-ending chorus of complaints and accusations that the affluent nations are pigging it by still exploiting the Third World countries. The central theme is the unquestioned dogma that the wealth of the United States and other industrial nations was acquired at the expense of the poor and undeveloped nations of the Third World. Constantly stressed are certain wide-ranging, guilt-by-association assumptions such as that three-quarters of the world's population live on one-fifth of the world income; that 800 million people in Asia, Africa, and Latin America are destitute and 30 million children under the age of five die from starvation each year; that the United States, for example, consumes 40% of the world's energy output, while the Third World countries are now $500 billion in debt, just trying to survive in a world where fuel and energy are increasingly expensive; that 90% of the total manufacturing capacity is located in the wealthy industrial nations, which increasingly block imports of Third World goods . . . ad infinitum, ad nauseam.

The large majority of these undeveloped countries are basically anti-American and pro-Soviet in their foreign policies. They are also opponents of liberal free-enterprise capitalism and preachers, if not practitioners, of Marxian socialism. This seems to be an inexplicable situation. Why should the Third World be so hostile to the countries which provide foreign aid—so critical of the United States, which has contributed over $172 billion of its own wealth to help the undeveloped lands to become a better world to live in? Henry Kissinger has provided a trenchant comment on this paradoxical situation:

By one of the ironies of history Marxism has proved attractive to the developing nations, not because of the economic theory on which it prides itself, but because it supplied answers to the problems of political legitimacy and authority—a formula for social mobilization, a justification for political power, a means of harnessing the resentments against western cultural and political dominance and of fostering unity. . . . By a historical joke, a materialist philosophy [Communism] that has solved no country's economic problems, has spread because of its moral claims; while the West professing an idealistic philosophy has bemused itself with economic and technical remedies largely irrelevant to the underlying political and spiritual problems of the Third World.[9]

In the immediate postwar years, Stalin refused to have anything to do with the new nations, which were the former colonies of the European powers. He regarded the liberated states as "imperialist lackeys,"[10] still under the influence of their former colonial masters. After Stalin's death in March 1953, Nikita Khrushchev told his colleagues on the Politburo that this attitude had been a mistake. Soon thereafter Khrushchev began making overtures to India, Egypt, and later the other new states in Africa and Asia. By 1958, Sékou Touré, leader of liberated French Guinea, made the first approach of the new black African states for a political relationship with the Soviet Union.

The Third World countries have, in effect, told the First World of developed nations: "It's none of your business what we do with the foreign aid assistance you give us; how we spend that money is our own affair!" That is the blunt message of the Declaration on the Establishment of a New International Economic Order (NIEO), pushed through the General Assembly of the United Nations in 1974. This stated: "Every country has the right to adopt the economic and social system that it deems to be most appropriate for its own development and not to be subjected to *discrimination of any kind* as a result." (Italics added.)

In plain English, the phrase "discrimination of any kind" means simply to cut off foreign aid. Thus if the United States objects to a Third World country's using its foreign aid funds to support a government that is anti-American and pro-Soviet in its policies and practices, its hands are tied, or so Washington believes. To take any action—and cutting off the flow of foreign aid is the only effective remedy—is to risk being stigmatized as a "moral outlaw" and being "anti-UN."

Incidentally, apparently in a fit of absentminded masochism, the United States delegate voted for this resolution, as did the British representative.

[9]Kissinger, *The White House Years.*
[10]Edward Crankshaw, *Khrushchev* (New York: Viking Press, 1966).

Another very successful ploy to perpetuate the flow of foreign aid is to stimulate the "guilt complex" of the western nations, particularly the United States as the richest and most powerful of this bloc. In fact, a cottage industry has grown up in the United States, Great Britain, Canada, and the Scandinavian countries to promote the aims of the Third World bloc. It is mainly recruited from the ranks of the opportunistic and bleeding-heart liberals. Their pseudo-anguish over the plight of the hungry and helpless millions blithely puts the blame for their wretched existence on the backs of the industrially developed nations. As Prof. Thomas Sowell wryly pointed out, "the poor are a gold mine. By the time they have been studied, advised, experimented with and administered to, the poor have helped many middle class liberals to attain influence with government money."[11]

The principal instruments of the propaganda campaigns are the information media—the press, television, news magazines, etc.—in these countries. Typical of the overheated rhetoric used to impress their readers, generally uninformed about Asia and Africa, is an article titled "How We Oppress the Poor" in the publication *Christianity Today* (July 16, 1976). The Rev. Ronald J. Sider writes on "the stranglehold the developed West has kept on the economic throats of the Third World," and claims that "we are participants in a system that dooms more people to death than the slave system."

Across the Atlantic in London we find such gems in the press as: "A quarter of the world's population lives, quite literally, by killing the other three-quarters."[12] And: "It is a wonder that the white man is not more thoroughly detested than he is. . . . In our dealings with every single country, greed, masked by hypocrisy, led to the unscrupulous coercion of the native inhabitants. . . . Cruelty, greed and arrogance characterized what can be summed up in one word, exploitation."[13]

The latest chapter in the North-South dialogue has been the issuance of the Brandt report—a "Program for Survival." Commissioned by Robert S. McNamara, while he was still president of the World Bank, this is another doomsday, bleeding-hearts study of the urgent necessity that the industrial "North" countries underwrite a massive "share-the-wealth" program to help the less-developed countries. Its preamble states categorically: "Reshaping North-South relations has become a crucial commitment for the future of mankind. We

---

[11]Thomas Sowell in the *New York Times*, Aug. 6, 1976.
[12]Jill Tweedie in the *Guardian*, Jan. 3, 1977.
[13]Cyril Connolly in the London Sunday *Times*, Feb. 23, 1969.

believe it to be the greatest challenge to mankind for the remainder of this century."

So far, so good. However, the methods proposed to solve this grave international problem fly in the face of knowledge and experience of foreign aid programs gained since the end of World War II.

The *Wall Street Journal* (Aug. 28, 1980) put its editorial finger on the basic flaw of the "Program for Survival":

When Social Democrats like Willy Brandt, former Chancellor of West Germany,[14] and Olof Palme, former Prime Minister of Sweden, get together to publish a report on the Third World with the word "survival" in its title, one knows instinctively some new assault on the private pocket-books is about to be launched. In this the Brandt report does not disappoint. Written by Social Democrats for Social Democrats, this report closely follows the party line throughout its 304 pages.

The Social Democrats, for example, have unshakable faith in the curative powers of income transfer: "If the Social Democrats who wrote the Brandt report took time off from lecturing others on how to manage world affairs, to put their own house in order, the Third World—among others—would benefit immensely."

The Brandt report, which now incorporates the demands of the Third World nations into one document, calls for an increase in loans and financial grants from the industrial nations of $50–60 billion a year instead of the present $20 billion being given the less-developed countries. In addition, to increase food production in the "South," an additional $8 billion a year in financial aid is necessary. To keep the money coming to the less-developed countries on a regular basis, and not subject to the controls of the affluent industrial nations, the Brandt report demands a mandatory levy of taxes on world trade, airline tickets, international arms sales, minerals recovered from the ocean floors, and other possible international sources of income. In addition, the poor countries would be given representation on the boards of the World Bank and the International Monetary Fund, whose capital assets have been provided by the United States and

---

[14]Willy Brandt resigned as West Germany's chancellor in 1974 after it was discovered that his principal aide and secretary had been an East German Communist spy. Brandt was made the chairman of the Social Democrat Party to lessen his public disgrace. He has since taken on leadership of West Germany's *Ostpolitik*, a movement calling for political and economic *rapprochement* with the Soviet Union. His espousal of the Third World is consistent with his growing anti-Americanism. Twenty years ago he was 110% pro-American as he stood practically arm in hand with President John F. Kennedy, when the president made his famous *Ich bin ein Berliner* speech in West Berlin. Willy Brandt is a successful opportunist, always trimming his sails to meet the prevailing winds.

other industrial nations. This would ensure that a steady flow of loans would go to the less-developed countries. In the final analysis, the "Program of Survival," if ever put into operation, would require the rich industrial nations to submit to an *arbitrary* sharing of their wealth.

However, not only is the transfer of money from the North to the South involved in this master plan, but also the handing over to the developing nations of the technology of the North.

In the years ahead to A.D. 2000 the most serious challenge to the United States as a superpower will arise out of a simple but frightening development: the population explosion in the Third World. It has crept upon us with little advance warning; its wide-ranging implications have largely escaped the attention of the world media. Yet this population explosion, coupled with mass unemployment and shrinking food supplies, will have drastic global repercussions, causing social, political, and economic disruption of world stability in the foreseeable future.

For centuries past, the populations in these Third World nations have been kept within supportable limits. There could be no "population explosion"—as we have witnessed since World War II—because of the yearly decimation of the ranks of their ragged and starving millions by hunger, malnutrition, crop failures, droughts, and the occasional death-dealing visits by cholera or other ravaging diseases. Birth and death rates kept to an uneasy equilibrium. However, since 1950, the population in the Third World countries has climbed dramatically, from about 1.7 billion in 1950, to 3.3 billion in 1980—and by the year 2000, it is expected to reach or exceed 5 billion. By contrast, in the industrially developed countries—mainly United States and Canada, Europe, and Japan—the population was about 900 million in 1950 and has slowly climbed to about 1.2 billion by 1980. It is expected to level off at about 1.3 billion by the year 2000.[15]

The Third World's population is about three-quarters of the global population of somewhat more than 4 billion—no exact figures are available to the demographists. However, what is now happening in the two most heavily populated nations in the world, India and China, gives us a clue as to current population trends and problems. After completing the largest census in history, the Peking government announced in October 1982 that China had a population of 1,008,175,288—or almost one-quarter of the estimated global population of 4.5 billion. India has recently completed (Jan. 1, 1981) a new

[15]Figures from *Scientific American*, September 1980, in a special global demographic survey.

census, the results of which have been described as a "demographic disaster."[16] This sprawling subcontinent, where starvation has always been the specter haunting every village, now has a population of 700 million. That is an unexpected jump up from the 550 million which the government estimated to be the population in 1979. On May 25, 1981, Indian Prime Minister Indira Gandhi called for a concerted national effort to curb the runaway population expansion. She appealed to all political parties and social and industrial organizations to make the concept of a small family a "people's movement." J.R. Tata, a leading Indian industrialist, proposed that every woman who came to a birth-control clinic should receive a $25 bonus. He pointed out that this bonus would be a good investment by the government, considering that it costs $1,000 for every child that is born, including the expenses of its childhood.

The key to this population explosion is to be found in the declining infant mortality rates in the Third World countries, not in the fact that the adults are living longer—though that is a factor also. For example, in Mexico before World War II, only two or three babies out of every ten born survived to reach their twentieth year. In 1981, seven out of every ten born in 1960 were alive and entering the Mexican job market. Perhaps what is even more surprising is that the overall birth rate has fallen since World War II. This situation below the Rio Grande explains the population explosion that is occurring in varying degrees throughout the Third World.

This expanding Third World population wants its share of the world's goods and food, plus a better standard of living. It needs and clamors for economic and technological aid and assistance, not only to improve the lot of its own peoples but as a matter of national pride. Nobody wants to be the poor boy on the block. The less-developed countries seek ways to exploit their own native resources, especially their minerals, which are needed by the industrial countries. They want to expand their food production far beyond the ox-and-wooden-plow stage of agriculture. And the pressure on their economies is heightening as their populations continue to climb sharply. In contrast, the birthrates in the affluent industrial nations, including Japan, are coming into line with their annual death tolls.

It is now becoming clear that in the Third World countries today, newborn babies are not dying in a matter of days, weeks, months, or a few years after their births, as was the norm in prewar times. This means that increasing millions of young men and women are reaching

[16]*Economist*, March 28, 1981.

adulthood and are coming into the labor market of the Third World to compete for the diminishing number of jobs available. For these new postwar nations in Asia, Africa, and the Orient have not as yet developed industrially or agriculturally to productive levels that would provide work for the swelling ranks of young men and women. Even menial labor is now highly competitive. If they can't find work at home, they must be prepared to travel, for example, to the Persian Gulf countries, which are spending their oil millions on vast construction projects. So the hopes of these new generations to find gainful and secure employment in their homelands, employment that will provide better living standards in the coming years, is decreasing in direct ratio to population growth.

Millions in the Third World are without jobs and without any form of economic security for themselves and their families. In the United Nations a figure of 300 million unemployed adult males is reported for the Third World bloc of countries. And these men and their families have no vision of a better future, an improvement in their barren and impoverished existences. These are the grim facts of life for hundreds of millions of the poor and the uneducated, those without the strength or the will to reach upward and grasp the next rung of the ladder to improve their lives. Out of this despair and misery, revolutions and terrorism are fashioned.

In most of the Third World countries, the economy is in retreat rather than advancing toward a better way of life for all. (See the following chapter.) The West German financial newspaper *Handelsblatt* (Sept. 30, 1981) reported: "The alarming increase in food shortages in some developing countries, especially in Africa, means that they are well on their way back to underdevelopment." Coupled with this trend is the growing conviction of bankers and government officials in the free world that the uncoordinated financing of the vast deficit spending of the Third World bloc, together with continuing foreign aid assistance, has gotten out of control. As of Jan. 1, 1981, the Third World owed more than $500 billion for loans from commercial banks, western governments, and international financial institutions, such as the World Bank and the International Monetary Fund.[17] The nine largest U.S. banks alone have loaned almost $40 billion to Third World states. Any major wave of defaults on these credits could trigger off a worldwide financial crisis in the western world.

The lessons to be learned from these facts stare us right in the face: If the great majority of Third World countries can't manage to

[17] *Wall Street Journal*, Jan. 28, 1981.

feed their own peoples in some of the most fertile lands on earth, how can they be expected to manage their own economies, to industrialize, and to compete in the world's export markets? Second, it should now be painfully obvious that foreign aid is not the answer to improve the lot of these poor and backward countries. Siphoning off the wealth of the affluent industrial nations to satisfy the political blackmailing of the Third World can only serve to extend the life of the disease which it is supposed to cure. Third, if there is no change in these depressing projections for the years ahead, the Third World countries would seem to offer great opportunities for the advancement of Soviet Russia on a truly imperial scale.

Lenin, one of the most farsighted of the twentieth century's movers and shakers, first used the exhortation "Workers of the world, unite!" when he began to preach global revolution. Later he sensed the broader dimensions of the basic social and economic conflicts between the industrial nations and their colonies, which would become the nucleus of the Third World after World War II. Lenin restated his revolution thesis as "Oppressed peoples, rise up!" He struck a responsive chord that is still reverberating around the world.

The problems besetting the Third World are basically economic and social—not political or military. They have endured two decades of instability and insecurity and a steady decline in their already depressed standards of living. Change and improvement can be brought about only by a return to orthodox economic policies and practices. Though the Russians have the power and the influence to make political mischief on a grand scale in the Third World, they cannot exert a lasting influence in these countries. The Russians have military force and an ideology—one that has failed in its promises to put bread on the table—as their only weaponry in the struggle for the minds and hearts of the teeming millions of the Third World. Conversely, this state of affairs can be transformed into an unparalleled opportunity for the United States and other enlightened industrial nations. For they, and not the Communists and their allies, have the appropriate tools and the resources to exploit the development potentials of the Third World.

CHAPTER THREE

The Darkening Continent

. . . Africa lies open, like a vacuum, and is almost perfectly defenseless—
the richest prize on earth.
> —JOHN GUNTHER, *Inside Africa*
> (New York: Harper & Brothers, 1954)

Africa is already in a catastrophic condition, most of the countries of
tropical Africa . . . are in reality bankrupt, reduced to a state of permanent beggary.
> —RENÉ DUMONT, French agronomist and
> U.N. consultant on African affairs,
> *Chicago Tribune*, Sept. 27, 1981

Our ancient continent is on the brink of disaster . . . sinking into the
dark night of bloodshed and death. . . . The prospects of future development are gloomier still. . . . It is clear that the economy of our continent
is lying in ruins.
> —EDEM KODJO, secretary general, addressing
> the 1978 meeting of the Organization of
> African Unity

BEFORE Ghana became an independent state in 1957, it was known as the Gold Coast, one of the richest and most progressive colonial domains in all of Africa. It possessed alluvial gold fields and substantial deposits of manganese, bauxite, and diamonds, and was the world's largest exporter of cocoa. Ghana had a healthy agriculture; "the land could support the people in moderate comfort."[1] At the time of its liberation, Ghana had the largest foreign exchange reserves of any black African country.

Today, Ghana is a land of hungry people; food has to be imported, its money is all gone, its debts have passed the $1 billion level, an impossible fiscal burden for a nation of only 10 million indigent people. The economy is in shambles. Its credibility and its credit have evaporated on the international money markets. For all practical purposes, Ghana is a ward of the World Bank, its last port of call this side of complete bankruptcy. The political side has been equally disastrous: five military coups since 1960 and several more which didn't quite succeed. The successive native governments have regressed from a free market democracy to a tinpot despotism, disguised as an African version of Marxist socialism, followed in turn by a series of military juntas whose mandate was the gun instead of the ballot box and, in 1980, a return to civilian government, which is always looking over its shoulder for the next military coup. Quite understandably, after almost a quarter century of independence, the 10 million Ghanaians are a despairing and dispirited people. They have little to show for

[1]*Encyclopaedia Britannica*, 1971 edition.

67

their "liberation"; their faith in their future is flickering. Ghana is an example of what has happened to most of the newly liberated states of postwar black Africa. With few exceptions, standards of living in these countries, which were former colonies, have declined since their liberation. Their economies have been in a state of disarray and tribal warfare without cessation, and they have been governed largely by uneducated "hit-and-run" political adventurers whose main objective is to gratify their egos through the exercise of power and to fatten their bank accounts through graft and corruption. In short, the new African states have developed to a fine art the technique of jumping from the frying pan into the fire, after gaining their freedom from their former colonial masters.

The Republic of Ghana owes much of its independence and its subsequent downfall to one man, Kwame Nkrumah, a charismatic leader whose lofty ambitions were corrupted by a love of power and a growing Swiss bank account. Nkrumah was the archetype of the postwar African ruler. Before gaining control of the newly liberated Ghana, he promised to provide "a government of the people, for the people and by the people . . . a People's Republic!"[2] He came to public office as an ardent nationalist, professing democracy as his political philosophy. But once entrenched in the seat of power, he organized a one-party totalitarian rule. He and his lieutenants treated the Republic of Ghana as their own private property, to do with as they liked. That led to Ghana's first military coup, when a junta of high-ranking army and police officers seized control of the government while Nkrumah was on a state visit to Red China in 1966.

Kwame Nkrumah was born in 1909 in a small village in the deep bush country. His father was an artisan who made trinkets; his mother was a "mammy trader"—a small shopkeeper. He received his early education in a Catholic mission school and then became a teacher. An uncle gave him the money to attend Lincoln University in Pennsylvania, where he received four degrees. Nkrumah was active in black affairs and for a while was president of the African Students Association of America. He completed his postgraduate studies at the London School of Economics, where he sat at the feet of the guru of textbook socialism, Harold Laski. Like so many other young Africans of promise, he was contacted by the Communist Party in London, wined, dined, and indoctrinated. Then in 1947 after twelve years abroad, he returned to the Gold Coast to become the secretary of the chief na-

[2]During his studies in America in the 1930s, Nkrumah had become an admirer of Abraham Lincoln. Years later, when he returned to campaign in Ghana's first postliberation election, Nkrumah frequently quoted from the Great Emancipator's Gettysburg Address.

tionalist party, the United Gold Coast Convention (UGCC), to work for the liberation of the colony from British rule. In 1948, Nkrumah was arrested following damaging riots in Accra, the capital city. The police found an unsigned Communist Party card in his wallet. However, Nkrumah denied he was ever a Communist but described himself as a "Christian Marxist."

Nkrumah and the other black nationalists did not have to fight too hard or too long to "liberate" the Gold Coast from British rule. In fact, the Colonial Office in London had been making preparations since the late 1940s to surrender the Gold Coast and other African colonies to qualified native governments, as soon as they could be legitimately installed in office. A government White Paper issued in London laid down the fundamental principle that "a European system cannot be imposed arbitrarily on an African society."

This decision of the British government not to contest to the bitter end the possession of its colonies worried Nkrumah. He thought the UGCC was being too cautious and not pushing hard enough against the yielding British. So he formed his own ultranationalist party, the Convention People's Party (CPP). To focus the attention of the Africans on this new political instrument, he called for an illegal general strike. For this action, he was convicted and sentenced to two years in prison.

Meanwhile the first general election was called to ratify a new Gold Coast constitution—a development initiated by the British and drawn up by a panel of educated Africans. The CPP won this election by a large majority, though Nkrumah and his lieutenants were still behind bars. The British governor-general, Sir Charles Aden-Clarke, was a realist; he saw no purpose in postponing the inevitable. He freed Nkrumah and his colleagues from prison and authorized them to form the first native government since creation of the Gold Coast Colony in 1874. Kwame Nkrumah assumed the office and title of prime minister in March 1952. In 1957, the Republic of Ghana became fully independent. Nkrumah's hold on the machinery of government, particularly the security forces and the treasury, was hard and fast. The foreign exchange reserves of almost $250 million piled up in London were his for the taking—and take them he did.

Nkrumah came to the leadership of Ghana with ambitions that far outstripped the resources of his small country. He wanted to play a big role on the international stage, as the architect of an awakening Dark Continent. His goal was to create a federation of "socialist" states out of the European colonies, once they were liberated. If this objective could be realized, Nkrumah expected to emerge as the dominant figure of this new constellation of African nations. At this preliminary stage he was acutely conscious of his need to acquire prestige, so as to attract attention and support both for himself and for his dream of a socialist coalition spanning Africa from the Atlantic to the Indian Ocean. The speedy transformation of the former Gold Coast Colony into a new and dynamic Ghana would be the instrument to carry out his plans.

Nkrumah and his political lieutenants launched a spending spree. They had the substantial annual revenues from cocoa sales, plus the government foreign exchange reserves, as well as the annual grants of U.S. foreign aid, which totaled $293 million while Ghana was one of the recipient nations. First on Nkrumah's shopping list were some expensive prestige projects: creation of a national airline and a national shipping line, sports stadia, new government buildings and residences for top officials, fleets of Mercedes and Cadillac limousines, boulevards, and financing of the industrialization of this predominantly agricultural state with new factories and other infrastructure. The centerpiece of the industrialization program was a $1 billion hydroelectric project to dam the Volta River and reap its energy potential. Kaiser Engineers of California was given the contract to develop the bauxite reserves and produce aluminum in Ghana with the cheap electrical power from the Volta.

The Ghanaian leader operated on an age-old political principle: "To the victor belong the spoils." The machinery of government expanded to give jobs to Nkrumah's coterie and its followers. Thirty-two government ministries were formed, a huge mushroom compared to the lean colonial administration which preceded it. The seeds of decay were sown early, as graft and corruption flourished like weeds in this fast-spending atmosphere. Agriculture was neglected as the emphasis shifted to industrialization and thousands of Ghanaians left their small plots to emigrate to the populated areas where better-paying jobs were available. Soon native food production dropped and Ghana, which could once support its population "in moderate comfort," had to spend its dwindling supply of dollars to buy wheat on the world market.

Political opposition began to develop as a result of the widespread graft and corruption. Proclaiming the need to maintain "law and order," Nkrumah began jailing his critics, imposing full censorship on the press and tightening his hold on the infant republic. In 1964 he held a referendum to give himself dictatorial powers. With this victory in hand, the Ghanaian parliament approved legislation making the country a one-party state and electing Nkrumah president for life. He gave himself the title of "Osayfeygo" (the Redeemer) and settled in for a long tenure. Inasmuch as the trade unions were controlled by Communists, the transformation of Ghana from a democracy into a totalitarian state was carried out relatively smoothly. However, this development triggered the flight of white managers and technicians who had been employed in public and private jobs, as well as thousands of educated Ghanaians who emigrated to Great Britain and the United States in search of better opportunities and more lucrative employment.[3]

Chinese and East German teachers and technicians were brought in to fill the gaps caused by the exodus of the managers and technicians, both white and black, who did not see any future in Ghana for themselves. But productivity, output, and efficiency continued their downward slide, while the Nkrumah government kept on squandering its wealth, a substantial percentage of which was squirreled away in Swiss bank accounts.

As 1966 dawned, Nkrumah's plans were going awry. His dream of an African federation, with himself as its leader, was foundering. His prestige was sinking as his capabilities as a statesman and leader of a government were being ridiculed by the leaders of other new black African states. The blatant malfeasance of his administration, together with the visible decline in the living standards of the people of Ghana, also further damaged his already-tarnished public image. Then in February he made a serious mistake; he paid a state visit to Red China to bask in the reflected aura of Mao Zedong, the acknowledged leader of the Third World bloc. In his absence from Accra, a junta of military and police officers took over the government. They swiftly deposed Nkrumah from his life presidency, in the first of four successful coups against the government in Ghana. Nkrumah returned to Africa to become an exile in neighboring Guinea under the protection of its president, Sékou Touré.

The legacy which Kwame Nkrumah bequeathed to Ghana and its native population was economic disaster and political chaos. After his ouster, Ghana was ruled by four successive military juntas during an eleven-year period. The last military junta, headed by Flight Lieutenant Jerry Rawlings, discovered, as had its predecessors, that the generally uneducated army officers could not cope with, much less under-

---

[3]In his book *The African Condition* (Cambridge, England: Cambridge University Press, 1980), author Ali A. Mazrui emphasized that "the significant wave of migration from Africa to America . . . will include some of the most sophisticated Africans in history. The brain drain will be gathering momentum in the 1980s. . . . The migrants are what might be called the black Pilgrim Fathers, running away from the crisis of political habitation in Africa."

stand, the many political and economic problems that beset the nation. So in September 1979, Rawlings called for a general election, which chose Hilla Limann, a former diplomat, as president and head of a new civilian government. However, before relinquishing the reins of power, Rawlings ordered the execution of three former military heads of state and five other officials on charges of corruption, and also to forestall other coups. As Ghana limps into the 1980s, the damage inflicted on this once economically self-sufficient country seems almost irreparable. For example, Harry Sawyer, Ghana's civilian minister for communications and transportation, described the problems he must try to set right: "I inherited a lot of sick babies—rotten railways, corrupt airways, undisciplined shipways. . . . Our government has inherited a corrupt system."

The brief experiment with civilian government ended abruptly on Jan. 1, 1982, when Rawlings staged his second coup d'état in an attempt to bring some order out of the continuing misrule and chaos in the country. Rawlings charged that the civilian government "had brought nothing but repression" to the 12.5 million Ghanaians. At this writing he is still heading the government in Accra.

Elsewhere the Ghana landscape is littered with economic wreckage. A few factories are running at 30% of capacity; others are shut down for lack of raw materials, spare parts, technicians, or markets for their output. Exports are crippled. Cocoa, the foundation of Ghana's thriving economy before Nkrumah took power, is in the doldrums. The government's Cocoa Marketing Board sets a low domestic price, which it pays the farmers for their cocoa beans, because it wants to reap the benefits of the higher world prices for its own treasury. As a result, private producers are smuggling a substantial tonnage of cocoa across the border to the neighboring Ivory Coast or Guinea, where it is sold for hard currency that does not return to Ghana. Diamonds and gold also are smuggled out. Meanwhile the government had abandoned its faltering industrialization in favor of new support for agriculture, but as yet no practical steps have been taken to increase cocoa or food production. Planners are studying a billion-dollar program to irrigate the Accra plains, but financing and management are in short supply. The current government budget deficit for 1981–82 is about $1.1 billon, a sum that is 30% of the country's GNP. Financially speaking, the Ghana government has very limited room to maneuver.

I have focused at some length on Ghana not because of its importance, or lack of it, in the African spectrum, or because what happens there will have wide-ranging repercussions throughout the Dark Continent. Rather, Ghana is a composite of the meaningful developments, trends, and personalities that are characteristic of most of the black African states that were formerly colonies of European powers. Ghana is also a synthesis of the basic problems that affect these black African countries, which include in their ranks twenty of the most economically undeveloped and politically unstable states of all the Third World nations.

Roughly speaking, there are three "Africas." There are the predominantly Arab states—Egypt, Libya, Tunisia, Algeria, Morocco—lying along the southern shore of the Mediterranean. These countries have been "Europeanized," so to speak, because of their age-old contacts with Europe spanning the Mediterranean over the centuries past. Then there is the last stand of "white man's Africa," that is, the beleaguered Republic of South Africa. This rich and industrially powerful state is determined to fight to the bitter end to resist the rising pressure of the blacks, who vastly outnumber the whites, to get control of this southern province of the Dark Continent. Finally, there is "black Africa," the forty states lying below the Sahara in a crazy-quilt pattern from the Atlantic to the Indian Ocean.

Under Kwame Nkrumah, Ghana gave promise of a bright and progressive future,[4] but that was as evanescent as a desert mirage. And this situation was to be duplicated in varying degrees in the other black African states newly liberated from their former colonial masters. The governments of these new African states had no traditions or experience—except their tribal backgrounds—to guide them in the formation and administration of a twentieth-century nation. With rare exceptions, they had no cadres of trained and educated native civil servants, bequeathed to them by the departing Europeans. So it was a case of first come, first served. Being the head of the government of a new black African state, or sharing in its administration, was a supreme prize. It opened the doors to personal power, prestige, luxury housing, expensive cars—Mercedes 600s usually won out over Rolls-Royces or Cadillacs because Germany was not considered an "imperialist power"—and sudden wealth. But it also triggered struggles for rulership of the former colonies that were savage, fratricidal, and bloody.[5] When the attractions of virtually unlimited political power,

[4]*Time* magazine featured Kwame Nkrumah for its prestigious Feb. 9, 1953, cover story on the basis that he was the outstanding black African personality of the postwar era.

[5]One fact generally overlooked in reports about postwar Africa is that the unabating conflict between states and within their individual boundaries has produced approximately 3.5 million refugees, uprooted from their homelands. They escaped with their lives but not much else, and they left behind uncounted thousands who were killed in the fighting.

coupled with ever-increasing graft and corruption, plus simple looting of the government's treasury, began to exert their inexorable influences, the slide into economic deterioration and political instability was swift.

A survey by the London *Economist* has disclosed that during a fifteen-year period (1951–76) the member states of the Organization of African Unity (OAU) have been subjected to thirty-eight successful and eighteen unsuccessful military coups, in addition to eleven full-scale domestic revolutions. Some of these former colonies proved to be extremely unstable politically after being liberated. For example, the Sudan has undergone one revolution and four unsuccessful and three successful military takeovers under a total of nine heads of government. The tiny state of Benin, formerly Dahomey, in the sixteen years of its so-called independence has been ruled by ten presidents and has been subjected to five successful coups. Africa has proved to be a most unsettled continent.

Most of these violent military takeovers are carried out under the banners of "peace-loving" Marxist socialists. At first glance this seems strange, considering the fact that the military coup-makers are generally uneducated and politically unsophisticated with no personal background or experience with European socialism and Communism. The appeal that Marxism has had for these newly liberated countries in black Africa was that it provided their new rulers with a political justification for seizing power by force or by misrepresentation. It also gave them a workable formula to disguise their own crude tyrannical regimes as "people's governments." The former colony gained its freedom and quickly identified itself as socialist or Marxist in character. This was the formula to legitimize the forced subjection of political and economic forces into a straightjacket of government control.[6] Those opposing the new leaders were shot, imprisoned, or, in many cases, just fed to the crocodiles in the neighboring rivers. Meanwhile their propagandists identified the "enemies" of the new regimes as being "capitalists," "imperialists," together with the former colonial

---

[6]V.S. Naipaul, the Indian author and prescient observer of the Third World, offered some acute comments on developments in Ghana and other new black African states on a Public Broadcasting System TV talk show in December 1980: "These places are steeped in the lie. The lie begins when the metropolitan society [of Western intellectuals] decides to be good and not talk about what is wounding. The people deceive themselves with encouragement from the outside. Nkrumah's supporters in Ghana bent backwards to explain Nkrumah's behavior. The lie takes over then for the nicest reasons." Then, discussing the proliferation of dictatorships in the new black African states, coupled with the destruction of the institutions inherited from the colonial powers, Mr. Naipaul stated: "The lie comes in again to cover up that there is nothing to put in their place but personal power."

governments, all following the lead of the United States, the nemesis of all newly liberated states. Then after a period of consolidation of their power, the new petty dictators had virtually unlimited rein to exploit their positions and to enrich themselves and their followers.

"On the basis of all economic projections we have seen so far, Africa in the year 2000 will not be in the ditch where it is now. It will be in the bottom of a deep black hole." That is the gloomy forecast made in 1980 by one of Africa's most respected economists, G.E.A. Lardner, executive secretary of the United Nations Economic Commission for Africa (ECA). Lardner was addressing his warning to the heads of fifty African governments, who were to meet in Lagos, Nigeria, in April 1980, to consider how to forestall this economic collapse which involved all their countries. The heads of state held their meeting in Lagos, shuffled their paperwork impressively, agreed on some platitudinous conclusions concerning economic and political questions of their agenda, and then returned home, hoping for the best.

However, after that meeting, with very few exceptions, things have continued to slide downhill for these black African countries. After struggling for years to rid themselves of the white man's colonial rule, they finally obtained their freedom. In many instances they established model "democratic" governments, with constitutions, parliaments, free elections, and high hopes for the future. But freedom was fleeting, a brief phase in the short histories of these new black nations. The attractions and the prizes available to those who got the control of the government of a fledgling democracy, as well as the vendettas of tribal warfare that extend far back into the hazy past of the African peoples, led inevitably to military coups and revolutions. The "rascals" on the outside conspired to throw out of office the "rascals" on the inside. One tyranny succeeded another. Graft and corruption, coupled with mismanagement, remained the only constant factors on the ever-changing political scene. As of October 1981, thirty-four of the black African states were ruled by military juntas, or one-party governments.

And wealth in the form of native resources, such as oil and minerals, only seems to compound the problems. Consider the case of Nigeria. As the richest—in 1980 its oil revenues topped $25 billion—and the most populous—an estimated 80 million inhabitants—this former British colony is the acknowledged leader of the black African states. By comparison to its political siblings, Nigeria is a giant. Yet today Nigeria is suffering from its own self-made economic crisis.

What has ensued is truly a case history of what is going wrong in black Africa in the last quarter of the twentieth century.

The British colony of Nigeria—it was the largest remaining colonial domain of the fading empire—became an independent republic in 1960 with virtually no opposition or foot-dragging on the part of her majesty's government in London. Sovereignty was handed to the Nigerians on a platter; not a shot was fired in anger. But after "liberation," a wave of political instability set in that has continued unceasingly ever since. It arises out of a witch's brew of tribal conflicts, which has its roots in the dim distant past, that makes the feuding of the legendary Hatfields and McCoys seem as mild and public-spirited as a neighborhood softball game. There are about two hundred distinct native tribes, each with its own language. They are loosely divided into three ethnic groups: the Hausa-Falanis in the north, who are Moslems; the Yorubas in the southwest sector; and the Ibos in the southeast third of the country.

The British colonial administrators had previously maintained political stability because they dealt directly with the individual tribal chiefs. Enjoying unchallenged control, the British were able to reward or punish the heads of various tribes for their success or failure in keeping their restive subjects in line. However, when a native parliamentary-type government was installed in 1963 as the first stage of Nigerian self-rule, the tribal rivalries and conflicts quickly surfaced. Deep-seated tribal differences, plus bitter dissension over spoils and government jobs, led to coups and political assassinations as the struggle for the political control of the new republic gained momentum. Then in 1967 the Ibos seceded to form their own Republic of Biafra. The Ibos had been rated by the British as an intelligent and industrious people, described by some as "the Jews of Africa," as a tribute to their energy and talents in the marketplace. Outnumbered in the Nigerian parliament, they bitterly resented the success of the Hausas and Yorubas in imposing their political decisions on the 4 million Ibos. Another factor that contributed to the secession was that most of the major oil deposits in Nigeria were found in Ibo territory, in the delta of the Niger river and on the coast of the Bight of Biafra. That was the big prize at stake in the fierce civil war that followed. The Yorubas and the Hausas joined forces, but it took three years of fighting and over a million casualties before the Ibos surrendered. From that point on, Nigeria was ruled by a military government headed by General Yakubu Gowon from the Moslem-dominated northern territory.

To heal the wounds of the savage fratricidal civil war, Gowon began to spend the country's oil revenues in a lavish fashion. He embarked on a massive public-works program, which involved airports, sports stadiums, roads and highways, office buildings, theaters, etc. As was to be expected, a small elite of businessmen, civil servants, and military skimmed off vast amounts of money allocated by the government's Nigerian National Petroleum Co. for industrial development. Government officials got rich on bribes connected with government spending. Imports climbed drastically, rising an average of 64% a year, as speculators brought in thousands of tons of goods to sell to the government. At one point in 1975, there were almost five hundred ships at anchor in Nigerian harbors, all laden with cement, because of uncoordinated and duplicated procurement orders. The adverse effects of this bottleneck took years to erase.

Because he could not or would not carry out the much-needed economic reforms, in 1975 General Gowon was overthrown in a bloodless coup, headed by a Brigadier Murtala Ramat Mohammed. In turn Mohammed was murdered in a 1976 coup, led by a drunken physical training officer, a Major Dimka. He and his co-conspirators were executed by a successor ruler, General Olusegan Obsanjo, an honest but ineffective man. His program to restore order out of economic chaos and corruption failed in its mission. Obasanjo admitted in 1977: "We are fast becoming a nation of agents and middlemen with the attendant easy money and corruption. Our uncontolled consumption has lost the nation valuable resources. In spite of our efforts, the Nigerian society is not sufficiently disciplined . . . because of our unusual love of grandeur."

After recognizing its inability to halt the economic deterioration, the Supreme Military Council stepped aside in 1979 to allow a civilian government to take over. In a national election Shehu Shagari, a prominent member of the Hausa-Falanis, was chosen as president. Hardly had he moved into the presidential office when a major scandal erupted. It involved the state-owned oil company which now accounts for about 95% of Nigeria's exports and provides 92% of the government's revenues. In 1979 an audit of the books of the Nigerian National Petroleum Co. (NNPC) disclosed that unidentified groups of government and/or army officials had siphoned off over $4 billion of high-grade crude oil, surreptitiously sold it on the world market, and banked the proceeds in London. The government tried unsuccessfully to sweep the "Oilgate" scandal under the rug but finally was forced to cashier all the top-ranking officials of NNPC. However, an official investigation which followed announced that no criminal action had been involved; the missing funds were only "temporarily misplaced" because of a "bookkeeping error." That may or may not be the final answer to the $4 billion gap in oil revenues, but the investigation also disclosed that the NNPC just doesn't really know how much oil is sold on a day-to-day basis. A major reorganization is in the works.[7]

Before oil was discovered, Nigeria had a comparatively prosperous agricultural economy, producing cash crops for exports, such as cotton, palm oil (for soap-making), cocoa, rubber, and peanuts, as well as sufficient food to support a population of about 80 million. But oil and the industrial development program inaugurated by General Gowon introduced some drastic and adverse changes to the Nigerian economy. Hundreds of thousands of Nigerians left their farms to get better-paying jobs in the cities, where the oil revenues were being lavishly spent on a wide variety of development projects. Domestic food production has suffered accordingly. Nigeria, once an exporter of agricultural products, now is importing food at the rate of $2.5 billion a year, including frozen chickens, wheat, canned goods, corn flakes, etc., from the United States.

President Shagari is well aware that the declining food production is a serious threat to Nigeria's future. He has embarked on the third program—the promise of a $13.5 billion "Green Revolution" to regain self-sufficiency in food crops. But it will take more than just money to remove the obstacles, such as shortage of trained manpower, mismanagement in government bureaucracies handling seeds and fertilizers, inadequate transport, lack of credit institutions to finance the small farmers, and lack of schools, public utilities, and other services that would attract more of the unemployed workers back to the farms. Nigerian officials admit that "there is a lot of money involved in the importing of food." For example, a 100-pound bag of rice costs about $55 when unloaded on the Lagos docks. But the time the rice has passed through the middlemen, wholesalers and retailers and street vendors, the rice costs the Nigerian housewife around $4 a pound.

[7]Finding the bedrock truth about events and developments in Nigeria—and in virtually every other black African state—is a heavy burden borne by foreign diplomats, businessmen and journalists. On January 23, 1982, the *Economist* of London published a detailed and lengthy survey of Nigeria, prefaced by the following comment:

"It might as well be admitted from the start. This is the first survey published by the *Economist* in which every single number is probably wrong. There is no accurate information about Nigeria. Nobody knows, within a margin of error of about one third, how many people the country contains, where they live or how much they produce. . . . Here is the latest annual report of the central bank of Nigeria on the government's acounts:

'At the time of the writing of this report (April, 1981), no actual data on the federal government's revenue and expenditure was available for the whole of 1980: the situation as usual was worse for the state governments. External trade data for 1980 similarly was unavailable . . . the data situation has continued to deteriorate rather than improve.'

"By the end of 1981, the bank—and the electorate—was none the wiser."

And much of that rice comes from the United States, which is now exporting over $500 million worth of food annually to Nigeria.

If there were a middle class in Nigeria and in other black African nations, there would be solid hope for their future. A middle class would play a decisive role in the industrial, commercial, and financial lives of the newly liberated countries. A middle class would bring two much-needed qualities to a black African government: stability and a measure of accountability. But those disciplines are sadly lacking in all but a few of former colonies. In Nigeria, Ghana, Kenya, Zambia, Tanzania, Zaire, and the other successors of former European colonial domains, there is only a small elite—and not necessarily an educated elite, at least by western standards—at the top of the social pyramid. Far below them are the millions of illiterate natives eking out a subsistence living. In a wide majority of cases, their daily existence is worse than it was when they lived under their European masters. One thing is plain: They are not eating as well as they did formerly.

The control which the elite exercises over the political and economic affairs in Nigeria and other former British colonies has been facilitated by an administrative instrument which the English left behind when they pulled down their Union Jack and departed. At the outset of World War II the British created separate commodity agencies to handle the marketing of the various cash crops. These agencies paid the individual farmers for their crops and then sold them on the world market, or withheld them so as to obtain the best prices available and to keep the prices as high and as stable as possible. In effect, these were crop cartels in operation. And when the former colonies were given their freedom, the various commodity agencies continued to function. For example, when Ghana became independent in 1957, its Cocoa Board gave Nkrumah an instrument with which to fasten more tightly his despotism on the inhabitants of Ghana, essentially dependent on its agricultural products for its subsistence.

In Nigeria, for example, the country's faltering agricultural production is further encumbered by a bureaucratic holdover of commodity agencies: a Rubber Board, a Cocoa Board, a Palm Produce Board (palm oil), a Cotton Board, a Groundnuts (peanuts) Board, and a Grains Board. They have long outlived their original purpose; they are counterproductive. They pay the absolute minimum price to the individual farmer for his cash crop, while reaping the current world prices for the various commodities. They are instruments of exploitation of their own peoples in Nigeria and in other former colonies.

One of the most robust myths of our time has been the assumption that the British manipulated the agricultural productivity of its

West African colonies to the detriment of the natives and to the profit of the entrepreneurs by the development of these cash-crop economies. Dr. Nkrumah, who was a front-page personality in the '50s and '60s, described western capitalism as "a world system of financial enslavement and colonial oppression and exploitation by a handful of so-called civilized nations."[8]

In all the years when he had the attention of the world press, Kwame Nkrumah never publicly acknowledged the true historical facts about Ghana, and also about Nigeria and other British colonies— what they had once been before the white men arrived and how they were transformed by the British. For hundreds of years before the Europeans settled in as colonists, the Gold Coast, as Ghana was then known, together with Nigeria and other West African territories, had a flourishing export trade of a single commodity—black slaves. The English came to this desolate corner of Africa—known as the "white man's graveyard"—to break up the slave trade. They stayed on to build up new agricultural economies. For example, the British imported cocoa trees from South America; before the turn of the century this bit of flora was unknown to Africa, but it took root and flourished on the Gold Coast and elsewhere. After World War I the Gold Coast had become the chief producer of cocoa on the world market. Finally when Ghana gained its independence, its accumulated wealth of some $240 million in foreign exchange reserves, earned by the Cocoa Marketing Board, which had been founded and operated by the British, was handed over to Kwame Nkrumah and his gang of spoilsmen. As "colonial exploiters," the English seemed to be getting a bit soft-headed. However, in reality, the English operated on the principle that to reap solid benefits from a colony it must be made as self-sustaining as possible. This policy line was universal. For example, before World War I, the British were able to smuggle some rubber plants out of Brazil. They were transplanted in Malaya, which in a relatively short time became the chief rubber producer of the world. The British also transplanted Chinese tea bushes in India, where tea soon became a major cash crop, principally marketed in London, where it piled up foreign exchange earnings.

Nigeria's almost complete dependence on its oil production makes it particularly vulnerable to the ups and downs of the world petroleum market. The high point was reached in 1977 when the country's GNP was $33 billion, of which 92% was due to its oil ex-

[8]Kwame Nkrumah, *Africa Must Unite* (London: Heineman Ltd., 1963).

ports. Only white-dominated, mineral-rich South Africa with a GNP of $36 billion surpassed Nigeria in the gross revenues of all African states. Then in June 1981, Nigeria, together with Algeria, Libya, and Gabon, raised the price of its high-grade crude to $40 per barrel. This was done in the face of an increasing worldwide oil glut that shook the OPEC oil cartel to its foundations. By the end of summer 1982, Nigeria was able to market only about 600,000 barrels per day, well below its break-even point of 1.7 million at a price of $28 per barrel. Nigeria had total reserves of about $10.2 billion in December 1980, but these reserves have since dropped to about $4 billion or less.

This unforseen development bodes ill for the $131 billion five-year development plan, including the $13.5 billion "Green Revolution," which was announced in the spring of 1981 with great fanfare. Widespread unemployment is developing in the crowded cities as the many construction projects quietly come to a halt

Even merely to get by in the coming years, Nigeria is going to borrow heavily from big western banks, as well as spend the last of its once-substantial foreign exchange reserves, to meet its balance of payments deficits in the years ahead.

Looming on the distant horizon is a very uncomfortable economic fact of life: Nigeria will exhaust its oil deposits about the year 2000. In any event, its future national income from crude oil will be in the millions instead of the billions of petrodollars of these halcyon decades. How is Nigeria going to feed its tens of millions of natives? How will the government keep them profitably employed when the petrodollar income begins to dry up?

Consider the Sudan, Africa's largest country, almost one-quarter the size of the United States, which potentially could be the "bread basket of the Middle East." As agricultural production declines in Africa and the Middle East, any substantial increase in food supplies could have a tremendous impact, political and economic, on that crisis-ridden sector of the globe. Yet as Africa enters the decade of the 1980s, the Sudan's once rosy future seems to be disappearing over the distant horizon. Circumstances and events beyond its control are contriving to play havoc, both politically and economically, with this great block of strategic geography that straddles the Nile River for 1,300 miles in a north-south direction.

The Sudan has the greatest potential for agricultural development of any country in Africa. With the completion of the projected Jonglei Canal over 400,000 acres of land in northern Sudan can be transformed from a burning desert to a lush and green farming area. By doubling the width of the canal, an additional 5 million acres can be added to the agricultural output of the Nile River Valley.

Several hundred miles below Uganda the Nile River enters the flatlands of southern Sudan and then disappears into the Sudd. This is a giant swamp about 40,000 square miles in area, choked with floating vegetation, flies, and mosquitoes and virtually impassable for any water transport except native canoes. Like a giant sponge, the Sudd yearly absorbs—and loses through evaporation—about 4 billion cubic meters of water that could be better utilized to irrigate expanded farming areas, not only in the Sudan but also farther north in Egypt. The Jonglei Canal project involves draining the Sudd by digging a 230-mile-long trench, at a cost, estimated in 1979, of about $500 million. Yet each year it could provide about $3.5 billion worth of extra water for agricultural use along the whole Nile Valley north of Khartoum.[9]

In 1974 when escalating oil prices aroused angry reaction in the United States, there was some talk that the Americans might use their agricultural surplus as a "food weapon" to counter the OPEC "oil weapon." The Arabs then took a sudden interest in the agricultural potential of the Sudan, which lies across the Red Sea from Saudi Arabia. The Saudi government gave the Sudan a $300 million line of credit to be used for agricultural development. Yet ironically, while helping the Sudan with one hand, the Saudis were damaging its economy by intensive recruitment of Sudanese workers for the many industrial development projects along the Persian Gulf coast. The Sudan had a population of about 18 million at the beginning of the 1970s. Since that time it has lost about a million of its best workers to the oil-producing states of the Persian Gulf area. The migrants have included teachers and technicians, drivers, cooks, skilled and unskilled construction workers, etc. This loss of manpower has become a major obstacle in the Sudan's own economic development. It has thrown the country into a decline, at a crucial period in its relatively short life. For example, it was originally planned to complete the Jonglei Canal by 1984; now 1994 is a more likely date, if ever the canal-digging can accelerate its present snail-like progress. But insoluble shortages of labor and money make this unlikely.

The labor shortage has also caused a decline in production: Cotton is down by 30%; peanuts, another stable cash crop, is also reduced

[9]Statistics on the Sudd from *Business Week*, Sept. 17, 1979.

by 18%. The Sudan is in default on payments for about $4 billion of loans from U.S. and European commercial banks. It depends on financial handouts from the World Bank and the International Monetary Fund for its basic financial needs. The Sudan has become, or shortly will be, an economic cripple, when with luck and good planning it could have been the "Jolly Green Giant" on the banks of the Nile River.

Mineral-rich Zaire, formerly the Belgian Congo, presents another facet of the economic and political deterioration that has set in for many of the former African colonies after they have gained their independence. René Dumont, French agronomist and consultant to the United Nations on African developments, has described Zaire as "the most mismanaged country in black Africa." Bribery, graft, and corruption are so rampant that "the Zairean form of government is described . . . as a 'kleptocracy,'" according to the *Wall Street Journal* (June 25, 1980).

Ostensibly Zaire is a capitalist country; in reality it is a tyranny, with every aspect of its political and economic life subject to the authoritarian rule of President Mobutu Sese Seko, reportedly the richest man on the African continent. There is a parallel between President Mobutu and King Leopold II of Belgium. In the 1880s, with the assistance of explorer Henry Morton Stanley, Leopold acquired vast tracts of land in the Congo Basin for his own personal possession. The monarch's own private colonial preserve earned him a large fortune by the ruthless exploitation of its mineral wealth and rubber plantations. Finally in 1908 the wave of international criticism that resulted from Leopold's harsh treatment of the natives caused the government to annex the Congo. It was held as a colony until 1960, when King Baudouin gave the territory its independence, as the Republic of the Congo. The name was changed to Zaire in 1971. Today Mobutu rules Zaire with the same iron hand exercised by Leopold II. And it has enriched him with millions of dollars, as it did the Belgian monarch.

When Mobutu took control of Zaire in 1965, the former colony was in good shape economically. It had a strong currency, a small foreign debt and a 7–8% annual growth rate, substantial foreign exchange reserves, and a bright future. It was and is the world's largest producer of cobalt, vital to the construction of modern jet engines, to space exploration, and to the machine-tool and oil-drilling industries. Zaire is also a major producer of copper and industrial diamonds, as well as zinc, manganese, gold, silver, and platinum. Its mineral resources make Zaire one of the most important African countries to the western industrial nations.

But today the economy of Zaire is in a shambles, verging on bankruptcy. The country has piled up a debt of $6.4 billion. Its agriculture has been woefully neglected, while the transportation system is a disaster. When the Belgians left there were 85,000 miles of paved roads; now only 21,000 miles are usable. The cheapest protein food, locally produced beans, cost $0.35 a pound, in a country that once could feed its own population and still have a surplus of food for export. Chronic malnutrition is widespread while the country has to import $400 million of food supplies from South Africa.

In 1981, as a result of the spreading epidemic of *le mal Zairois*—the sickness of Zaire—the per capita income of the 27 million inhabitants of the country was only $117, one of the very lowest GNPs of any of the African nations. The average for the entire continent was $490.[10]

Mobutu, however, has one characteristic which Zaire does not possess: He is able to survive and get stronger while his country becomes more enfeebled. Mobutu appeared on the scene in the second year of Zaire's independence as the instigator of a coup which restored President Kasavubu to power. In the first five years of its existence, Zaire was almost torn apart by rebellion, secessionist movements, and tribal warfare. In 1965 Mobutu staged a second coup, but this time kept all power for himself and his followers. He banned all political parties but his own, the Popular Movement for Revolution. Today, every Zairean is enrolled as a party member, even babies at birth. Mobutu has been unchallenged in office. He rewards his loyal followers by allowing them to profit with impunity from the graft and corruption that are endemic in all phases of daily existence in Zaire. Second, he continually shifts his lieutenants from one post to another, so that few have the opportunity to build an independent base of political power that could be the nucleus of an opposition movement. Needless to say, the Mobutu government is protected by an all-pervasive intelligence-cum-security network throughout the country.

Mobutu also survives because he is a pragmatic man. He does not hesitate to reverse policies that are damaging to his regime. For example, in 1972 he embarked on a "Zaire for Zaireans" program, a nationalization of employment. All the foreigners who had been running the country's industry, business, and farming had to hand over their

[10]Data from a United Nations Report, 1981.

jobs to Zaireans. As an immediate result of this replacement of qualified foreign technicians and administrators by untrained and un-educated political supporters of Mobutu, the production in these three fields of the economy began to drop drastically. Mobutu called a halt and canceled the nationalization program as it related to the employ-ment of foreigners. But too late; the damage had been done to the weakening economy. For the period 1974–80, Zaire's national income dropped 22%, and agriculture by 65%; industry is now operating at only 20% of capacity, because of shortages of fuel, spare parts, and raw materials; real wages fell below the levels of 1910. The only plus mark has been inflation, running at the rate of more than 60%.

When Zaire became a sovereign state in 1960, the retreating Belgians left it without any trained civil service to handle the govern-ment's operations. Nor was there any cadre of educated natives. In the newly liberated state, there were only sixteen black college graduates. The Catholic missionary schools had been the principal fount of edu-cation. But they could provide only a smattering of primary school training to hundreds instead of the thousands upon thousands of young blacks who needed some education to enable them to cope with the rude and hostile world into which they had been born.

It is easy to find scapegoats which will explain the inability or unwillingness of Zaire to develop its economic and political potentials, based on its mineral riches. For all practical purposes, Zaire has be-come a tribal empire under control of one man, Mobutu Sese Seko. Tribal organizations in Africa do not lend themselves to adaptation in the twentieth century. Yet, in the final analysis, Mobutu is not an anachronism in this day and age. He sees himself in the role of a great tribal chief such as Chakka, the feared and militant head of the Zulu nation in South Africa, who waged his own wars against the British as well as the truculent Boers. He wears a leopardskin cap and carries a carved swagger stick—twin symbols of his power. He acts in the man-ner of a tribal king. He visits villages in his domain to distribute gifts to the natives. He styles himself "Father of the Nation." He was born Joseph Desire; the name he chose for himself after independence, Mobutu Sese Seko, means "bold and mighty warrior." Mobutu makes no secret of his great wealth. It is in the African tradition for a chief to be the richest and most powerful man in any tribal society. In pre-colonial times such wealth was measured in cattle, concubines, and other tangible assets; today a numbered account in a Swiss bank, villas in Europe, and Mercedes 600 limousines are adequate substitutes.

Mobutu is important to Washington, London, Paris, and Brussels—and he knows it. He also is aware that the western industrial nations have no other candidate to replace him, to guarantee continuous shipments of cobalt, copper, and other vital minerals. He is no reformer of his government, nor does he pretend to be any protector or guardian of public morality, in or out of government. He does not consider it a part of his duties to educate his subjects, to broaden their limited political and economic horizons. That is also not in the tradition of the great tribal chieftains of Africa. Mobutu's role is to rule his people as he sees fit to do so. The only effective veto on his power can be his assassination.

Zambia, formerly the British colony of Northern Rhodesia, was born in 1964 with a copper spoon in its mouth and has proceeded to squander its rich inheritance away in its short existence as an independent state. This country is also a contender for the title as the most mismanaged state of black Africa, in competition with its northern neighbor, Zaire. Zambia has joined the beggars' queue of other Third World countries who line up each year for monetary bailouts from the World Bank and other western financial institutions and thereby sustain the illusion that they are not bankrupt. Zambia proves once again that with few exceptions the black African states have regressed, instead of progressed, since gaining their independence after World War II. Their leaders in general have shown immaturity and the lack of education and competence necessary for the administration of their respective governments and for profitable utilization of their resources so as to be self-sufficient.[11] The following situation exemplifies this national deficiency.

A country of some 6 million people, Zambia is blessed with a mild climate, fertile soil, and plenty of water, all of which permit food production twelve months of the year. "If we cultivated even half of the arable land we would be feeding Africa," says James Wood, director of the commercial farmers' union. Yet at present, Zambia is cultivating only 5–6% of its arable land. The reasons are not hard to find. The government controls agricultural production—the state is the sole purchaser of farm produce and also sets the price to be paid to the individual farmer. There is no open market in Zambia. The government also handles the distribution and marketing of the agricultural produce. Often the fruits and vegetables rot before they reach the buying public because of the makeshift nature and inefficiency of the government's monopoly on agriculture.

[11]The author is well aware that this criticism smacks of a racist point of view. The facts are simply that black Africa comes late to the twentieth century. For example, the concept of the wheel for transport purposes never appeared in equatorial Africa until after the white man arrived.

Corn is the staple item in the Zambian diet, and the government keeps the price low to placate the workers and those living in the crowded cities. However, this low price discourages the farmer from expanding cultivation of food crops. Thousands of young men also leave the farms, seeking better-paying jobs in the cities and in industry. It all adds up to a growing food shortage. The result is that Zambia is spending almost $100 million yearly of its scarce foreign exchange to buy South African corn at $25–27 per 100-pound sack, while it pays less than $15 a sack to local farmers. Zambia's total food imports are costing about $350 million for 1981, a very high price to pay for its neglect of its domestic farming.

Zambia was a prosperous country in 1964 when it became independent. For its first decade, exports of copper and cobalt, its two most important and valuable mineral resources, enabled the Zambian government to spend its multibillion-dollar income, as well as its foreign exchange reserves, as if there were no tomorrow to worry about. The government nationalized about 80% of all industrial and commercial enterprises in the country. This program enabled President Kenneth Kaunda to give well-paying jobs to his political followers, as well as to gain almost full control of the economic structure of the nation. One result was that this 80% bloc is now so badly managed, overstaffed, and inefficient that it provides only 20% of all the corporate earnings in Zaire. "Less than a half-dozen officials in the financial field have any concept of what they are doing," an economist stated. "If you are not careful you find yourself dealing with a Donald Duck."[12]

Following their nationalization, the productivity and viability of these enterprises have fallen sharply. For example, the nitrogen chemical plant, taken over by the state, now produces fertilizers at two and a half times the current world price. A local Fiat plant assembles cars at such inflated costs that the government has to provide a subsidy to make its prices competitive on the Zambian market. Meanwhile industrial unemployment has risen to 35% while the crime rate has soared to 300% of the 1980 figure.

The economy of Zambia is also seriously affected by a slump in world copper prices, from a recent high of $1.42 a pound in 1980 to $0.78 a pound in September 1981. Copper production has been declining from 900,000 tons a year in 1972 to 600,000 tons in 1980 and probably down to 300,000 tons in 1992. Zambia's reserves of copper are expected to run out by the year 2010, according to officials at Roan Consolidated Mines. Copper and cobalt account for 96% of Zambia's

---

[12]Ray Moseley in the *Chicago Tribune*, Sept. 20, 1981.

hard-currency earnings. Zambia shares a mini-cartel in the production of cobalt, together with Zaire. The two states have about 40% of the world's cobalt reserves between them and generally control of the world price of $25 a pound for this rare metal, vital to U.S. defense needs.

However, the prime cause of Zambia's skidding economy is Kenneth Kaunda, its first and only president since the country became independent in 1964. The son of a black missionary of the Church of Scotland, in his earlier days he described himself as a "Christian humanist," later changed to "humanistic socialist." This fuzzy and redundant phrasing is like the man himself. Kaunda is a chameleon, changing loyalties and political dogmas to match his changing circumstances. He came to the presidency as an avowed democrat. A few years later when opposition developed against his regime, he transformed Zambia into what he labeled a "one-party anticipatory democracy." That is another way of describing a rather sloppy and inefficient autocracy, in which only the friends of the president have access to the levers of power. Those who oppose this form of government go to jail.

The opposition to him is growing. Kaunda has just about exhausted his credit and credibility with the western powers, so he has taken the initial steps to open up a new relationship with Moscow and the Communist bloc. Once an outspoken anti-Communist, Kaunda recently signed a treaty with Moscow for over $100 million in assorted arms and other services, including East German security experts, which form a new Praetorian guard to protect the frightened missionary's son from being ousted from his presidential palace in a coup. In return, Moscow gets shipments of cobalt, a critical raw material which the Russians have had to import in recent years.

In the postwar rise and fall of black Africa, Tanzania is unique. This East African state is the only one of the new black African nations which has been subjected to a Marxist-style collectivization. As a result this former British colony is now a terminal case, in the final stage of political and economic bankruptcy.

On emerging from their colonial cocoons, many of the black African states proclaimed themselves to be "people's republics." Their governments paid lip service, if not substance, to Marxist ideology. This was a not unnatural reaction of these countries, just liberated from their former colonial masters. However, in general, the new rulers of the black African states were much more concerned about securing uncontested political and economic control of their new domains. Their first priority in most cases was to consolidate their power and to acquire as much wealth as was there for the taking. They had little time or inclination to attempt to convert the millions of their subject peoples to Marxist doctrine and practice.

Not so in Tanzania. Since gaining its independence in 1961, this country has been ruled by Julius Nyerere, a former teacher and a compulsive social reformer. Nyerere is one of those single-minded men uncorrupted except by power. He believes that he has discovered how to solve the major political and economic problems not only of Tanzania, but of the entire Third World. He is intolerant of those who challenge his opinions or his actions. They are his enemies, and prison or execution is just punishment for their lèse majesté. He is messianic in his conviction that he must reform and restructure the whole of Tanzanian society. He must cure his countrymen of all their social ills, even if they are unable to survive the rigors of this treatment. Julius Nyerere is a reformer cast in the same mold that in other years produced a Cotton Mather or a Torquemada. Thousands of Tanzanians have died as a direct result of his social engineering; thousands upon thousands more families have been uprooted and impoverished by Nyerere's unsuccessful efforts to create his utopian state, flying the banner of "African socialism."

Tanzania is a merger of Tanganyika—Ernest Hemingway's Africa of "The Short Happy Life of Francis Macomber" and "The Snows of Kilimanjaro"—and the island of Zanzibar, once the greatest slave entrepôt in all of Africa. The only industry, so to speak, endemic to Tanzania was slavery. The Arabs began to mount their slave raids into East Africa in the eighth century, not only into what is now Tanzania but deeper into equatorial Africa. Tanzania was on the main supply routes to the slave markets in Dar es Salaam and Zanzibar. The slave trade continued well into the twentieth century before the British were able to wipe it out. The hunting of wild game has since supplanted the hunting for humans on the Tanzanian landscape.

With an area twice the size of California, Tanzania's population of 19 million is spread thinly throughout the countryside. Most of the land is marginal and semiarid; hence comparatively large areas are needed to support individual families. The scarcity of potable water has been one of the occupational hazards for the native farmer. Electricity has been virtually nonexistent for the rural areas. Shortly after World War II the British government subsidized a large-scale program to produce peanuts in Tanzania, but it was a fiasco of wasted effort and money because it was discovered too late that the land was unsuitable for this crop. Production of sisal is the principal cash crop of this country.

In 1967 Nyerere launched a program of "*Ujamaa*—the Basis of African Socialism." (*Ujamaa* is Swahili, best translated as "family-hood.") Nyerere wanted to create a nation where everybody was a member of a big family, all, theoretically at least, sharing equally in its work and its income. The program called for the mass collectivization of the entire countryside with its desperately poor peasants trying to scratch a meager living out of their marginal farmlands. The scattered natives were to be moved out of their farmsteads and resettled into *Ujamaa* villages, from which each morning the able-bodied would go forth to cultivate the new state-owned farms. The scheme promised the new residents safe drinking water, medical clinics, and schools for the young. But the whole program flew in the face of the accumulated wisdom of the natives, who knew from experience that farming can't be concentrated, but must be spread out to gain any sustenance from the poor and arid soil. The natives balked at joining the *Ujamaa* program.

In 1973 President Nyerere, angry at his erring children, ordered all the farmers to move into the collective villages. Army units rounded up the peasants like cattle and trucked them into the popu- lated centers. Those who fought back saw their huts bulldozed or set on fire. Hundreds and thousands died in the next two years as about 11 million natives were forcibly resettled in the new collectivized villages. What might have been foreseen by anyone not violently partisan came to pass. The food output began to decline sharply. By 1981 the govern- ment was forced to admit that only 2% of the collectivized land of each *Ujamaa* was being cultivated. René Dumont, a French agronomist attached to the UN, has pointed out that since the peasants are forced to live in central villages rather than on their own homesteads, they must walk additional miles each day to reach their fields. He cited one woman who had to make forty 10-mile trips to harvest her fields and bring the produce back to the *Ujamaa*.

"The upheavals created by the forced relocation and nationaliza- tion have pushed Tanzania's economy towards bankruptcy. A lack of consumer goods has encouraged well-organized smuggling. Huge quantities of Tanzanian coffee, tea, cotton and cattle clandestinely find their way to free markets in neighboring Kenya," reported *Time* maga- zine (March 13, 1978).

W. David Hopper of the World Bank in a special report has criticized the Tanzanian government for pushing collectivization of agriculture, which has worked against the improvement of living stan- dards. "The government's attempts to bring about a social transforma- tion," Mr. Hopper stated, "have been responsible for a major decline in the national food output. . . . In this case, the ideology of social reform has fully replaced any drive for economic growth. As long as food aid (or long-term loans for the purchase of food) is supplied to Tanzania by industrial nations, the social experiment will continue."

Mr. Hopper's comments are all the more surprising considering that Tanzania has been described as "McNamara's favorite African country." While president of the World Bank, Robert McNamara approved a steady flow of loans to Tanzania, and the former whiz kid of the Ford Motor Co. appears to have swallowed Julius Nyerere's "share-the-wealth" philosophy hook, line, and sinker. However, McNamara's political and economic opacity concerning Tanzania is understandable. As U.S. Secretary of Defense during most of the disastrous war in Vietnam, he was constantly seeing the light of victory "at the end of the tunnel," a mirage which was never to become reality.

President Nyerere manages to hold off at arm's length the official bankruptcy of his country because he has been able to extract billions—a total of $3 billion in the 1970s—in foreign aid, grants and loans, from the industrial nations, the World Bank and the International Monetary Fund. The country owes $1.5 billion to its foreign creditors and has not a prayer of being able to make any payments on this mountain of debt. In 1982, two-thirds of the annual Tanzanian budget was provided by foreign aid funds and the country had funds in hand sufficient to meet the government's expenses for only one month's operations. As Nyerere admitted recently in the *Wall Street Journal* (Aug. 27, 1982) on the twentieth anniversary of Tanzania's independence, "We are poorer now than we were in 1972."

On a per capita basis, Tanzania receives more foreign aid than any other black African country. President Nyerere is the most articulate of the Third World leaders in his incessant preachments that the rich countries of the world have a moral obligation to share their wealth, technology, and resources with the underdeveloped poorer nations of the Third World. He successfully appeals to the "guilt complexes" of the McNamaras of the industrial nations, convincing the gullible that their good fortune was acquired at the expense of lowering the living standards of a primitive Swahili tribesman and other natives of the African jungles and bush country.

An example of Nyerere's thinking is his 1967 speech in London when he called for the imposition of "a ceiling on the wealth of individuals and nations, as well as deliberate action to transfer the resources from the rich to the poor countries, within and across international frontiers." He has also demanded the reorganization of the

World Bank and the International Monetary Fund, so that the poor nations like Tanzania would have an equal say in how the billions of dollars which the United States and other industrial nations have contributed to these financial institutions should be allocated to the Third World bloc. In short, Nyerere and his ilk want to take over the World Bank and the IMF as their own fiscal agencies.

Nyerere is obsessed with the fact that inequality seems to be the rule, rather than the exception, in the world we all live in. As the London *Economist* (March 18, 1978) pointed out in a special survey of Tanzania:

Three types of inequality worry him in particular. The inequality between countries of the third world—like Tanzania—and those of the industrial world; the inequality within Tanzania between those who live in the countryside and those who live in towns; and the inequality between those town dwellers who are rich and those who are poor. The first has proved harder to tackle than the second, which has proved harder than the third.

Ujamaa, the collectivized village, is supposed to be the equalizer between town and country. But only a small percentage of the villages have safe drinking water—polluted water is the prime cause of diseases that riddle the native population—or the schools or medical clinics promised by Nyerere. The president even admitted as late as 1978 that more than 10 million of the 13–14 million natives living in the country "are still using dirty water and walking long distances to get it."[13]

Nationalization of commerce and industry, including the banks, is the other side of "*Ujamaa*—the Basis of African Socialism." First, there was not much to expropriate from private ownership. The *Economist* described it as the "nationalization of the commanding anthills of Tanzania's pathetically underdeveloped economy."

In the place of private corporations have arisen some four hundred state-owned agencies which now dominate and interfere in every aspect of Tanzania's economic life. Corruption is rife; virtually nothing gets done without the initial lubrication of bribery. The bureaucrats squeeze down the farmers in payment for their crops. This in turn further encourages smuggling. It is estimated that 30% of the coffee crop is smuggled to Kenya and there earns six times the official price paid in Tanzania.

Finally, there has been the abortive attempt to create a native industry in an environment virtually without any incentives whatsoever, except for the government bureaucrats given the factories to operate. The only growth industry in Tanzania has been the prolifera-

[13]From the *Economist* survey, March 11, 1978.

tion of an army of bureaucrats manning a plethora of state corporations. Industrial productivity is in a steady decline; profits are nonexistent. However, the Nyerere regime can boast of one solid accomplishment: It provides well-paying jobs and "perks" for the faithful adherents of the president and his one-party tyranny. But on second thought, perhaps due credit should be given to the World Bank, the IMF, and the gullible foreign nations, particularly Sweden, the sources of the lavish foreign aid which brought us the unique "*Ujamaa*—the Basis of African Socialism."

It's not all doom and gloom in black Africa, thanks to a policy of enlightened self-interest of the French government. At least four—the Ivory Coast, the Cameroons, Gabon, and Benin—if not more of the fourteen former French colonies are probably the only countries in black Africa which enjoy higher living standards today than they had before being granted their independence. And therein lies a lesson for the United States and the other affluent industrial nations to ponder concerning their present and future relations with the Third World.

At the end of World War II it was becoming clear that the colonial era was drawing to a close. The Africans wanted self-government, not a government imposed on them by white Europeans. To the educated blacks, numerically few though they might be, colonialism was an arbitrary division of society, an enforced segregation, with the whites on top and the millions of blacks below them. However, in Africa the blacks were not a social minority; they were the overwhelming majority in every colony. They wanted acceptance as co-equals with the Europeans.

The French had read and understood the handwriting on the wall with greater perspicacity than other Europeans with a stake in Africa. The French accepted in principle the possibility that they might lose control of their African colonies by granting them their independence. But they wished to keep them in the family, so to speak, by special incentives and relationships, and thus retain a maximum of political and economic influence in their former African possessions. A master plan was formulated in a special but little-publicized "Brazzaville Conference" which took place in the capital of French Equatorial Africa in 1944 and was attended by General Charles de Gaulle, then leader of the Free French government in London. The participants, who were pro-French natives and the Free French leaders, reached agreement on some surprising innovations in France's future relations with its restive colonies, once the Allied forces had defeated the Axis powers in Europe and the Mediterranean theaters of war.

A new constitution was promulgated in Paris in 1946 by de Gaulle which gave French citizenship to the native peoples of *France d'Outre Mer*, France Overseas. By this literary expression, France extended its European frontiers to include the French colonies in Africa and Asia. In theory, a black of the Malinke tribe in the jungles of the Ivory Coast was as much a citizen of France as was Jacques Dupont of the Paris suburb of Le Vesinet, co-equal in rights and privileges and with the franchise to vote in the national elections of metropolitan France. In reality, voting rights were extended only to French-speaking Africans who had an official *carte d'identité*. However, this resulted in actual black African representation in the French national assembly and senate. In 1951, for example, there were 59 of the 626 deputies— almost 10%—who were black Africans, enjoying the same rights and privileges as the native-born French deputies. Black Africans also held important posts in the French government. Felix Houphouët-Boigny was a minister in President de Gaulle's cabinet before he took over as president of the Ivory Coast after it became independent in 1960. Felix Eboué, a black who was born in French Guiana, had a long and distinguished career in the colonial service, culminating in swinging the allegiance of Equatorial Africa away from the Vichy government to the Free French forces. Eboué was the organizer of the Brazzaville Conference in his capacity as governor-general of the Chad. After the liberation of France, he also served in the French cabinet as a minister. Leopold Senghor was a prominent member of the French national assembly before he became president of Senegal.

The broad objective of the French colonial policy in the postwar years was to assimilate the cadre of educated natives and to transform them into *black Frenchmen*, as far as circumstances permitted. From this small group in each colony would come the political leaders as well as the businessmen and traders. The goal was to persuade the elite corps of educated blacks to remain pro-French in their thoughts and actions.[14]

Michel Pasquier, first secretary of the French embassy in Libreville, Gabon, has pinpointed this process as "cultural imperialism." It meant educational opportunities for the natives, creation of a racially integrated society—"if you eat with them, you sleep with them" was the current French maxim governing relations between the whites

---

[14]The official language was subjected to change, so as to create a new image of interracial relations. No longer was the word *indigène* ("native") used; instead the black Africans were identified as *autochtone*, roughly translatable as "original inhabitants" of the land. The word "colonies" was replaced by *France d'Outre Mer*, France Overseas, as opposed to *France Métropolitaine*, or France in Europe.

and blacks—and, in theory, social integration and equal access to political power for the blacks. These were the pillars of this "cultural imperialism" program that began to be implemented as soon as General de Gaulle took control of the French government after the liberation of his country in 1944.

In the late 1950s, the French government offered their African colonies their independence, together with membership in an economic union with France, in the French African Community, or CFA, plus military protection from outside aggression or inside threats to national security. This economic arrangement has provided the former colonies with a steady market for their export goods and raw materials into France and—after the Treaty of Rome was signed in 1957—into the European Common Market. In return, French products enjoy a favorable competitive position in these new countries as against the imported goods and services from other industrial nations. Most important, it has given these former colonies a common currency—the CFA franc—which has a guaranteed fixed convertibility rate with the French franc. And France acts as their central banker.

The economic union also provided a continuation of French technical services to man the infrastructure of the former colony—to operate its public utilities and transportation, industry, communications, banks, and commercial services and, in a large degree, to take part in the administration of these new African states. There was to be no mass flight or expulsion of whites as had happened in other African countries to the serious and irreversible economic damage to these former colonies. For example, in 1981 there were about 22,000 French civil servants teaching in African schools and holding administrative positions in government offices. In the Ivory Coast, the most economically stable and prosperous of the former French colonies, there were about 60,000 French businessmen, technicians, and government officials at work, six times more than were there when this colony got its independence.[15] In Gabon, there are 25,000 Frenchmen employed, compared to 3,000 twenty years ago.

This new pseudo-familial relationship with France—President de Gaulle often referred to the colonies as "our children"—has spared these newly liberated countries from many of the trials and tribulations that affected other ex-colonies in their early years.

French Guinea on the west coast of Africa was the only liberated colony that refused to join in the economic union with France. In view

---

[15]The World Bank further estimated that 80% of the jobs in the Ivory Coast requiring college degrees were held by Frenchmen.

of Guinea's large iron-ore and bauxite deposits, President Sékou Touré decided he could go it alone with the help of the Russians, so he cut the umbilical cord with France. In swift reprisal, the French stripped the country of most of the modern industrial equipment which they had brought into the colony: machinery, trucks, railroad rolling stock, and communications networks, including the telephone system. Touré tried to create a Marxist-Leninist state, but rhetoric and ideology alone cannot put together a functioning governmental apparatus; Guinea was woefully short of the necessary working parts. By the late 1970s it was apparent, even to the most hidebound Marxist ideologue in Conakry, that Guinea was unable to develop its iron-ore and bauxite resources without western capital and expertise. President Touré began overtures to Paris for a reconciliation and a restoration of old economic relations with France. The future arrangements are still in the diplomatic pipeline.

Sékou Touré, who for years was one of the most strident critics of the United States and its foreign policies, appears to be doing an about-face politically and economically. In February 1982, David Rockefeller, chairman of the Chase Manhattan Bank, was welcomed at Conakry by Touré with the fanfare normally reserved for heads of state. The following July, Touré "unofficially" visited New York and Washington, where he was received by President Reagan in the White House. The president of Guinea is frankly appealing for United States investment and other economic assistance. In the process he appears ready to be weaned away from the Soviet Union, provided the price is right.

Black Africa is awash in paradoxes and anomalies. None are more surprising or unexpected than those to be found in the so-called people's republics that were formerly French colonies. The gap between the Marxist-Leninist ideology that is preached officially from the government's pulpits and the free-enterprise capitalism that is openly practiced in the marketplace has to be seen to be believed.

The tiny state of Benin, population 2.5 to 3 million, enjoys one of the highest living standards in black Africa. Its $420 per capita income is roughly the same as that of its neighbor to the east, oil-rich Nigeria, whose income is measured in the billions of petrodollars. In theory, Benin is a Marxist state. However, the ex-colony is governed not by a "dictatorship of the proletariat" but by a military junta. Yet in reality Benin is actually administered by about a thousand Frenchmen who run the civil service, the banks and industries, and the restaurants and shops, and direct the spending of the $20 million annual foreign aid grant that is received from Paris. The result is that Benin is a shopper's haven for businessmen and diplomats, who stream across the border each weekend to buy the latest in French luxury goods and food and wines that are unavailable in Nigeria. There is also a lively traffic in smuggling Benin's stocks of French goods into neighboring states, all of which brings a substantial cash flow of hard currency. Benin is prospering because its lively commercial instincts have full freedom to operate.

A somewhat similar situation exists in the People's Republic of the Congo, which proclaimed itself to be the first Marxist-Leninist state in Africa in 1963. It lies to the north, across the great Congo River, from Zaire, the ally of the western industrial nations because of its great mineral resources. The Congo "People's Republic" has a per capita GNP of over $500, compared to Zaire's $130 a year, and it is too rich to qualify for U.S. foreign aid, though Zaire is eligible. Though pledged to operate along Marxist lines, the Congolese government supports a free market capitalist economy because it brings in money. Business operations are free of controls by the government. President Denis Sassou-N'guesso invites foreign investment and promises there will be no government interference in any foreign-owned project that qualifies for approval. There is quite substantial "foreign investment" already in the People's Republic of the Congo, the profits of the smugglers from Zaire. The leading producer of industrial diamonds in the world is Zaire, but the Congo, which has no known diamond deposits, has become the world's leading exporter of industrial diamonds. While no hard figures are available, it has been estimated that about 40–50% of the Zairean diamond output is smuggled across the Congo River, where these gems sell for two to three times the price offered by the state diamond monopoly in Zaire. These smuggling profits are banked in Brazzaville, capital of the Congo, and do not return to Zaire. There is also widespread smuggling of cobalt from Zaire to the Congo.

The Congo People's Republic is about one-seventh the size of Zaire, and its population is only about 2 million compared to Zaire's 27 million. Wages in the Congo are double and triple the wages paid in mineral-rich Zaire, while consumer goods are two to three times lower in price on the north side of the Congo River than in Zaire. The Congolese are, for all practical purposes, enjoying the blessings of a free market economy with its improved standards of living. Zaire, the friend of the democratic western nations, operates on a totalitarian basis, with controls fastened on its economy.

The Ivory Coast is an island of stable prosperity surrounded by its black African siblings struggling to survive politically and economically. A French colony until 1960, the Ivory Coast is a viable marriage of two differing ethnic cultures, European and African. It is one of the very few success stories of the Third World. For two decades since becoming independent, the Ivory Coast has enjoyed an annual increase in its GNP of 8%, the highest in black Africa. Then world prices for cocoa and coffee, two major cash crops for the Ivory Coast, began to drop, while oil prices began to rise, and the economic health of this former colony seemed seriously threatened. Its annual bill for imported oil had reached the $1 billion mark. But simultaneously with these adverse developments was the discovery that the Ivory Coast possessed major oil deposits in its offshore waters. This tended to confirm its new status as the "Switzerland of Africa."

The Ivory Coast owes much of its stability and prosperity to its president, Félix Houphouët-Boigny, one of black Africa's most intelligent and shrewdest political leaders. He became the chief executive in 1960 when the colony gained its independence and has been its unchallenged benevolent and autocratic ruler into the 1980s. Houphouët-Boigny was one of the few black African leaders who really understood and profited by the postwar realities facing the former colonies on becoming sovereign states. First, he had an intimate knowledge of and long association with the French. He had been educated in Paris and after the war served in President de Gaulle's cabinet as minister for colonial affairs. He had also been a member of the national assembly in Paris, so he was completely *au courant* regarding the political and economic affairs of the French government of the postwar period, especially concerning colonial policies and practices.

But more important, Houphouët-Boigny was the son of a tribal chief who became a wealthy plantation owner. He knew the importance of a healthy agricultural economy for the future of the Ivory Coast. This former colony did not have the mineral resources that other black African countries fell heir to, such as Zaire with its rich copper and cobalt reserves, Ghana with its gold and diamonds, Zimbabwe with its chromium and other minerals, etc. Oil had not yet been discovered, nor was there any hint that it might lie within the boundaries of the Ivory Coast. So Houphouët-Boigny had to make do with the assets the Ivory Coast possessed, its cocoa and coffee plantations and farms, and its fertile soil for growing food crops.

The president took positive steps to develop the agricultural sector. In the Ivory Coast, as in other former colonies, the government maintained its practice of being the sole purchaser of the crops, for the domestic and export markets. However, there was no squeeze on the farmers. Instead, the Ivory Coast government paid good prices and maintained support levels, despite the price fluctuations on the world markets. This has brought about a rapid growth of small farms, and they were further assisted by an adequate system of roads, as well as by bringing electricity to the small farming villages. The result of these innovations was bigger crops. Agricultural exports tripled and the economic growth expanded 7% a year. A liberal investment policy encouraged foreign firms to establish industry in the Ivory Coast, whose political stability was recognized by all as favorable to business.

There is no food shortage in the Ivory Coast, despite the fact that thousands of young men drifted to the urban centers to get better-paying jobs. Higher standards of living in this country have brought in 2.5 million migrant farm workers from neighboring black states, where unemployment and hunger are rife.

Finally, Houphouët-Boigny knew that the Ivory Coast, if it was to develop its full economic potentials, could not get along without the French, their administrators and technicians, their money and their expertise. Working together, the French and the blacks have produced political stability and economic development on a broad scale that is unique in the Third World. Though the Ivory Coast is not without its deficiencies, today it is the brightest star in the constellation of black African countries because it alone has learned how to profit by doing what comes naturally.

A short generation ago black Africa closed one door on its colonial past and opened another door to a future that seemed bright and promising. But in the turbulent years that followed, the Africans, with few exceptions, have never really gained what their freedom promised. The expectations that they could be masters of their own destinies have not been realized. Nor have the Africans attained a place on the world scene that matched their burgeoning ambitions and self-esteem. They have also been unable to exploit their own natural resources profitably. Independence has not brought with it a corresponding rise in the living standards of the 360 million blacks, except for a few small pockets of economic stability and growth. The daily existence in the great majority of the new nations is going from bad to worse. "Since 1960 the gross domestic product (GDP) per person has grown less than 1% a year in nineteen African countries; in fifteen other states it has failed to grow at all in the last decade. One child in five dies before the age of one and only a quarter of the people in black Africa have access to safe water."[16] In short, one could say that in exchanging colonial

[16]*Economist*, Oct. 10, 1981.

status for sovereignty, most of the black African countries have traded their birthright for a mess of pottage.

The black African governments spend lavishly from their slim resources to buy guns, tanks, and other military equipment. They have even used their foreign aid loans and grants to protect their regimes against the threat of coup or revolution, or to engage in bush warfare with their neighbors. However, in their frenetic search for security and for political dominance, some few governments are making the painful discovery that true power and international influence do not grow out of the barrel of a gun—as the followers of the late Mao Zedong have also learned in recent years. This is especially true in black Africa, where everybody's neighbors are also rearming as fast as their finances and circumstances permit.

In 1956, Benjamin Fairless, chairman of U.S. Steel, was asked by President Eisenhower to examine the underdeveloped countries (UDCs)—they were not known as the Third World in those days. The purpose of the global survey by Fairless and a distinguished panel of experts was to determine how U.S. foreign aid could make these UDCs as economically self-sufficient and politically stable as circumstances permitted. On the last leg of his trip Mr. Fairless discussed his major finding to a group of German businessmen in Düsseldorf's Industrie Club.

He said that the trouble with the new nations in Africa and Asia was that they "all want to have big development projects—a large steel mill, a national airline, a big football stadium, a skyscraper—all the hallmarks of a modern industrial state. They are necessary as status symbols of their new nationhood. The trouble is they don't have the manpower or the capabilities to operate such projects. Nor do they have the markets lined up for the products of the new industries—if they build them. Industrial development to them is largely a symbol of prestige and national power; not of serious and sustained economic growth. To be more specific, they don't really understand economics."

Almost two-thirds of black African investment in the last two decades has been allocated to industrial projects—and with little positive effect on general economic growth. There is a wealth of statistical and documentary material, including a special report of the World Bank,[17] to support this finding. The prime reason for the lack of economic growth has been a general failure to grasp the economic realities facing the black African nations on becoming masters in their

---

[17]World Bank's report: "Accelerated Development in Sub-Sharan Africa: An Agenda for Action," September 1981.

own houses. Their rulers did not realize that "agriculture is the key to African development, both for earning the foreign currency to buy fuel, machinery and raw material and for boosting real incomes at home."[18]

Almost three-quarters of the native populations are at work on the land, raising crops of one sort or another. Yet the farm output dropped from 2.3% in the 1960s to 1.3% by 1980. At the same time the population is growing rapidly at the rate of 3% per year. Despite the high infant mortality rate of one in five births, African fertility is in full bloom with 6.6 live births per adult woman. Hence black Africa's population of about 360 million in 1981 is expected to total 1.4 billion by A.D. 2020. Distilled out of these World Bank statistics is the grim fact that each year the African nations as a whole have to import 9% more of the food they eat than they can grow on their local farms. To keep the cities and towns—where the most volatile segments of the populations live and where the coups and revolutions originate—from getting politically restive, the governments keep down the cost of food. This is done by squeezing down the incomes of the peasant farmers, who must either sell their crops at government-dictated price levels or try to smuggle their produce abroad. The peasant farmers can't cover the costs of cultivating their crops; their sons leave the farms for jobs in the cities and towns, or seek work abroad.

Yet, as the Ivory Coast has demonstrated, giving the farmers fair and stable prices for their crops boosts production, both for home consumption and for exports. This has brought wealth and stability to a nation whose government had a clear grasp of economic realities.

Kenya, formerly the scene of savage guerrilla warfare between the white farmers and the landless black tribesmen, is another state which now understands the prime importance of agricultural development. In the 1960s President Jomo Kenyatta, once the hunted and feared ruler of the Mau-Mau terrorist gangs, lifted most of the government controls on small farms. As a result agricultural output began to jump 4% a year, until a long spell of drought upset all farm production. Similarly, Cameroon, a former French colony, is now self-sufficient in food, while its coffee and cocoa crops have done well on the world markets.

Zimbabwe, formerly Rhodesia, is another bright spot on Africa's agricultural front. Its president, Robert Mugabe, a self-proclaimed Marxist though anti-Soviet in his foreign politics, is encouraging food production by giving farmers greater freedom from government con-

[18]*Economist*, Oct. 10, 1981.

trols. As a result, a record harvest of 112 million bushels of corn, the staple food for the natives, was achieved in 1981. This also provided a welcome surplus of 45 million bushels. The 4,000 white farmers who remained in Zimbabwe after Mugabe took over produced some 67 million bushels, aided by modern agricultural machinery. Some 750,000 black farmers with no machinery accounted for 45 million bushels of the year's harvest. The corn surplus for 1981 is sufficient to meet the food shortages in Mozambique, Zambia, Angola, Zaire, and Malawi. This demonstrates that Africa's agricultural potential really hasn't been scratched as yet.

For the great majority of black African states, the future looks dire indeed. However, those countries which adopt *ecopolitics*, rather than an arsenal of weaponry or a foreign ideology, as the basic instrument of governance have a chance not only to survive but also to prosper in the foreseeable future. For a black African state, ecopolitics means simply giving top priority to economic development above all political, social, or military considerations. It means freedom for private business entrepreneurs, domestic or foreign, to develop the country's natural resources—oil, coal, minerals, agriculture, etc.—to the fullest extent possible. In short, it means introducing free enterprise capitalism as the only feasible and practical system to enable these Third World countries to become truly self-sufficient and independent. It is also the only knife sharp enough to cut the umbilical cord of foreign aid, on which they have depended for sustenance ever since gaining their freedom two decades ago.

It is paradoxical that some leftist governments in black Africa are veering away from Marxist dogma and are becoming more interested in how the free enterprise system works. In varying degrees this trend is gaining force in the former Portuguese colonies of Mozambique and Angola, in Zimbabwe, and in the former French colonies, notably the Republic of Congo, Benin, and Guinea.

Mozambique, which is a good example of this unexpected transition process, is "steering a common-sense, middle course between Communism and free enterprise."[19] Symptomatic of the country's changing mood is a poster which adorns the facade of the central bank of Mozambique in the capital, Maputo. In 1980 this poster proclaimed: "Down with Capitalism." In 1981 this was changed to: "Down with Racism." When the Portuguese decamped in 1975 after almost 450 years of ruling this East African colony, they stripped the country of its quick and movable assets such as cars and trucks, its

[19]*Business Week*, July 14, 1980.

treasury, and virtually all its skilled technicians. Left behind was a new pro-Soviet regime, headed by President Samora Machel, and a native population that is 98% illiterate. He and his colleagues took control of every aspect of Mozambique's economy, even to nationalizing the barber shops and funeral parlors.

President Machel has become aware that Marxist ideology won't feed the 12 million Mozambicans, though the former colony is incredibly fertile and its 1,800-mile coastline is a veritable fish chowder of edible seafood. Machel has had to spend over $200 million of his diminishing foreign exchange reserves to import food. Though he has several thousand Russian, Cuban, and East German advisers, mainly concerned with Mozambique security forces, they can't provide him with the technicians or training of natives for the operations of the industrial plants, transportation facilities, public utilities, etc. Though he is a bitter opponent of South Africa with its racial apartheid policies, Machel has strong economic links with the detested Afrikaners. South Africans operate the port of Maputo and are under contract to expand its shipping facilities. Mozambique's government sends thousands of its natives to work in South Africa's gold mines. Their hard-currency earnings are remitted directly from Johannesburg to the Mozambican treasury. This indentured black labor accounts for 50% of Mozambique's foreign exchange income.

In a four-and-a-half hour speech given in March 1980, President Machel openly admitted that the name-brand socialism forced on the country had been a failure. He placed the blame for this on the corrupt and inefficient officials who manage the state enterprises which cover every productive, distributive, and service industry in the country. He promised major reforms, such as decentralizing agriculture, stimulating industrial productivity by forcing state-owned companies to show a profit, and reviving the moribund private sector of business. The president also invited the Portuguese and other foreign businessmen and technicians to return to Mozambique, promising noninterference in their affairs and their investments. He did not blame socialism itself for the economic chaos that has followed on the heels of the departing Portuguese and the imposition of rigid, non-African ideology on the country.

However, Machel and his lieutenants are discovering for the first time some of the virtues and values of capitalism, long hidden and distorted by Communist propaganda and Marxist-Leninist dogma. The free enterprise system offers Machel something he desperately needs: a key to unlock the storehouse of unexploited natural resources which the country possesses in abundance. "By most accounts,

Mozambique's potential is enormous."[20] The country is so rich in minerals that coal sprouts through the topsoil; so fertile that fruit drops from the trees. Its numerous rivers can generate an estimated 13,000 megawatts of hydroelectric power. Below ground is an estimated 45 billion cubic meters of natural gas, as yet untapped.

The government has drawn up a blueprint for a ten-year, $1 billion industrial development program. This includes coal mines, iron and steel industries, aluminum plants, textile mills, cement plants, fishing fleets, etc. But at present the blueprint is just a dream. Mozambique cannot take the first faltering steps toward large-scale industrial development until it gets outside help from the industrial nations—the tools, the technicians, and the western expertise that can make this program become a reality. President Machel recognized the true dimensions of this vital problem when, in his 1980 speech, he stated unequivocally: "Private industry has an important role to play in our country."

Few observers of the African scene are so sanguine as to expect Machel to abandon socialism in favor of free enterprise capitalism in the foreseeable future. But he is gradually edging away from the clutches of the Russian bear. Recently Machel turned down a request from Moscow to establish a naval base for Russian warships on patrol in the Indian Ocean. And, unwittingly or not, President Machel and his colleagues are moving away from socialism toward an *ecopolitical* stance. First, nationalism is becoming stronger than socialism as the determining factor in government policy. Second, he sees the future of Mozambique in the exploitation of its wealth of natural resources. This in turn, of necessity, portends a closer relationship with the western industrial nations, both as sources of technology and investment and ultimately as major markets for Mozambique's exports of raw materials, agricultural products, and finished goods. These goals are the very essence of ecopolitics. And if similarly applied in other black African states, ecopolitics may bring light to the long-shrouded Dark Continent.

[20]*Wall Street Journal*, Dec. 29, 1980.

CHAPTER FOUR

The New
"Long March"

China? There lies a sleeping giant. Let him sleep, for when he awakes he will move the world.
> —NAPOLEON BONAPARTE

How can any men or any method govern one billion people successfully?
> —ROBERT KEATLEY in the *Wall Street Journal*,
> Jan. 19, 1981

Practice is the only test of truth.
> —DENG XIAOPING, 1980

China today is not a full-horror police state, but it is a neighborhood committee state, and a shop-steward state and a mother-in-law state, which may at times be as bad.
> —NORMAN MACRAE in the *Economist*,
> Dec. 31, 1977

$\mathbf{T}$HE People's Republic of China, which contains roughly one-fourth of the earth's population, is a Third World all by itself, literally and figuratively. As such, it is a mirror, clearly reflecting the deep-seated and chronic problems which beset the nations of the Third World. China also illustrates the inescapable fact that economic growth, rather than military or political power, is the basic requirement of the less-developed countries if they are to advance toward wealth, stability, and security.

However, there is a major difference between China today and the other Third World countries, apart from their respective sizes and populations. China is the oldest nation in the world, going back three thousand years to the threshold of recorded history. It had a functioning civilization centuries before the Roman Empire came into being.[1] When the European continent was populated by quarreling barbarians living in the forest, China already possessed a cohesive stable society, speaking the same language, bonded together by the same culture and traditions and political identification. China has its own peculiar ethnology, that it was created to be the "middle kingdom," inhabited by a superior race of people and suspended midway between the gods in their heavens and the "barbarians"—that is, all the other human beings on earth, except the Chinese.

As a veteran British diplomat commented:

---

[1]The Han dynasty (202 B.C.–A.D. 221) was "now an empire, rivalling, if not exceeding, Rome in size, and probably also in wealth, power and prestige," and it dominated virtually all of Asia (*Encyclopaedia Britannica*, 1971 edition).

China fits none of our ready-made categories. As a nation, it is *sui generis:* a Third World country whose leaders deal with their First World counterparts without a trace of psychological inferiority. China's present poverty and industrial weakness are an accident of history: culturally and intellectually China is a permanent member of that group of great nations whose stature is recognized by a seat in the Security Council of the United Nations.[2]

As a race, the Chinese are experts in the fine art of survival. They are conditioned by their long and turbulent history. They and their ancestors have experienced in full measure the woes and misfortunes visited on mankind: wars and civil conflict; famines and floods; the harshest of tyrannies at the hands of their foreign conquerors, or their own emperors or warlords, interspersed with periods of enlightened and benevolent government; decades of intense poverty and deprivation, contrasted with years of prosperity and peace. As a result the Chinese have developed a resiliency and an endurance which have enabled them to surmount the calamities and catastrophes inflicted on them during the centuries of their existence. Through the last three millennia they have retained their basic character[3] and social structure largely intact, as well as their own traditions and culture, while the "barbarians" of the world have seen the rise and fall of many nations and empires.

The Chinese were "Chinese" for hundreds of years before the Italians, Germans, French, English, and Russians emerged from their tribal communities to become separate nations. In short, because of their long experience and background, the Chinese know, perhaps to a greater degree than any other racial or national group, how to survive in a hostile and materialistic world. The "sons of Han" have become supple and subtle pragmatists down to their fingertips, a quality which they absorb from infancy with their mother's milk.

On Oct. 1, 1949, from the balcony above the Gate of Heavenly Peace fronting on Peking's Tiananmen Square, the victorious Mao Zedong proclaimed the formation of the People's Republic of China. From that day forward China became the second power in the Communist world after the Soviet Union. The writ of Karl Marx ran from the Elbe River in Germany to the Pacific Ocean; from the frigid wastes

---

[2]David Garside, *Coming Alive: After Mao* (New York: McGraw-Hill, 1981).

[3]David Bonavia, for many years Peking correspondent for the *Times* of London, summed up the qualities of the Chinese in these words: "They are admirable, infuriating, humorous, priggish, modest, overweaning, mendacious, loyal, mercenary, ethereal, sadistic and tender. They are quite unlike anybody else. They are the Chinese." From *The Chinese* (New York: Lippincott & Crowell, 1980).

of Arctic tundra to the steamy jungles of Indochina. Or so it seemed to the governments in Washington, London, and other western capitals.

Today, like a snake shedding its worn-out skin, the People's Republic of China is trying to escape from the Marxist straitjacket that it has been wearing for the first quarter century of its turbulent existence. In the last few years since the death of Mao in 1976, the struggle for the body and soul of China has intensified. For it has become apparent that the People's Republic was not going to achieve the superpower status which its geographical size and its billion population count would seem to guarantee. Nor would the daily lives of its citizens be radically improved or the national security and stability be assured by an alien political ideology that had originated in distant Europe and then had been transplanted in ancient Cathay.

Tiananmen Square became the principal stage prop for the revolutionary People's Republic. From the Gate of Heavenly Peace, Chairman Mao and the key governmental and military personalities—an ever-changing cast of characters except for Mao—showed themselves to China and the world at large, reviewed parades, gave their blessing to other political spectacles, and made their speeches. Until as late as the summer of 1980, at the east and west sides of the square were grouped giant pictures of Karl Marx and Friedrich Engels, Vladimir Lenin and Josef Stalin. These huge pictorial displays were a tribute paid by the People's Republic to the fathers of Communism who had provided the philosophy and the format for China's revolution. At the same time they were constant reminders to the sometimes xenophobic Chinese that once again the pattern and the character of their government had been imported into the "middle kingdom" from the lands of the "barbarians."

Mao Zedong first read the *Communist Manifesto,* written by Marx and Engels, in 1919–20 when as a young man he plunged into intense study of the theories and tactics of revolution and social change. Marx's doctrine on the inevitability of the fall of capitalism in an industrial society, to be replaced by the "dictatorship of the proletariat," was hard for Mao to grasp. He had been raised in feudal agricultural society; he knew peasants in the field but had little knowledge of or experience with the workers in China's factories. However, Lenin's Bolshevik revolution, which overturned the autocratic government of Czar Nicholas II, was something that he could readily grasp as fundamental and applicable to postwar China. In Mao's eyes, Lenin was the architect of the world-shaking Russian revolution while Stalin was the executor who transformed Lenin's plans into reality.

Mao reasoned that if Marxism as a theory could be the sustaining chord of a revolution in backward autocratic Russia and if Lenin with a mere handful of men could capture control of this giant of a nation, then this could be repeated in China, with its three-thousand-year history of emperors and kings, warlords and foreigners with their gunboat diplomacy.

As Ross Terrill has acutely observed, Mao

lived long enough to be the Marx-Lenin-Stalin rolled into one of the Chinese Revolution. . . . More than fifty years ago he was China's Marx, as he analyzed the ills of feudal China carved up like a melon by foreign intruders. He became a Lenin as he led the rebellion that seized power by a crablike encirclement from the countryside. After 1949 he put on a third hat as Stalin and took trowel and bricks to build a new socialist China.[4]

Mao Zedong was a multifaceted personality who proved to be one of the greatest movers and shakers of modern history. His talents were more wide-ranging than those of other revolutionary leaders, such as Lenin, who tended to be single-minded men, fanatical and ferocious to achieve their ends. Mao was a military strategist with few peers in his specialty, the art of guerrilla warfare. He molded an army from the rough cadres of illiterate and primitive Chinese peasants, and defeated the superior forces of the Japanese and the Nationalist Chinese under Generalissimo Chiang Kai-shek.

He was a self-educated man, the son of a farmer who took delight in discussions of philosophy and ancient and contemporary history. He surprised West German Chancellor Helmut Schmidt on the latter's visit to Peking in 1975 by a lively conversation about the works of German philosophers Hegel and the relatively unknown Haeckel, as well as the views of Karl von Clausewitz. The Chinese leader was also a poet from his youth to the end of his life. Military action, defeats and victories, problems and events, the varied Chinese landscapes—all inspired him to compose poems, written in his sprawling calligraphy. His literary output was surprising throughout his life, produced in the classical style of ancient China.

Withal, he was a man of action; he said his bowels never worked better than when he was in combat. He relished struggle; he seemed obsessed with the need for constant revolutionary change. No sooner was one Communist goal accomplished than a new revolutionary task must be imposed on the nation and its peoples, who longed for some respite. Mao was not the type to consolidate or to administer the revolution once victory was achieved. Basically he distrusted the

[4]Ross Terrill, *Mao* (New York: Harper & Row, 1980).

human material which he had to lead and to work with. He believed that unless continually prodded, the Chinese would lose their revolutionary fervor; the spirit of reform to cleanse and make perfect the social structure of postwar China would gradually die out. As a result, Mao pursued an erratic and inconsistent course in the governance of China from 1949 until his death on Sept. 9, 1976.

In 1956 the revolt against Communist rule in Hungary alarmed Mao, as it did the Soviet overlords in the Kremlin. Mao believed that the Communist bosses had so isolated themselves from the people that they did not know or appreciate what were the weak spots in their totalitarian systems. But Mao was determined this would not happen in the People's Republic of China, so he launched the new campaign to "let a hundred flowers blossom and let a hundred schools of thought contend."[5] This was an invitation to the public, particularly the educated classes, to freely publish or communicate their criticisms and complaints about the government in public meetings, in the press, or in wall posters, the typical Chinese forum. The response was overwhelming and frightening to the government. The complaints and criticisms largely fell into two broad categories: China belonged to the Chinese people and not to the Chinese Communist Party; and the Communist Party and the government exercised too much control over the private lives of the millions of Chinese. Within a matter of weeks this brief experiment in freedom of expression and of the press was found to be too politically unsettling. So the "hundred flowers" wilted on the vine and the "hundred schools of thought" closed their doors as the heavy hand of censorship resumed its grip on the organs of public communications. Those who had shown the courage to criticize Mao's government publicly later paid dearly for their temerity. Reportedly about 300,000 were arrested for being "rightists"—that is, enemies of the regime. Others lost their jobs and suffered other penalties. After this *volte-face* by Chairman Mao, the members of the intelligentsia would never again stick their heads out; it was too dangerous to speak one's mind.

Revolutionary leader *par excellence*, intellectual, poet, military strategist, charismatic politician—all these Mao was. But economist he definitely was not. It is a curious paradox about Communist leaders throughout the world. In general, they are worldly, educated men.

---

[5]During the Western Chou dynasty, from the sixth to the third century B.C., there was a movement labeled the "hundred schools of thought" in which a large degree of freedom of opinion and information was permitted. It is possible that Mao was influenced by this period of history in his attempt to probe the mass mind of the Chinese people.

They have to be, to maintain their position. They are, however, functionally illiterate, so to speak, concerning economics. They appear to be ignorant of the marketplace and how it works, of the ever-valid laws of supply and demand and how they affect the daily lives of virtually every inhabitant of this planet. Instead, the Communist leaders accept the untried and unproved thesis that Marxist socialism has the remedies for all the economic ailments of mankind. The thesis of Communism is essentially economic, to provide for man's basic needs: food, shelter, secure employment, fair distribution of the goods of the world. Communism blithely ignores or closes its eyes to how mankind has satisfied these needs in the four thousand years of recorded history. If Mao had possessed any understanding of basic economics, comparable, for example, to his keen interest in history and its lessons for mankind, he could have avoided the disaster of the Great Leap Forward. This was a Mao-inspired program to more than double the rate of economic growth of industry and agriculture in a few short years. But no economic planning went into this Great Leap Forward. It was Mao's vision of a better world, untainted by any grim reality or statistics. It was presented as a crusade; the Chinese people were called on to gird up their loins and with their primitive tools to increase drastically both industrial and agricultural production.

The Great Leap Forward virtually ignored the potentials of Chinese light industry for producing consumer goods and the crying need for agricultural tools and machinery in favor of emphasis on heavy industry.

China's farmland—and only 15% of the total land area is arable—today supports a population of more than six times that of two hundred years ago. Yet farming techniques have advanced only slightly in the intervening decades. But the Great Leap Forward did not envisage any measures to make it easier to increase production through modern machinery, etc. The whole program was amateurish and conceited almost beyond belief. For example, Mao was certain that China's steel output could be drastically increased if virtually the whole nation got involved in steelmaking. To this end, thousands of small and crude pig-iron smelters and blast furnaces were set up in the agricultural communes, on the campuses of universities, and elsewhere that space permitted. These primitive backyard smelters and furnaces were manned by inexperienced peasants, students, and other workers unskilled in the arts of steel production. Meanwhile the demands on the nation's transportation system to haul the components necessary to build and operate the thousands of backyard smelters—the firebrick, coal, iron ore, etc.—constituted a much greater drain on the national economy than the comparatively few tons of poor-quality steel and pig iron produced were actually worth.

Mao kept up with the steady stream of exhortations, platitudes, slogans, and poems, almost religious in their invocations, to give rhetorical momentum to the Great Leap Forward. China was plastered with giant posters, promising, "We shall create a new heaven and earth for man," and "We shall teach the sun and the moon to change places." The whole weight of the Communist Party apparatus was brought to bear to convince the millions of Chinese that it was their moral and patriotic duty to spend their free time and energies enthusiastically carrying out the objectives of the Great Leap Forward without any additional rewards or wages from the government.

A major phase of the Great Leap Forward was the sudden collectivization of the farms of 125 million peasant families into 24,000 communes. This was the initial stage of "agricultural reform." Mao was certain that the Chinese peasants, who make up about 80% of China's population, could and would participate wholeheartedly in the Great Leap Forward. However, the majority found it strange, frightening, and hateful. Families were broken up and family life—the linchpin of Chinese society—was seriously threatened by government decree to impose communal living in place of individual households. Hundreds of thousands of peasants revolted, as the post-Mao government has disclosed. Instead of surrendering their grains and vegetables to the communes, they took their produce to the cities and sold it on the open market in open defiance of the government decrees.

Old China hands have evaluated the Great Leap Forward as a giant lurch sideways. It was economic dislocation, not economic development. The calendar of progress was set back many years by the damage inflicted on the Chinese economy through the whims and ignorance of Mao.

The Great Leap Forward (1958–60) resulted in the emergence of the first serious opposition to Mao in the top ranks of the Peking government. It was led by Liu Shaoqi, chief of state and a veteran comrade of Mao since the earliest days, and Deng Xiaoping, secretary-general of the Communist Party and also a veteran of the "Long March" of 1934–35. Liu had been a co-worker of Mao's since they first met in the Hunan coal mines in 1921. In the succeeding years Liu had risen in the Communist ranks until after the revolution he was the No. 2 man just behind Mao. Liu and Deng were essentially pragmatists and politically were to the right of Mao. They sought to consolidate the gains of the revolution—not to continue it into every phase of Chinese life, as Mao wanted—and to get on with the growth and strengthening of China as a nation. But they could accomplish little as long as the nation's economy was being bulldozed by the Great Leap Forward, set in motion by Mao. When the serious damage that this program had caused became apparent to the Politburo in Peking, it was reined in. Gradually some semblance of order was restored out of the chaos created by Mao's impulsive and unplanned decision-making.

Deng's pragmatic attitude was best expressed in his encouragement of private farming by the peasants as the only means to increase production of food, which the mass collectivization was seriously disrupting. Deng told the Politburo: "Private farming is all right, as long as it raises production; just as it doesn't matter if a cat is black or white, as long as it catches mice." This was political heresy to Mao, who countered with the rhetorical question: "Which emperor said that?"

The real lines of the ideological struggle for the body and soul of postwar China became apparent in the mid-1960s as the Great Leap Forward was phased out with little explanation of its manifest failure. Mao was placed on the defensive for the period 1961–65. To the outside world he was still the unchallenged leader of the People's Republic. However, behind closed doors in the corridors of power, his position as No. 1 and his claim of political infallibility were challenged by the pragmatists.

André Malraux, the noted French writer, who was a sympathetic observer of the Communist revolution in its earlier days, gives us a revealing vignette of this ideological rift in his book *Antimémoires*. He called on Liu Shaoqi to present the chief of state with a letter from President Charles de Gaulle. Mao was standing apart from the members of the Politburo in the Great Hall. He later remarked to Malraux, "I am alone with the masses—waiting," an obvious reference to the strained relations then existing at Politburo level.

As the reins of power began to slip from his fingers, following the disastrous Great Leap Forward, Mao became convinced that *his* revolution was being sabotaged by the "capitalist roaders," his term of contempt for pragmatists, as well as the party bureaucrats. He was correct in his opinion that his opponents were giving priority to economic development at the expense of revolutionary political and social goals. In short, the revolutionaries were becoming bourgeois, in his estimation.

Liu and Deng had taken over the day-to-day administration of the People's Republic, with Chou En-lai handling foreign affairs. The heavyhanded control of the peasants and the farms was eased. Private markets were permitted to operate. The communes were given greater autonomy to handle their own affairs. Meanwhile, in the factories the local managers enjoyed more leeway and less interference from government agencies in their daily operations. There was a definite retreat from "scientific socialism" as preached by Mao. To combat this trend, Chairman Mao launched his Cultural Revolution in 1966 to purge the ranks of the Communist Party, as well as the government, of all those who did not support his concept of continuing revolutionary social changes. This movement was intensely nationalistic and "anti-foreigner" in its outlook. This marked the rupture of the Moscow-Peking alliance. Mao did not conceal his opinion that the Khrushchev regime in Moscow was "revisionist," the ultimate in Communist invective to denote heresy among the followers of Karl Marx. Henceforth, as Mao made clear, Red Russia could no longer be the monitor and guide of its junior partner in the East, Red China, on the road to the long-awaited "workers' paradise."

One day in 1966, Chairman Mao personally pinned up a poster on the door to the offices of the Central Committee in Tiananmen Square declaring political war against the political hierarchy of Red China. In its symbolism it was comparable to Luther's break with the Catholic church.[6] This two-hundred-word manifesto, with the provocative headline "Bombard the Headquarters," was the opening gun of Mao Zedong's Cultural Revolution. It was to bring this ancient nation to the brink of civil war, as the last climactic act of the bitter and deep-seated struggle for the body and soul of Red China between the radical leftists and the pragmatic moderates.

Mao did not resign from the Communist Party; rather, he cast himself in the role of the true socialist revolutionary and reformer, going into action to cleanse the party of those individuals and factions that were sabotaging the revolution. His opponents were "capitalists," "revisionists," "deviationists," and others who had forsaken the spartan code of Marxist socialism and had been seduced by materialistic gains and perquisites of officialdom. Mao was able to muster enough political clout to persuade the Politburo to remove his two principal antagonists, Liu Shaoqi and Deng Xiaoping, from high office. Liu was arrested and imprisoned, publicly denounced as a "scab, ren-

---

[6]On Oct. 31, 1517, Martin Luther nailed his provocative "Ninety-five Theses" to the large oak door of All Saints Church in Wittenberg. With this gesture of defiance to the long-established Catholic Church, Luther launched the Protestant Reformation, which shook Europe to its foundations then and in succeeding centuries.

egade, and traitor," and expelled "forever" from the Party. He died in 1973. Deng went down with Liu and was publicly denounced as "even more sinister and dangerous than Liu." Among the many ideological sins he was charged with was riding around the country in special trains, playing bridge with his cronies. The crowning indignity inflicted on Deng was to parade him through Tiananmen Square wearing a dunce cap. He was later sent to Hopeh, where he worked as a waiter in a Party mess hall. But Deng was to survive, thanks to friends. He finally emerged at a 1973 banquet in Peking given for Prince Norodom Sihanouk of Cambodia. This was after the Cultural Revolution had run out of steam and the adverse reaction was setting in.

To carry out the Cultural Revolution, Mao was able to mobilize millions of young men and women, including teenagers, who were organized in the semimilitary "Red Guards." They operated under a broad mandate from Chairman Mao that "to rebel is justified. . . . Today the world is ours, the nation is ours, and society is ours." On eight separate occasions, Mao reviewed a total of 11 million fanatical and delirious youths in Tiananmen Square. They poured into Peking on special trains—free passage provided by the government—to salute Mao in Tiananmen Square and then to fan out throughout the country on their destructive rampages. These open-air demonstrations took place at dawn, to coincide with "rising of the Red sun in the east—Mao Zedong." Another theme constantly pounded on the new apostles of destruction and rebirth was the exhortation: "Do away with the Four Old Things: old thoughts, old culture, old customs, and old habits." It was the justification for the mob rule that followed throughout China's twenty-five provinces.

Old temples, monuments, museums containing the artifacts of imperial China, libraries, palaces, gardens, works of art, etc., were the first targets of the Red Guards. They began to burn, pillage, destroy, and deface the physical remnants of the past. Then came the harassing and killing of individuals. Any person or group suspected of harboring "capitalist" or "revisionist" tendencies or tolerance for the old order and its treasures and ways of life was considered open game. What began as reform became mob rule in uniform, as the Red Guards escaped all control and discipline from the government. The politically uneducated youth set themselves up as judge and jury to punish veteran party members as "capitalists" when, for example, the Red Guard units could not even define the character and nature of capitalism. And there was no appeal from their decisions. The Red Guards were also destructively xenophobic in their fury. Foreign-made articles in shops were seized and destroyed or looted in a wave of nationalism.[7]

The Red Guards got out of hand in their mindless crusade against phantoms created by Mao Zedong and his closest associate and chosen successor, Lin Biao, to spur them on. Units of the People's Liberation Army in some of the provinces were sent into action by their local commanders to restore law and order. Armed clashes between the PLA forces and the Red Guards were mounting as the latter sought to seize power in many of the provinces and cities. It was estimated that about 400,000 people were killed in the fighting as the destructive crusade got out of hand.[8]

In a tour of the Yangtze River area in August and September 1967, Mao was shocked by the chaos and destruction caused by the conflict between the Red Guards and those who fought off their grab for power. "I think this is civil war," Mao is reported to have said. Only years later after Mao's death has the full story of the Cultural Revolution come to the surface, detailing the full extent of the wholesale economic disruption, the collapse of public order and private morality, the suspension of the public education system above primary schools, and other serious damages sustained by the People's Republic and its billion inhabitants.

Ross Terrill in his master study of Mao Zedong capsulized the Cultural Revolution in a succinct comment: "In France the Revolution ate its children. In China the children nearly ate the Revolution."[9]

The Cultural Revolution unleashed by Mao Zedong ravaged China's higher educational system as the bubonic plague decimated medieval Europe. The universities almost ceased to function for the period 1966–70 and remained in an enfeebled state for another six

---

[7]The Boxer Rebellion of 1898–1900, in the last years of the Manchu dynasty, was an earlier outbreak of Chinese xenophobia that was somewhat similar to the anti-foreign reactions stirred up by the Cultural Revolution in the 1960s. The Boxers—their Chinese name was the "Righteous Harmony Fists"—were mainly young men, whose battle cry was "Protect the country; destroy all foreigners!" They were encouraged by the Dowager Empress Tzu-hsi to attack all the Europeans and their legations in Peking, so as to divert public attention from the ineptitude and corruption of the Manchu court. The foreign missionaries and their flocks of "rice Christians" were also prime targets of the Boxers. The defeat of the Boxer Rebellion by the armed forces of Great Britain, Germany, the United States, Japan, and Russia was followed in 1911 by the revolution which overthrew the Manchus, instigated by Sun Yat-sen, and the formation of the first Republic of China. However, in intensity, casualties, and amount of damage done and chaos created, the Cultural Revolution was greater in scope than the brief dislocation caused by the "Righteous Harmony Fists."

[8]Figure from Agence France Press and Associated Press, Feb. 3, 1979.

[9]Terrill, *Mao.*

years. Their dark night of disruption and chaos ended only in 1976 with the death of Mao and the arrest of the Gang of Four, who had kept this destructive aberration alive. The universities and later the secondary schools were under direct attack by gangs of Red Guards. They harassed and pilloried the professors and teachers as "stinking intellectuals," driving them from their lecterns, putting them in prisons, causing many to commit suicide. This was one of the lowest points in the long history of Chinese culture. Academic authority and discipline were blown away by a political typhoon which sought to denigrate higher education as the instrument of "capitalism" and the servant of "decadence." The litany of abuse was as vicious and vulgar as it was wide of the target. Even in the middle schools the teachers were humiliated by being forced to sweep their classrooms and perform other menial labor, while being subjected to constant taunts and insults by the Red Guards and the incited student body. This storm of anti-intellectualism permeated the youth of the land, as the last tidal wave of revolutionary socialism swept across the nation. As a result China has lost a generation of thinkers, teachers, and scientists, which it now badly needs for the painful process of rebuilding the economy. And this deficiency will adversely affect China's growth and development for many years to come. However, the Chinese youth have apparently realized the mistakes of the past, in which they shared in the degradation of the educational system. They are now applying to attend the universities in record numbers; some 5 million young men and women fiercely compete each year for the 300,000 undergraduate places.

Entrance exams have been revived as the prime qualification for admission. Regular four-year terms have been reinstated, as well as academic discipline and order. It seems clear that the Cultural Revolution has been repudiated more decisively in education than in any other field of social activity. The youth of the land now see that a higher education is the route to a better way of life, which the Cultural Revolution promised but could not make into reality. It is all a part of the slow reappraisal by the Chinese of the world they live in and of their standards of value.

The culmination of the abortive Cultural Revolution coincided with the beginning of Mao's decline in power and influence. It began in February 1967, when the Red Guards seized control of Shanghai. They proclaimed the formation of the People's Commune of Shanghai, patterned after the original Paris Commune of 1871 at the close of the Franco-Prussian war. The Red Guards made a nationwide appeal for the establishment of other independent communes throughout Red China. But this was the last straw, for this move was a direct threat to the very existence of the central government in Peking. At this juncture, Mao reportedly lost his nerve. He called for retreat. The Shanghai Commune was forced to dissolve itself. The storm was nearing its end, as Mao swiftly changed sides. He publicly criticized the Red Guards. The Chairman announced publicly that "if anyone continues to oppose, to fight the PLA, to destroy the means of transportation, kill people or set fires, he is committing crimes . . . and will be annihilated." To remove these troublemakers, millions of the Red Guards were banished to the countryside, compelled to earn their living as workers in the agricultural communes.

"The Great Helmsman" walked off the quarterdeck, relinquishing the navigation of the ship of state to less demonic personalities. His new role was that of the "elder statesman" rather than the dynamic revolutionary. The curtain was not lifted to reveal his feet of clay; he remained aloof from the arena of politics. In the words of one observer, "Mao behaved like a Buddha and was treated like one."

In retrospect, the Cultural Revolution was the decisive battle in the long ideological struggle for the control of Red China. Mao had been convinced that the nation was in danger of being taken over by the "capitalists," or at least that the rightist elements would drastically alter socialist plans for its future development. Hence he unleashed his battalions of Red Guards. But their excesses and amateurish bungling were counterproductive and self-defeating. China escaped complete socialization because obviously the country was not in the mood to accept the hard and heavy-handed domination of the leftists and the bullying Red Guards. The army fought back, and so did the provincial and city governments and their supporters. The Cultural Revolution never recovered its initial momentum and persuasion. However, the struggle was to simmer on just below the surface until the death of Mao in September 1976. The Cultural Revolution was then interred with him in his crystal sarcophagus, inside a $1 million mausoleum in Tiananmen Square.

Mao's death was followed by the arrest of the Gang of Four headed by Jiang Qing, actress wife of Mao and the "Jane Fonda" of Red China. This group of conspirators had taken over the leadership of the radical left, gradually elbowing the ailing chairman to the sidelines while trying to keep alive the Cultural Revolution. They had succeeded in ousting Deng Xiaoping from the corridors of power. However, they were unable to accomplish their objective of getting complete control of the party and government. With Mao's death, Hua

Guofeng, his anointed successor as party chairman, swiftly removed the Gang of Four from the scene by a successful coup d'état. Deng came back from his imprisonment to resume his post as vice-chairman. The pendulum began to swing from the left to the right.

A 180-degree turn was decreed by Deng, who was, by virtue of his experience and capabilities, the new helmsman of the ship of state. His first task was to dismantle as far as possible the power structure and ideology set up by Mao in his long years of dominance. Mao's system of government had two criteria of leadership: political reliability and the will to carry out policies to achieve his revolutionary socialism. Mao did not regard socialism in the same light as Marx, Lenin, and other ideologues. They viewed it as a "science," a proven formula to fulfill the economic needs of the lower classes: guaranteed employment, free medical care, cheap housing, free schooling, etc. Instead, socialism was more of a religion to Mao, as a way to develop *better* human beings, more socially responsible to their fellow men. That explains his growing disenchantment with the so-called "laws of socialism," the "Marxian dialectic," and other high-flying concepts, which originated in Europe and which Mao thought did not satisfy the needs of the Chinese. Mao's ideology had something in common with the Roman Catholic doctrine. He did not believe that the penitent sinner who promised to mend his evil ways would stay "reformed" for very long. He would soon sin again, a victim of his basic impulses. Man essentially was a weak reed to lean upon. He must be constantly prodded, threatened, frightened, persuaded, bribed, or otherwise cajoled to remain faithful to a moral code or to a political ideology. Mao believed that his followers would backslide into capitalism unless they were forced to live in a constant revolutionary atmosphere or environment. And more important, he was firmly convinced that Marxist socialism in its European form had become stagnant and was no longer a living and stimulating force of social change. It was too rigid, too static—and, the greatest *sin* of all, too bureaucratic!

The diminutive (four feet eleven inches) and feisty Deng Xiaoping, after more than sixty turbulent years as a Communist worker in war and peace, has finally reached the top of the heap. Deng was the obvious successor of Mao to the leadership of both the party and the government. Though he does not hold the titles of chairman or premier, he is unquestionably the dominant figure and will probably remain unchallenged until his own retirement or death. Deng's strength rests on three qualities. He is a veteran whose career as a

Communist activist few in the party can match. Born in 1904, he became a Communist as a teenager and has served through the stormy decades that followed. He made the Long March with Mao in 1934 and then helped to set up the highly effective guerrilla forces which harassed the Japanese. After the war he held important posts, culminating in his appointment as secretary-general of the Party, and member of the Politburo's executive committee.

A very ambitious man, Deng is a fighter in the party councils as well as on the field of battle. He stood up to confrontations with Mao Zedong on many occasions. His pugnacious nature belies his name, which in Chinese means "Little Peace." It could also appropriately mean "little peace" for his enemies or opponents.

Finally, Deng is a self-made man, so to speak, whose strong convictions have grown out of his own experiences and background. His views on how China should be governed are not based on an ideology, or a set of abstract concepts. His philosophy of government reflects what he thinks the Chinese need and what they can give their support to. A thoroughly pragmatic man, he nevertheless seems to share one thing in common with Mao: He does not believe an ideology imported from Europe can provide solutions for China's manifold problems. Rather the growth and development will depend largely on the Chinese people themselves and on how they are motivated. Deng believes what will truly and successfully activate the hundreds of millions of Chinese will be giving them the opportunity to better their way of life, through their own efforts. Deng's grand strategy is to harness the consumer hunger of China's hundreds of millions for an improved standard of living as the motor for economic growth. In other words, give the Chinese incentives of materialistic gain rather than political exhortations, and they will again put their shoulders to the wheel to get the nation moving.

Deng Xiaoping, perhaps unwittingly, is following in the footsteps of the late Prof. Ludwig Erhard, the architect of the amazing postwar economic recovery of West Germany. Professor Erhard formulated the *Soziale Marktwirtschaft*—"socially responsive free market economy"—and imposed it on the defeated and devastated country as it was emerging from Allied occupation to its own statehood. Wage and price controls, as well as rationing, were lifted as the struggling new postwar government gave its people complete freedom to rebuild their own lives again, largely governed only by the inexorable laws of supply and demand. The results were startling. In the space of a quarter of a century, West Germany was transformed from a bankrupt and physically gutted nation into the No. 1 economic power in Europe. As

Erhard had confidently predicted, the recovery was powered by man's acquisitive instincts, given full freedom to operate.

Deng Xiaoping has created his own "brain trust" out of the Academy of Social Sciences in Peking. In a landmark address in July 1978, its president, Hu Qiaomu, highlighted the thinking of Deng's pragmatic administration in the field of domestic economy. He emphasized the basic importance of economic laws and their effects on the government and on the lives of the Chinese. He stated that these laws "determine the human will, the consciousness and intentions of men." The Academy president reminded his listeners that socialism carries no guarantee that an economy will develop in a planned fashion and more quickly than it will in a capitalist society. On the contrary, no socialist country has ever equaled the per capita labor productivity that has been achieved in a capitalist nation. Also, a capitalist economy has built-in mechanisms to limit the impact of its mistakes, and this is something a socialist economy lacks. Hu advised the Chinese to study the operations of the advanced capitalistic countries, paying special attention to the "highly efficient planning and other managerial functions carried out in today's big corporations. . . . It is precisely in respect to this first function of the management of the capitalist enterprises . . . that the proletariat can and must learn from the capitalist class."

Since the death of Mao, China has been in a state of ferment. The nation is undergoing a transition in which the old order of things and hierarchy are being dismantled. However, the blueprints for the new post-Mao China have not as yet been completed on the drawing board. The various forces on the right and left are pushing and shoving the Party and the government so as to affect the design for the future. The result to date is something of a stalemate. Despite the general revulsion to the Cultural Revolution, there is no rush to abandon socialism in favor of a western-style "democracy." Nor is there any drastic reform of the economic structure as yet under way. The government and the party are not about to jettison the cornerstone of their socialist economy: the public or collective ownership of the means of production. The Chinese are groping for political and economic formulas which will effectively substitute for the failure of "European" socialism applied to an ancient Oriental nation, with its radically different culture and outlook.

The Chinese look overseas to three countries in particular which seem to have the answers to their own political and economic problems: Yugoslavia, Romania, and the United States. Yugoslavia is an example of an *independent* Communist state, which under Marshal

Tito developed an economy that is a working mixture of socialism and free enterprise. Romania is an example of a Communist satellite which has cleverly created a large measure of freedom for itself from Moscow's controls while also having friendly and fruitful relations with the western nations, especially the United States. And the United States looms large in the eyes of Peking, because it is the biggest and most powerful capitalist nation in the world, and the source of much of the modern technology which China must have to develop into a superpower.

However, as Deng and his pragmatic colleagues have discovered, a change in itself in the membership of the Politburo and its policies does not always accomplish the government's objectives. For example, when Deng took over in 1978, the government plunged into a bonus incentive scheme to stimulate lagging productivity in industry. Extra pay for better work was expected to remedy this chronic shortcoming. But there were hidden reefs ahead. The incentive scheme got snagged on the "iron rice bowl" system, a metaphor for job security. Inasmuch as the "iron rice bowl" means that the Chinese worker has an assured job plus a reasonable ration, there is little incentive for him to be more productive or more efficient. There is overemployment in the factories because of the labor surplus, and this also militates against efficiency and productivity. The workers can take it easy on the job and not risk the loss of their employment.[10]

Second, added wages don't mean so much if there are shortages of consumer goods on which to spend this extra income. A left-wing economist, Liu Zizhen, publicly criticized Deng's plans to encourage productivity by getting rid of redundant labor. Liu argued that if necessary, China should accept the situation where five men do the work of three and five people live off the rations designed for only three. "Everybody must have both food and work. What's wrong with this?" he wrote in the daily press.

By the end of 1980, Deng's program of economic reform was encountering difficulties—not from the Chinese people, but rather from the entrenched opposition in the Communist Party and government. The bureaucrats, a large percentage of whom were still Mao loyalists, as well as some of the generals in the army joined forces with the still remaining radicals, to block or slow down the reforms. They saw these changes as endangering their well-feathered niches in the

---

[10] In April 1981, the government began experimenting with a new form of "labor discipline" in which unproductive workers receive warnings, demerits, pay cuts, and eventually dismissal if they do not apply themselves to their tasks in the factories. However, Chinese officialdom is moving very slowly on this socially explosive reform.

administration, and loosening the traditional economic and political controls which Peking has exercised on China for centuries. The opposition has succeeded in restoring the government's right of final approval of all major investments and the allocation of vital raw materials. One sure sign that the controversy was serious came in the failure of Deng to convoke the 12th Annual Party Congress scheduled for the 1980–1981 winter period. It was finally convened in September 1982, after Deng had his party colleagues in agreement on major policy issues.

However, looking back to 1949 when Mao and the Communist Party took power in the name of the People's Republic, it is not surprising that Deng's government was creeping on its way to economic reforms. The *Economist* of London sent a panel of experts to China recently and has summarized the situation facing Deng and his colleagues as follows (*Economist*, Dec. 29, 1979):

For the past three years (1977–80) China has been run by a government of radical moderation—"moderation" because it is consciously pulling back from its predecessor's disastrous extremism; "radical" because this has meant digging down to the roots of what went wrong before. These three years of radical moderation follow 17 years of experimental Maoism from 1949 to 1966 with its intermittent foretastes of the horrors to come, and then 10 years of all-out Maoism, when the old chairman unleashed and then lost control of the cultural revolution, with consequences which China and the world are only starting to measure. Can such a government, with such antecedents, find the alternative that China can live with?

To achieve their goal—a politically stable and economically secure China—Deng Xiaoping and his new team must experiment, introduce change, and take risks. They are working against time. Within the span of two to five years they must show definite progress. Otherwise the opposition will make a strong bid to restore the Communist bureaucracy to all its former power. However, the Chinese are not expected to accept a return to totalitarian rule as readily as did the Russians when Khrushchev was ousted and Brezhnev and the old-guard party-liners resumed their iron-handed control from the Kremlin.

After Stalin's death, the reign of terror and police rule was temporarily relaxed. For a few years there was a liberalization of Communist governance. Serious consideration was given to Professor Liberman's program of economic reforms, so as to better the Soviet standard of living and to make industry more efficient and productive. But Brezhnev and his aging colleagues on the Politburo saw in this decentralization of planning and overall management control of the

Soviet economy by Moscow a direct threat to their own power structure. So the Liberman program was scrapped and the totalitarian straitjacket reimposed on the nation's economy. And this has led to a steady, inexorable decline in the living standards of the Russian people ever since.

However, today the Chinese no longer look to Moscow for guidance and direction in their political and economic affairs. With their own national identity, culture, and traditions that go into recorded history for over three thousand years, the Chinese are more self-confident. Also they are a more politically sophisticated and individualistic race than are the Slavs.

Maybe that is why the Soviet Union—a much younger nation by several millennia than China—suffers from a chronic social illness. The deep-seated insecurities which affect the behavior of the Russians are reflected in the widespread alcoholism that is virtually endemic in the motherland of socialism, the promised cure for all man's problems. Alcoholism has never been a social problem in China, for the Chinese certainly do not suffer from the doubts about life and how it should be lived that grip the Russians. For that reason alone, China's long-term future is considerably brighter than Russia's, despite the disparity in their respective military establishments.

In his book *The Chinese*, David Bonavia provides a revealing insight concerning China's superiority complex toward the Russians. For example, the Chinese have always resisted Russians' claims to contested border areas along their 4,300-mile common frontier. The Russians are always unwilling to give up any territory which they have taken over in their decades of geographical expansion. In 1969 the Russians argued that China's northern frontier since the fourth century (Chou dynasty) had been defined by the Great Wall and that all areas north of the Wall were not historically subject to China's sovereignty. At its farthest point from today's Chinese-Russian frontier, the Great Wall is over 800 miles distant; from its closest point approximately 550 miles distant. The implication was broad, if unspoken: The Russians had as much right to these lands in between the frontier and the Great Wall as did the Chinese. To this Russian point of view, a Chinese historian sarcastically commented: "Where, one may ask, were the frontiers of the *Russian* state in the fourth century B.C.?"[11]

What gives hope for China's future lies in the pregnant slogan which Deng and Co. have proclaimed to be their basic guideline:

[11] Bonavia, *The Chinese*.

"Practice is the only test of truth." For a Communist official to understand and to accept the implications of this thesis is to live dangerously. It means jettisoning large chunks of doctrine and dogma concerning Marxist-Leninist "scientific socialism" because it failed to deliver on its promises. And it further means that the definite criterion for a government's policies and operations will be simply: Do they work? If they do, they are acceptable and useful. And that is an extremely pragmatic approach to political and economic affairs. In fact, the more one thinks about this slogan, the more truly revolutionary it is in reality. In China it opened the door to ecopolitical policies and actions.

It is ironic that both Deng and Mao—though opponents in recent years—had the same basic objective: a made-in-China formula for the regeneration of this great nation into superpower status. Their methods were different. Mao sought the impossible: the transformation of the Chinese into permanently motivated revolutionaries, so as to accomplish his goal. Deng explores the possible: how to mobilize the talents and the strength of the billion Chinese to make their country a superpower by the year 2000.

To achieve superpower status, China is almost completely dependent on its economic potential, rather than on its political power or military muscle. Moreover, it must focus the talents and energies of its people on economic growth and development with the same intensity that it once applied to imposing the foreign doctrines of Marx and Lenin after the revolution was won in 1949. For the hardest, most complex problems that will confront the Chinese in the years ahead— barring an unexpected war with the Soviet Union—will be essentially economic in character and not political or military.

Consider this Mount Everest of a national problem looming up on the horizon. Sometime in the 1990s, the People's Republic will have a labor force of about 500 million literate and healthy Chinese men and women, between the ages of twenty and forty-five years, the most productive sector of any society. This group, or conglomerate of labor, will be double the work forces of the United States, Europe, and Japan combined. This nearly boundless supply of human energy is China's greatest economic asset—if the 500 million Chinese can all be properly fed and profitably employed. However, it can also be China's greatest liability if the population outruns industrial growth or the availability of food. The social explosion that could follow is almost impossible to calculate.

At present there are about 20 million workers unemployed in China. The population is increasing at the rate of 12 million annually.

And the middle schools (comparable to U.S. high schools) are graduating 12 to 15 million students into the job market each year. However, the Chinese are a resourceful and self-confident people. Since Mao's death they are now—broadly speaking—providing adequate and equal food supplies to the billion-plus Chinese. Simultaneous with the increasing food production, they have reached almost full *rural* employment—and about 75% of China's people live outside the big cities and towns. The *Economist* of London (Dec. 31, 1977) has described this startling development as follows:

> In China's entrepreneurially communized countryside . . . China has achieved the biggest macroeconomic reforms of our lifetimes. . . . It has created rural full employment by the extraordinary device of making possible a village Keynesianism through giving each of its agricultural communes of over 10,000 people its own private secondary currency (called work points) which the commune itself can create.

At present China's rural population is largely concentrated in about fifty thousand communes, scattered throughout the country. The average commune has a population of about ten thousand and is usually based on a small market town and its environs. The commune not only farms the adjacent land, but also engages in local construction projects such as flood controls and irrigation, and in small manufacturing of agricultural machinery, paper mills, etc. The commune also directs local consumer services, such as repair shops, chicken farms, furniture making and repair, food stores, clinics, and other consumer services. In short, the commune is a complete miniature economy on its own, operating all its commercial activities. Every able-bodied person, including the elderly who can volunteer, is given a job in line with his or her own individual capabilities. All workers are paid in work points, which can be redeemed in cash at regular intervals, as percentage shares of commune's total income. In effect, a jobholder's take-home pay is directly tied to the general prosperity of the commune. It is somewhat analogous to the stockholders of a business corporation, whose equities rise or fall with the income and profits of the business enterprise. Hence, virtually the entire adult population of a commune has a personal stake in its economic growth and development.

In addition, every member of the commune is entitled to cultivate his own private plot of ground—a small part of an acre—and then sell what he raises on the open market for whatever the traffic will bear. Private plots and other sidelines, such as raising pigs, will augment a peasant family's income by about one-third. The Peking government is now increasing the amount of acreage allocated to private farming, now about 7% to 10% of all arable land. For it has been shown that here, as in Communist Russia, private farming, handicapped though it may be by size, is far more productive per hectare than the collectivized farmlands operated by the communes. And also, ideologically heretical though it may be, capitalist-style private farming produces more prosperity for the peasant and more food for the city dwellers and industrial workers.

Just how far the pendulum has swung away from the Communist policies and practices originally decreed by Mao Zedong can be seen in this surprising editorial comment in the Peking *People's Daily*:[12]

> The Chinese people want to get rich and their happy days for getting rich have already started. This is a trend which cannot be reversed. . . . To get rich together is our goal. However, it is inevitable that some will get rich faster than others.

The national newspaper was referring to the improved earning power of the peasants in farm communes, equalling in some instances the incomes of the better-paid industrial workers.

In December 1982, the Peking government took official action to substitute the "socialism of riches" for the "socialism of poverty." Labor Minister Zhao Shouyi announced that the government was actively supporting the expansion of a free market economy based on private ownership of industrial and commercial collective businesses. This was the opening gun of a new offensive against the "iron rice bowl" system of guaranteed jobs and wages for all Chinese workers, which drastically handicaps productivity and industrial growth. Mr. Zhao stated that henceforth those who oppose or criticize the development of privately owned and operated business operations are running counter to official government policy, according to the *People's Daily* (Dec. 8, 1982).

That change has the support of China's new premier, Zhao Ziyang, one of the leaders of the new school of pragmatic economics. From December 1975 until August 1980, Zhao was governor of the province of Sichuan (Szechwan in the old spelling), where he gave active encouragement and support to some daring and innovative experiments to test the validity of the pragmatic school of economics. Sichuan is China's most populous province—97 million—and potentially one of its richest provinces. It has become the laboratory for economic and social change in post-Mao China. Deng, a Sichuanese

---

[12]Cited by the London *Economist*, July 17, 1982.

himself, personally chose Zhao, one of the up-and-coming young Communists, to be its governor and to be the architect of change. Zhao's success is measured by the fact that in August 1980, he was named premier of the People's Republic and is a likely candidate to succeed Deng at the top of the political hierarchy in Peking.

In Sichuan, Zhao permitted a number of industrial enterprises, after they had fulfilled their regular quotas, to use their excess capacity to manufacture other goods which were in short supply. Profits earned on this overtime production were allocated to buy new machinery and for bonuses to the workers. Previously all profits had to be turned back to the state. Zhao's innovation was so successful that it is now being copied throughout China.

Zhao pushed through another trail-breaking experiment. He told the managers of five industrial plants that they did not have to transfer their profits to the state, but could use them as they saw fit. They would be responsible for the end results and would pay taxes levied by the government on their earnings. In the first six months, the five factories increased their output of goods by 51% and their profits rose by 90%, compared to the previous six months' operations.

In outlining his program of economic reform and change, Zhao has laid down the broad guidelines of China's economic development for the future. In the main, industry must be publicly owned, but there can be exceptions. Second, people will be paid "each according to his work. . . . As long as we maintain these two conditions, we should accept any structure, any system, policy, and measure, that can promote the development of productive forces."

As China's premier, Zhao has been given the task of gradually transforming the People's Republic from a socialistic economy to a more modern and efficient economy that can better serve the needs of the nation. The end result will not be completely a free enterprise system. However, it will incorporate some of the essential elements of a capitalist economy: notably, wage differentials for the workers to encourage productivity, and freedom for management to invest profits in new machinery so as to increase productivity, allowing new industrial and commercial enterprises to be established with a minimum of red tape. This new hybrid could be described with some accuracy as "state capitalism."

Under Zhao, Sichuan launched an all-out program to cut the population growth, which continues to nullify economic changes and reforms. The ultimate goal is to limit each family to one child. Those young couples who adhere to this discipline get a monthly allowance of cash or work points, as well as priority for housing, jobs, medical treatment, and schooling. However, if the couple has a second child, all those benefits must be paid back. Those having a third child are further penalized. The child does not qualify for free medical care, housing space, a private plot, etc.

The unplanned growth of so-called "urban collectives" is another example of Chinese adaptability to do business under difficulties. They give jobs and income to unemployed workers, mainly the young and old, and have developed without any push or support from the government. For example, a group of young men will get together to establish a makeshift factory to manufacture fans, refrigerators, or any other popular item which finds a ready market. The participants share in the profits and in many instances earn more than they would if employed in an already established manufacturing plant. Also, they band together to offer a variety of consumer services, such as shoe repairs and tailoring.

These new urban collectives flourish in the big cities, such as Shanghai, Peking, and Canton. In Peking, for example, there were about three-thousand light-industry collectives, employing over 120,000 young men, at the start of 1980. The government looks benignly on these infant capitalistic enterprises, giving them considerable freedom of action. They fill the gap in the neglected consumer goods and services sector. The government's only concern is that they do not pile up capital, but rather distribute their profits to participants or spend it on new equipment. However, in general these new makeshift collectives fit into the pragmatic economics of Deng and Zhao. They constitute a fresh source of much-needed consumer goods and services to the public, which generally was a neglected sector of the economy under Mao. The urban collectives also give employment to the young and take some of the pressure off the government from the masses of jobless. In evaluating this development it is well to bear in mind that a similar haphazard and unplanned industrial and commercial development enabled Hong Kong and Singapore to become powerful and viable city-states after World War II. In both cases, the Chinese played a dominant role as innovators and developers of the economic potentials of the great Far Eastern metropolises.

Zhao Ziyang wants to experiment further on innovations arising out of the creation of "production teams" both in farms and factories of about a hundred men each. On the collective farms these teams are already working as separate economic units. Spurred on by competition and prestige, plus the additional work points they earn for the crops they harvest, ten such teams of a hundred men each are more productive than an uncoordinated mass of a thousand peasants sent into the fields to plant and harvest the crops. In recent years the Chinese have achieved a breakthrough in grain production. A recent survey showed that the annual yield was averaging close to 4 tons of rice per hectare (2.5 acres), exceeded only by Taiwan, North and South Korea, and Japan, but well ahead of other countries of Southeast Asia, which are averaging 1½ to 2½ tons per hectare.

Today, the Chinese government is being educated by the successes achieved by the urban collectives. These privately organized industrial and commercial "teams" produce a variety of consumer goods and services for the public, making a profit for themselves and increasing tax revenue for the state. At the same time they have escaped bonds of red tape that still restrict the operations of state-owned industries and commercial enterprises.

On Jan. 16, 1980, Deng Xiaoping addressed a special conference of ten thousand of the People's Republic's top officials. He outlined for them the three main tasks facing the Chinese in the 1980s: opposing the geographical and political expansion of the Soviet Union (China shares a 4,300-mile common frontier with Russia and is acutely conscious of this geopolitical problem); working for the return of Taiwan; and modernizing China's economy. However, in his address, Deng emphasized that this third objective takes priority over the other two as "the prerequisite for solving our international and domestic problems."

Thus the People's Republic becomes the first Communist power in the postwar world to embark on an *ecopolitical* course of action. For the first time, China's domestic and foreign affairs will primarily be governed by its economic objectives rather than political or military considerations. In other words, Deng has recognized that the only practical and feasible way for the People's Republic to increase its power and influence on the world stage, commensurate with its size and population, is through economic growth and development.

However, the People's Republic has a long way to go before it reaches economic maturity, a state of affairs in itself that is far short of superpower status. Deng, Zhao, and other pragmatists in Peking will be handicapped for years ahead by two millstones around their necks which will impede their planning and efforts. The first is the massive Communist bureaucracy in Peking, which for a quarter of a century has sunk its roots deep into the whole structure of government. Working for the government, with its security and its "perks," is the most coveted employment in China. It is also the only source of real power in China. Men in public office do not take kindly to suggestions that they surrender some or all of their powers, especially Communist bureaucrats, in Peking as well as in Moscow.

To these modern-day mandarins in office, the Deng-Zhao program of economic reform and change spells disaster. It means giving the managers of agricultural communes and factories more power—the power to decide what and how much to produce and what price to charge for their goods. Allocating such powers to these men also means giving them more independence, which in turn leads to more political autonomy—all of these changes at the expense of the bureaucrats in Peking. The ebbing away of their powers of regulation and control is a form of political dry rot, in the eyes of the bureaucrats, which eventually will eat away the structure of centralized government. So the reaction of the Communist mandarins in Peking will be to oppose and to sabotage where possible the pragmatic reforms of Deng, Zhao, and their colleagues.

That is the way Communists react when faced with economic reforms. Leonid Brezhnev and the Soviet Politburo summarily rejected the economic reforms of Prof. Liberman in the mid-1960s. The Dubcek government in Czechoslovakia was crushed for the same reason in 1968.

Now it is China's turn to consider in advance what will be the consequences of the economic liberalization introduced by Deng Xiaoping and Zhao Ziyang. The instincts of self-preservation run as strong in China as elsewhere in the world. Will the mandarins in Peking have the last word?

The second millstone is dual in nature: ignorance and inexperience concerning economic affairs. Political power may grow out of the barrel of a gun, as Mao Zedong once boasted. But it is equally certain that economic power does not. The Communists have a blind spot concerning economics; it is their most vulnerable point. Understanding of economics is not part of the Marxist indoctrination, except in a most negative and critical way. Capitalism is feared and hated by the sincere Communist for its many "sins" against the working masses. There is never a word about the benefits that a sound economy offers to any society. Equally important is the inexperience of the Communists in dealing with economic affairs. Since the Bolshevik revolution in 1917, the world has witnessed the inability of Communist countries to make their "planned economies" function, to provide a better standard of living for the masses than the capitalist world can. Whenever and wherever there is the lack of a profit incentive in an industrial enterprise controlled by the Communists, there is inefficiency, faulty planning and manufacturing, deficits and a wastage of assets and labor involved. This is valid not only for the construction of a steel mill or a bicycle factory but also for their subsequent operations. These twin disabilities—ignorance and inexperience—are now plaguing the attempts of Deng and Zhao and their pragmatic colleagues to transform the People's Republic into "a modern powerful socialist country" that can take its place "in the front ranks of the world" by the year 2000.

Hua Guofeng, the successor to Mao, announced with great fanfare the first phase of China's industrial modernization program in February 1978. This involved 120 large-scale projects, estimated to cost billions of dollars. Included in the list were ten iron and steel complexes, ten nonferrous-metals processing plants, eight new coal mines, ten oil and gas fields, thirty power stations, six new railways, and five new harbors. Contracts for the construction of these industrial installations were given out to leading international firms, including Krupp and Thyssen of Germany, Nippon Steel and Mitsubishi of Japan, Royal Dutch Shell and Compagnie Française des Pétroles, Rolls-Royce, Kaiser Engineers of California, etc. The Chinese were determined to buy the latest industrial technology. Now a few years later the whole modernization program is bogged down; many projects have been scaled down and others abandoned, and contracts have been canceled with penalty costs. China's credibility to carry out economic planning and reform according to modern-day standards has been damaged. What happened? Why?

The answers are not hard to find. Banal though it may be, the old cliché fits nicely: China bit off more than it could chew. Back in 1978, the officials who put together this program of massive industrial modernization had survived the ten years of economic chaos and disruption caused by Mao's Cultural Revolution. They were little prepared for the responsibilities that would be thrust on them. They had had little contact with the western world and had scant knowledge of modern industry and its needs. But they had confidence that they could buy the industrial modernization they required on the world market. They wanted the best of western technology and industrial equipment, despite the obvious fact that they were woefully lacking the skilled laborers to construct and to operate these expensive new installations.

The biggest single industrial project on the list was a $5.5 billion steel mill to be constructed at Baoshan on the Yangtze River, near Shanghai. It was to be the equal of Japan's most modern steel complex at Cita, operated by Nippon Steel. The Japanese were to assist in the construction of the Baoshan project, in connection with several leading European firms. The first stage of the Baoshan project is now in abeyance, as the whole steel complex is under review. The second phase has been abandoned. The total cost is escalating and may reach $14 billion before it is completed, if ever. What happened at Baoshan illustrates China's problems in modernizing its economy.

The Japanese consultants had first advised the Chinese Ministry of Metals to build a less complex and smaller steel plant, but the Chinese rejected this suggestion. Then it became apparent that the Chinese had not done their feasibility studies. For example, the Baoshan mill would need high-grade iron ore. The low-grade Chinese ore was not usable. Hence, the Chinese had to import more expensive ore from Australia. Then it was discovered that the large bulk-cargo ships could not unload their Australian ore at Baoshan because the Yangtze is not deep enough at that point. This required offloading before Baoshan into smaller vessels, adding to the costs of production. Then it was learned that if Baoshan was to operate at full capacity, its demands on the energy and transportation capacity of China would adversely affect other sectors of the economy. In short, it was one snafu after another, as if the planners had each worked without any contact or coordination with each other. For example, the Metals Ministry, which was responsible for the project, did little research regarding the raw materials, on the assumption that they would be supplied by other state agencies when needed. Nor was there any market research as to the ultimate consumers of the 6 million tons of steel that would be produced, because the ministry explained that it was only concerned with producing steel, not with its ultimate utilization. Finally, there seemed to be blithe unconcern with the ability to pay for Baoshan and the other 119 heavy industrial projects. Everybody seemed to assume that China's oil resources could finance the costly imports. The oil probably is there in the billions of barrels, but it is still lying below ground and not yet available on the world markets.

The Peking government has learned its lesson. It is lowering its sights from the development of heavy to light industry. In this field at least it has a cadre of experienced urban collectives now producing consumer goods on which to build. It is another stage in the slow passage of China from feudalism through revolutionary socialism to its own indigenous pattern of living that will be essentially Chinese in character.

In the early 1930s, Chiang Kai-shek's forces managed to break up the Communist Party organizations in China's major cities. The Party's center of gravity then shifted to the makeshift army which Mao

Zedong had gathered in the province of Kiangsi. Faced with the threat of extinction by Chiang's stronger armies, Mao, Deng, and the peasant soldiers began the famous Long March, a 6,000-mile trek around the great bend of the Yangtze to the caves of Yennan in distant Shensi province. From Yennan, Mao was to go forth to conquer the Japanese as well as to defeat Chiang and his nationalists decisively and ultimately to proclaim the revolutionary People's Republic from Peking's Tiananmen Square in 1949.

Three decades later, Deng & Co. have launched a New Long March. The Peking *People's Daily* front-paged this development: "We are setting out on our New Long March to conquer the mountains, seas, plains, oil fields, and mines of our motherland. We want to scale the heights of science and technology. We want to develop normal trade relations with other countries of the world."

These words may sound banal, inflated, and too optimistic. But they do reflect a basic change in the objectives and outlook of the Chinese government. This New Long March is essentially economic—not political. It is a far cry from Moscow's Marxian dialectic. Emanating from the leading Third World nation, it is a portent of a less dangerous and more progressive world of the future. China sets an example for other Third World countries to follow.

TWO men with fertile imaginations, an Arab and a Venezuelan, plus the Texas Railway Commission, formed an odd amalgam some years ago which produced the most daring and lucrative money-making system ever devised by the mind of man. The result of this rare and fortuitous set of circumstances was the Organization of Petroleum Exporting Countries—OPEC.

Since it became operational in 1973, OPEC has siphoned off well over $600 billion from the industrial nations and their poor cousin countries of the Third World. This represents the greatest transfer of wealth that the world has ever known in such a short space of time.

However, the creation of this economic colossus has come about in such a swift and unplanned fashion and involves so much money that it carries within itself the seeds of its own dissolution. The breakup of OPEC's stranglehold on the world's supplies of fuel and energy is inevitable—and will come sooner than expected. This will result principally from the Arab oil producers' ignorance of and inexperience with certain basic economic and political principles and practices.

OPEC[1] is a loose association of thirteen diverse, quarrelsome, and potentially unstable countries, many of which are so new to the world

---

[1]At the risk of confusing the reader, we must introduce a sister organization to OPEC. It is OAPEC, the Organization of Arab Petroleum Exporting Countries—that is, the oil-producing countries of the Persian Gulf and Mediterranean areas which are primarily Islamic. OAPEC comprises Saudi Arabia, Iran, Iraq, Kuwait, Libya, the United Arab Emirates, Qatar, and Oman. OAPEC actually controls more oil, but OPEC speaks for the oil cartel as a whole.

scene they have only first-generation governments. They have held together in the cartel arrangement, united by their large oil resources, their avarice, and their hatred and envy of the western nations, particularly the United States. Since OPEC became independently operational in 1973, their oil monopoly has become successful and profitable far beyond the wildest dreams of its two founding fathers, Abdullah al-Tariki and Juan Pablo Pérez Alfonso, plus the unwitting assistance of the Texas Railway Commission.

It is difficult, if not impossible, to apportion credit between these two men for the creation of OPEC. By an amazing coincidence, each separately arrived at his own ideas through a common but unshared education and experience. We know more about Juan Pablo Pérez Alfonso. His father was a prosperous coffee planter in Venezuela, and Juan Pablo was educated as a lawyer and then entered politics in 1938, imbued with liberal views. At that time Venezuela had become the second-largest oil producer in the world, after the United States, or, more specifically, after the state of Texas. In 1945, when Romulo Betancourt was elected president, Pérez Alfonso became the Venezuelan minister for oil. Pérez Alfonso recognized that Venezuela had a limited supply of crude deposits, unless new fields were uncovered.

Pérez Alfonso had been attracted to the operations of the Texas Railway Commission. This state agency in 1935 had been given the authority to regulate the amount of oil that could be pumped out of each wellhead each month, so as to keep the prices stable and to avoid a production glut.[2] This seemed to be an eminently sensible idea to Pérez Alfonso, and so he invited experts of the Texas Railway Commission to come to Caracas to advise him and his government on how Venezuela could best conserve its most prized national asset, and at the same time enjoy the fullest market potentials for its great pool of oil lying beneath Lake Maracaibo.

Pérez Alfonso quickly grasped the simple logic of the Texas oil industry operating through the Railway Commission: Control the rate of production and you can control the price and maintain a stable market. It was just what he had been looking for, and from that moment on Pérez Alfonso had found his cause.

---

[2]In the immediate postwar years, the United States was producing approximately 230 million tons of crude a year, most of which originated in Texas. In the same period, the oil pumped out of the Middle East states was only 34 million tons a year, while the total global output was 371 million tons annually, also covering principally Venezuela, Indonesia, and the Soviet Union, as well as America's 230 million tons.

However, in 1948 a military junta headed by General Marcos Pérez Jiménez took over the Venezuelan government, and it was not overthrown until ten years later. In that decade, Juan Pérez Alfonso went into exile, first in Washington and then in Mexico City. In this period he devoted his time to diagnosing Venezuela's economic problem as producer of oil, its principal source of wealth, of which it retained only 11% each year of what was pumped out of the ground. He also closely studied the U.S. oil industry and its world operations, and the mechanics of the Texas Railway Commission. In 1958, General Jiménez, with his stolen oil millions, was ousted from power in Caracas and Romulo Betancourt returned to take over as president. He immediately recalled Pérez Alfonso from exile to resume his post as minister of hydrocarbons and minerals.

Meanwhile, after World War II a young Arab, Abdullah al-Tariki, came to the United States to study oil engineering at the University of Texas. He was later employed by Texaco as a trainee, reportedly an experience which embittered him because of the treatment he received. Despite that, he married an American girl, but was later divorced. Young Tariki was fascinated by the size and the operations of the major U.S. oil companies and made a detailed study of the range of their activities at home and abroad. He also examined at first hand the purposes and the functions of the Texas Railway Commission and its regulation of the production of oil. Like his fellow explorer Pérez Alfonso, Abdullah al-Tariki grasped the central purpose of the Railway Commission's day-to-day control of Texas oil production. He was also a convert to the doctrine that the oil producer must regulate his output so as to maintain a stable market—not a new doctrine by any means, but in the hands of Tariki and Pérez Alfonso it was eventually to become an economic atomic bomb.

Before leaving the United States, Tariki also studied the U.S. congressional hearings of the 1950s, which explored in detail the covert practices of the major oil companies in their price-fixing, production quotas, cartels, and other market-restrictive practices. When he returned to the Middle East, he was the first real Arab "expert" in the petroleum field. He was appointed to be the adviser on oil affairs by the Saudi Arabian government.

Possessed with a fertile and imaginative intellect, he began to advocate the formation of an Arab oil cartel, which would operate along the lines of the Texas Railway Commission. He looked forward to the day when the Arabs would take over full control of the pricing and production of their oil reserves from the hands of the "seven sisters,"[3] the major international oil companies which owned and operated all the concessions in the Middle East of any importance.

Tariki and Pérez Alfonso met in 1959 at the first Arab Petroleum Conference in Cairo. This was the initial tentative and hesitant step of the Arab oil producers to explore whether they could work together to raise prices and supplement their then meager royalties from the foreign oil companies. This meeting had one momentous result. As Pérez Alfonso later disclosed, he made a secret agreement to work with Tariki.

A year later in Baghdad, largely at their instigation and buttressed by the detailed information they provided about how the Texas Railway Commission operated, as well as what went on behind the bland corporate facades of the great U.S. oil companies, the Organization of the Petroleum Exporting Countries (OPEC) was officially formed. The event went unnoticed in the world press and the *New York Times* gave it only a one-paragraph mention on its business pages.

Tariki and Pérez Alfonso were prophets before their time, whose ideas struck no responsive chords among their own countrymen. There was a world oil glut. The price dropped as low as $1 a barrel. There was a buyer's, not a seller's, market. Tariki in particular was regarded as a radical whose views were considered dangerous because they might invite some reprisals from the all-powerful oil companies. So in 1962 he was removed from office as Saudi Arabia's oil minister. His successor was his assistant, Sheikh Ahmed Zaki al-Yamani, who has proved to be a gifted and faithful disciple of the economic doctrines laid down by the founding fathers of OPEC—and the Texas Railway Commission.

In Vienna on Oct. 16, 1973, the oil ministers of Saudi Arabia, Iran, Iraq, Kuwait, Qatar, and Abu Dhabi, the leading oil-producing states in the Persian Gulf area, took control of the pricing of the petroleum production of their countries out of the hands of the major international oil companies. Then began a swift succession of price raises for crude oil, first from $3.01 a barrel to $5.11, and then in the following December to $11.65. With these independent actions, OPEC set its money-making machine into high gear. The millions and then billions of petrodollars began to pour into the treasuries of its members, the volume steadily rising with the frequent price hikes, until a barrel of oil

[3]Enrico Mattei, former head of the Italian state oil company, was the author of this descriptive phrase identifying the major international oil companies—as they are now known, Exxon, Texaco, British Petroleum, Shell, Gulf, Mobil, and Socal (Standard Oil of California)—for their stranglehold on global oil production. Mattei was their bitter opponent and teamed up with the Russians to sell Soviet oil in an attempt to break the seven sisters' monopoly of this market. Mattei was killed in a mysterious plane crash in Sicily in 1962, ending this phase of Russian oil exports to the West.

cost more than $40 in the spring of 1979 in the Rotterdam spot market.

For example, a prominent Arab banker[4] has stated that by the end of 1980, the leading Arab oil producers—Saudi Arabia, Kuwait, Libya, Iraq, and the United Arab Emirates—alone had amassed over $355 billion in "net foreign assets," deposited in foreign banks and overseas investments. Obviously this figure does not cover the several hundred billion dollars which have already been spent by these oil-producer states in their own modernization and industrialization programs.

However, this continuous hemorrhaging of America's capital assets and those of other industrial nations[5] caused economic carnage worldwide. Crude oil prices, which jumped from $3.15 a barrel in 1973 to over $40 a barrel in 1980, were largely responsible for America's double-digit inflation, its growing unemployment, the crippling of the nation's great automotive industry, and a host of other economic problems.

The major Persian Gulf oil producers had finally become convinced of the truth of a dynamic ecopolitical principle laid down by Gamal Abdel Nasser. As the leader of the revolution against Egypt's corrupt and decadent regime led by King Farouk, Nasser was the first great pan-Islamic figure of the postwar era. Nasser prophesied in his 1954 book *The Philosophy of a Revolution:* "Petroleum is the vital nerve of civilization, without which all of its means cannot exist." He further stated that the Islamic world could not achieve real power and influence on the international scene unless it exploited fully the political and economic powers inherent in the vast oil resources of the Middle East—until it had unsheathed its "oil weapon."

Sheikh Ahmed Zaki al-Yamani, the minister of oil for Saudi Arabia, is a well-known figure in the world press and television screens because he is the spokesman for the biggest oil producer in the Persian Gulf. He is a handsome man, with his trim beard below a usually smiling and friendly countenance. In any event, that is how the photographers portray him to the world at large. In his many interviews and statements, he gives the impression that he is America's only true friend in the contentious Islamic world, always seeking to hold down

[4]Hikmat Nuwayhid, financial and industrial manager of the Industrial Bank of Kuwait, as reported in the *Wall Street Journal*, Feb. 9, 1981.

[5]The major American and European banks have loaned out $190 billion to less-developed nations of the Third World to enable them to pay for their oil imports from OPEC suppliers. There is lively speculation in international financial circles about whether these loans will ever be repaid. If not, the leading U.S. banks will be left holding the bag. In addition there is about $300 billion from the World Bank and International Monetary Fund still outstanding.

oil prices as a political favor to the United States, the biggest single consumer of Saudi crude oil. But his real talent lies in another related field of information. American-educated (New York University and Harvard), he was the most effective propaganda minister for OPEC since its formation. It was his major role in life, though purely in an unofficial capacity. He was an expert on when to offer the carrot and when to apply the stick to the somewhat obtuse foreign ministers and oil executives of the western nations. They fawned on him; his visits were state occasions. He was in his own way more important than any one of the rulers of the Arab states. His only rival in the Persian Gulf for the attention of the western industrial nations was the late shah of Iran. The shah's well-publicized preachings and posturings to the world at large were enhanced by his imperial role as "King of Kings" (Shahanshah) with the fabled and bejeweled "Peacock Throne" as the seat of his power. Sheikh Yamani had more oil at his command; Mohammed Reza Shah Pahlavi had more guns and more regal ostentation to catch world attention.

Sheikh Yamani had the ears of New York and Washington, and he reveled in his role as the all-wise friend and soothsayer in advising the Americans how to solve their "energy problem." In the immediate years after 1973, when OPEC started the ball rolling by suddenly quadrupling the prices, Yamani made it clear that this was only "long-delayed justice." For years the big oil companies had been "grossly profiteering" on their oil concessions in the Persian Gulf. Then it cost them approximately $0.15 a barrel to deliver it from wellhead to oil tanker, later to be sold for $1.18 on the world market. Today the same oil costs perhaps $0.60 per barrel to put aboard a tanker and then is sold for up to $34 to the western industrial consumers—a mark-up of more than 5000%—in the summer of 1982. The gall that OPEC displayed in its profiteering is virtually unmatched in history.

When it became apparent that Yamani had to placate the rising temper of the Americans at the high cost of gasoline, he began lecturing to the United States that it "must conserve, cut down on its wasteful use of gasoline by the general public." Reduced U.S. consumption of gasoline would lead to stable world prices, he promised—a promise that was never to be kept.

Yet OPEC continued to meet once or twice every year, and each occasion brought forth a new and higher schedule of oil prices. However, Yamani was always quick to point out that "Western inflation" was to blame. He was always dutifully echoed by a Greek chorus of other Arab sheikhs that they had to face ever-increasing prices for their imports of Cadillacs, machinery, household appliances, desalinization plants, etc. To pay the higher prices for U.S. and European goods and services, they had to charge more for their oil. At first glance, it seemed a reasonable and logical explanation of continuing rounds of price increases of crude oil. Of course, Yamani & Co. never for one minute admitted that OPEC's escalation of crude oil prices was an immediate and direct contributor to the inflation spirals in America and Europe.

By the end of 1978 the propaganda barrage and camouflage of specious reasons for the never-ending and spiraling price increases for Middle East crude oil began to wear thin and shabby. This was clearly evident at the December 1978 conference of OPEC at Abu Dhabi, a small country but a major oil producer on the Persian Gulf. After several days of wrangling, the delegates reached a new pricing formula, designed to "squeeze the goose without killing it," as one U.S. oil expert commented.[6] Under this new agreement, the crude oil price would be jumped 2.5%, every quarter of each year, for an annual increment of 10%. Obviously, this formula bore no relationship whatsoever to the current and fluctuating levels of inflation, commodities, and other economic indices. It lasted only to the 1981–82 worldwide oil glut.

However, what followed the new OPEC agreement was a victory celebration which clearly disclosed how empty of content and sincerity were the protestations of friendship and commercial goodwill that the OPEC bosses had been directing toward their American and European customers. On the tennis court of the Abu Dhabi Hilton, alleged to be the leading hotel on the Persian Gulf, the OPEC delegates staged "The Dance of the Rifles," a traditional Arabic ritual to mark the decisive defeat of an enemy. Leading the procession were Sheikh Mana bin Said-al-Otaibah, Abu Dhabi's oil minister, followed by Sheikh Yamani, his Saudi Arabian counterpart, and their colleagues, all brandishing automatic rifles. Fortunately for posterity, pictures of this bizarre anti-western demonstration were captured by photographers of Associated Press and Black Star and were published in the world press in the last week of 1978. Sheikh Zaki al-Yamani's participation in this "Dance of the Rifles" clearly earned him the public relations booby prize of the year.[7]

[6]Morris A. Adelman, petroleum economist at Massachusetts Institute of Technology, quoted in *Newsweek*, Jan. 1, 1979.

[7]In the traditional Islamic order of things, the world is divided into two categories, *dar al-Islam*, "Moslem territory," and *dar al-harb*, "hostile territory." The "Dance of the Rifles" at the Abu Dhabi Hilton inadvertently lifted the curtain to reveal the true feeling of OPEC's Arab rulers concerning the western industrial nations. Another example of this phobia comes to mind. In January 1974, when OPEC quadrupled the price of oil to $11.53 a barrel, an Arab spokesman was quoted by the western press as stating exultantly: "This is our revenge for Poitiers!" In A.D. 732, the Frankish army of Charles "The Hammer" Martel defeated the invading forces of Islam at the Battle of Poitiers, then a small town in west-central France. It was a defeat that still rankles the militant followers of the Prophet Mohammed, for it ended their dream of the conquest of Christian Europe. The Arabs apparently never forget a defeat or forgive an injury suffered by them.

The Persian Gulf states are faced with a series of paradoxes—political, economic, social, and military—which appear to be insurmountable. The failure to find an escape from these interlocking quandaries could bring down OPEC's fragile house of cards in short order. Overshadowing the day-to-day operations of OPEC is the major paradox of how to impose—and make work—a wide-ranging, western-type industrialization of an ancient and theocratic society, with its roots buried deep in the barren sandy wastes of the Arabian peninsula. It is a society that has been tribal, nomadic, inbred, and virtually unchanged for the last thousand years, until oil was discovered. The rulers of the oil-producing Arab sheikhdoms want to create industries which can utilize the abundant and cheap oil and natural gas available. They want to invest some of the billions which are pouring into their treasuries in the industrial development of their respective states. Then when the oil and natural gas reserves run short they will have an industrial economy together with an urbanized civilization that can support itself. That is the master plan, outlined in the broadest of strokes. But where the troubles begin is in trying to adapt this plan to reality. In short, they are attempting to build "instant Pittsburghs," so to speak, on what was a few years ago sandy wasteland, populated by illiterate nomads and fishermen. They are, in effect, trying to make the transition from camel to bulldozer, from abacus to computer, in a single generation. Some of the Arab bureaucrats are aware that they may be engaged in an impossible venture. Others, like Ghazi el-Quisabi, the Saudi Arabian minister for industry, think it can be accomplished. In an interview with *Fortune* magazine (July 31, 1978), he stated: "Many economists tell us that we cannot compress the century-long process of development—the creation of infrastructure, manpower training, industrialization in a few short decades. But since no nation with our resources has ever tried to do so, nobody knows if it can be done. We shall try."

However, as we shall examine in detail, the Arabs have just two basic resources: oil and money. On paper these would seem to be very substantial resources indeed. But the reality is quite different and depressing. The deficiencies and obstacles are great and manifold. Just to name a few: small and illiterate native populations; no defensible frontiers; a work force, from managers to street sweepers, that is 75% foreign in composition; a public school system that is still in its infancy; and native populations just becoming acquainted with the tools and mechanics of modern industry and not showing any marked interest in this form of work. In effect, foreigners are running their countries. For example, there is an air of fantasy about the current state of education in Saudi Arabia and in the other Gulf states. Everybody pays lip service to the concept that education is the answer to the industrialization and modernization programs. However, official photographs show classrooms filled with empty desks. At the same time, the governments make fantastic claims about the number of children and adolescents in school. For example, in January 1978, the Saudi government reported that 928,000 students were attending primary and secondary schools, 23,000 were in the country's six universities, and another 10,000 Saudis were enrolled in universities and colleges abroad. When one considers that the basic population, excluding foreigners who are not eligible for this state-financed education, ranges from 3.5 to 5 million Saudis, it is a strain on one's credulity even to consider such figures.

About one-quarter of the students in Saudi Arabia's six universities are taking medical or engineering courses, and the rest are to be found in the social sciences. One must keep in mind another salient fact: About 90% of all the teachers are foreigners—Palestinians, Egyptians, etc. Though Moslems, they can hardly be expected to hew to a solid, unwavering pro-Saudi cultural, political, and economic line in their contacts with their students.

The universities teach social sciences, humanities, etc., but surprisingly only 3% of the students are enrolled in agricultural courses. Yet farming and the raising of sheep, camels, goats, and other livestock were the way of life for most Saudis before oil was discovered. Despite that fact, only 0.8% of the first five-year plan's funds were allocated for agricultural development. In the years ahead, the Saudis will become increasingly dependent on food imported from other countries.

Finally, what will be the cultural, social, economic, and political effects of an educational system with a staff which is now about three-quarters foreign—Egyptians, Palestinians, Lebanese, and other better-schooled groups of Moslems in the Middle East? It will produce students who will not fit into the mold that either their parents or their tribal leaders hoped for.

Massive education of the native Arab population will in the coming years possibly lessen the present dependence on the foreigner, at least in the top levels of their economic establishments. But too many of the young Arabs seek cushy government jobs after completing their studies. They show little desire to take over the jobs now filled by foreign technicians and managers. In fact, this holds true throughout the economic and social structure, raising doubts as to whether the Persian Gulf states can ever be truly the masters of their own establishments. A recent report on developments in the Gulf pointed out that "it is unrealistic to expect traders or nomads to respond enthusiastically to calls that they become engineers or operatives in industrial plants."[8]

Today, in 1981, the dimensions and nature of the economic crisis that looms over the Persian Gulf states are becoming clearer and more threatening, helped by the longer perspective that the passage of time provides. In the simplest of terms, the Arabs cannot have their cake and eat it too. Though their oil revenues increased by leaps and bounds from 1974 to 1980, the Arabs will not be able to carry out their industrialization and modernization programs, at least not as they had once so happily planned. Their multibillion-dollar incomes are creating more problems and obstacles than they are solving. One recalls the story of the legendary King Midas; everything he touched turned to gold, even the food he put into his mouth.

In short, the Arabs are operating on the assumption that their billions of petrodollars can buy for their use a fully functioning modern industrial economy, with all the trappings and amenities of a western civilization to go with it. It is an odd conceit, because in reality, they contribute precious little to the achievement of this goal, except the oil that is pumped out of their sandy wastes. Perhaps they can make substantial progress toward the industrialization and modernization of their petroleum principalities, but in the final analysis this will not be accomplished by the Arabs. It will have been planned, built, and operated by foreigners.

The world of Islam would still be sleeping through the twentieth century if Europeans and Americans hadn't discovered the oil deposits of the Middle East,[9] drilled the wells, and developed the oil industry and its vast infrastructure in the Persian Gulf. Even after the foreigners' oil concessions had been nationalized by the Arab governments, they still had to employ foreigners to handle all aspects of the vast and complicated infrastructure of the oil industry that has mushroomed since World War II. Foreigners also administer the governmental and business operations of these sheikhdoms—whose native-born populations are mostly illiterate—that have since expanded into giant enterprises. Arabs of all social classes avoid, if possible, menial

[8]May Ziward-Daftari, ed., *Issues in Development: The Arab Gulf States*. (London: MD Research and Services, May 1980).

[9]Major Frank Holmes, a New Zealand geologist, was the first to sniff out on the Arabian peninsula the presence of oil, which he discovered at Bahrain in 1923. He bought a drilling concession from the local sheikh for a few thousand dollars. He later offered the concession to Standard Oil of New Jersey (now known as Exxon) for $50,000. Walter Teagle, Standard's president, had the candor to admit that he had committed a "billion-dollar blunder" by rejecting Holmes's offer.

labor, as well as technical, clerical, and administrative jobs, especially if foreigners are available to fill them.

However, since 1973–74, with unfeigned enthusiasm and acquisitive agility, the Arab rulers have been concentrating their minds and their energies on harvesting the capital wealth of the oil-consuming nations, both rich and poor. Judging from the record, until just recently they have given little thought to the damage they have been inflicting, not only on the economies of the industrial and Third World nations, but also on their own economic futures, as we shall further explore in this chapter.

Prof. C. Northcote Parkinson, a witty and erudite English observer of man's follies in the administration of his governmental and business affairs, has propounded several laws which govern such conduct. While presented to us in a somewhat lighthearted vein, the Parkinson postulates contain some proven economic truths. One is that work expands to fill the time available for its completion. In other words, a simple development project tends to become more complicated and more expensive and to spread its operational boundaries as work progresses. The second and perhaps the more important of the professor's findings is that expenditures always increase in direct proportion to rising income. In effect, if more money is made available to spend, man seems unable to resist the temptation to spend it as fast as it comes into his hands, if not faster. Without such laws or principles actually functioning, the whole economy of "cost overruns," of which the U.S. naval construction and space programs are such splendid examples, would be inexplicable. Hence, Prof. Parkinson's observations are not only relevant to developments in the Persian Gulf area, they also explain what is happening and why the Arab oil producers are getting so mired down in their incredible Croesus-like prosperity.[10]

The glaring weakness that relentlessly stalks the Arab members of the OPEC oil cartel is their lack of native-born manpower in all categories of labor, from executives to street sweepers. A few examples will illustrate this dilemma. The street sweeping in Riyadh, the capital of Saudi Arabia, is under contract to an Illinois company, which employs Yemenis and Baluchis to do the actual work. The Saudi telephone system—free phone service is promised for every residence—was put together by a Swedish company and is now actually operated by Canadian Bell Telephone. An American management company

---

[10]Parkinson's laws are first cousins to another bugaboo of modern-day civilization, Murphy's law, which states that if anything can go wrong, it surely will. Hence it can be readily understood why the outlook is so unpromising for the jerry-built economic structures that the Arabs are attempting to impose in a part of the world once described as "the land that God forgot."

operates the hospitals, which are staffed mainly with Egyptian doctors and nurses. A leading hotel on the Persian Gulf is the Dubai Sheraton, built by Americans, managed by a Swiss, staffed with Filipino waiters and European chefs, with an Austrian string quartet providing the Arab guests with dinner music. Abu Dhabi, one of the oil-rich members of the United Arab Emirates—it produces about 80% of the UAE's 1.75 million barrels a day—has only about 30,000 native-born citizens. To protect their rich heritage, it has had to employ foreign mercenaries. About three-quarters of the 37,000-man defense force to protect Abu Dhabi is made up of neighboring Omanis. It is called the "weekend army," because a great number of the Omani recruits tend to slip across the border each weekend to visit their families.

This lack of native-born and skilled manpower is acutely embarrassing to the Arab rulers. The actual population figures are guarded as state secrets. Only estimates are given out by government spokesmen, never the exact results of the most recent census. As the London *Economist*'s survey of Arabia in 1977 commented: "Population is one of the central political issues of the region. It is so sensitive that censuses are secret and inflated totals are common. . . . 'Guess the population' is the favorite game among the diplomats in Saudi Arabia."

An even stronger criticism of the Arab cover-up of population data and of the reasons for this practice is offered by Prof. J. B. Kelly:

> To exorcise the demons of doubt and confusion that their hectic expenditure of oil revenues has brought in its train, the governments of these states have resorted to the hocus-pocus of statistics. To give credibility to their claims to rule over politics worthy of international recognition as independent states, they have put out figures for the size of their populations and then, alarmed by the proportion of resident foreigners that these reveal, they have subsequently doctored the figures to show a higher percentage of native-born inhabitants than actually exist.[11]

For example, one can never find a hard-and-fast figure for the population of Saudi Arabia. In most press reports and surveys it ranges from 6 to 12 million. However, those long resident in Arabia, as well as diplomats, believe the actual native-born population ranges between 3.5 and 5 million. The country is also host to some 1.25 million foreigners, who make up about 75% of all those employed in the Saudi government and on development projects.

The other oil-producing states in the Arabian peninsula— Kuwait, Bahrain, Qatar, the United Arab Emirates (a loose federation

[11]J. B. Kelly, *Arabia, the Gulf and the West* (New York: Basic Books, 1980).

of seven sheikhdoms), and Oman—have a total population today of about 4 million. Of this number, only about two-fifths, or 1.6 million, are native-born citizens. The other 2.4 million residents are foreigners: an exotic racial and ethnic mix of Americans and Europeans, Japanese, Egyptians, Iraqis, Lebanese, Baluchis, Pakistanis, Indians, Koreans, Yemenis, Syrians, Turks, Afghans, Filipinos, Chinese, Omanis, Dhufaris, Hadramis, Jordanians, etc.

Two other oil-producing states on the Persian Gulf are Iran, with a population of 34 million, and Iraq, with 12 million. While they do not suffer the acute shortage of unskilled labor that sheikhdoms on the west side of the Gulf do, they are obviously in need of western technicians in virtually all capacities. Iran and Iraq are not considered Arabic in character, though they are adherents of the two main religious groups of the Moslem world, the Sunni and Shiite sects. However, from a strictly racial and ethnic classification, Iran and Iraq are a mixed bag of tribal peoples, in a constant state of irritation with other tribal or religious groups, both inside and outside their national frontiers.

For example, the most important historical date to many Iraqis and Iranians is the battle of Qadisiya in A.D. 737. The warriors of Islam, sweeping out of the peninsula, defeated the imperial army of the Sassanian (Persian) king at Qadisiya. This ended Persian domination of the Middle East and their rule of the ancestors of the modern-day Iraqis. Today the quarrel is still perpetuated, because the Iranians are primarily Shiite in numbers, while the government of Iraq at Baghdad is controlled by a minority Sunni sect. The Ayatollah Khomeini of Iran is the acknowledged leader of all the Shiite Moslems in the Middle East, and seeks to arouse his religious followers in Iraq to throw out the "satanic infidels" of the Iraqi government of Saddam Hussein. The latter in turn evoked the folklore of the Qadisiya victory more than a thousand years ago to rally the Iraqis to support his attack on Iran in the fall of 1980. The current Iran-Iraqi war is the latest chapter in bitter internecine rivalry, which, however, is not a major factor elsewhere on the Arabian peninsula.

In any economic view of basic petroleum development in the Persian Gulf area, one must consider Iran and Iraq as separate and disparate entities. Each of these countries is an ethnic, political, and religious mix of tribes, sects, races, as easily ignited to conflict as dry grass on a wind-swept prairie. It is this population mishmash that distinguishes in great measure Iran and Iraq from Saudi Arabia, Kuwait, Oman, Qatar, and the collection of the sheikhdoms known as the United Arab Emirates, clustered in the southeast corner of the Arabian peninsula. These countries are Arabian in character and outlook, as Islamic as ever was Saladin of the time of the Crusades.

One of the striking and disturbing anomalies of the Middle East is that today it produces about 35.5% of the world's crude oil. Four of these states have a daily output of almost 23% of the world's production, and yet they have a total native population—excluding the hundreds of thousands of foreign workers who have flooded in—of only between 5 and 6 million people. They are Saudi Arabia, Kuwait, the United Arab Emirates, and Qatar. Before the oil glut, these four states enjoyed a total oil income of about $450 million per day, or about $165 billion a year. The other four Middle East oil powers are Iraq and Iran (suffering from reduced production because of war damage to their petroleum installations), Libya, and Algeria. Together these four are pumping out about 12.7% of the daily world production of crude and probably enjoying total oil revenues of $225 million per day, or about $82 billion a year.

Life is good if you are born a citizen of one of the Persian Gulf oil sheikhdoms. For example, the per capita income in Kuwait is about $16,000 per year. Of course, that amount is not handed out to the individual Kuwaiti, but every native-born male citizen—there are less than 100,000 of them out of a total Kuwait population of about 1.3 million—is guaranteed full-time employment, plus a pension, tied to income earnings. Food and housing are cheap, thanks to government subsidies. Education and medical care are free, as are utilities and telephone service, and there are many other spin-off benefits arising from the $21 billion annual income which Kuwait receives. This important oil sheikhdom, measuring only 6,880 square miles, sits on top of the Burgan field, estimated to be the world's second-largest deposit of crude oil.

However, this largesse is not extended to the foreigners who compose about 75% of the Kuwait's work force, from garbage collectors to laboratory technicians. Meanwhile the Kuwaitis occupy about 54% of all government jobs, so they keep control in their hands. The foreigners are paid only about half the wages that a Kuwaiti receives in any comparable position. For example, a Kuwaiti white-collar employee earns about $750 per month, in addition to all his other financial benefits from the government. The foreigner in the same job category—probably a multilanguage Egyptian or Palestinian clerk—will be paid only $350 and receive none of the fringe benefits that a native-born Kuwaiti is entitled to, such as cheap housing, free medical care, education for his children, etc. This rank disparity in living standards and access to public funds, which is the lot of the foreign worker, is found throughout the Persian Gulf states. Despite their almost 100% dependence on foreign workers and technicians, not only for today but for the years to come, the Arab oil-producing states make no effort whatsoever to encourage the foreigners to settle down and become permanent residents. Only rarely is a foreigner granted citizenship, and then only because he is in a special and nonpolitical category, such as medical doctors. The foreign laborers are secluded in their living quarters as far as possible from the native population, to lessen their contacts and their influence. The Arabs are fearful that allowing foreigners to intermingle with their own people will create new political issues and problems. For example, one of the reasons why South Korean firms have received substantial construction contracts in the Gulf area is that they bring their own labor force with them, and then when the project is completed all the South Koreans are sent back home. The net result of this discrimination against the foreigners, especially those in the worker classes, is to create a simmering pot of social discontent, which could boil over in the not-too-distant future. For, in the final analysis, too few Arabs in the Persian Gulf states control too much wealth, and this situation is a fertile field for political and social discord.

Kuwait is ruled by the al-Sabah clan, the hereditary sheikhs of this northwestern corner of the Persian Gulf. They are well aware of their vulnerability, having no natural frontiers to give them geographical protection. So the Kuwait government closes its eyes to the fact that many terrorists, especially the Palestinian PLO, find temporary refuge within its borders. Also the Kuwait government pays out between 6% and 8% of its yearly income in a "foreign aid" program, a euphemism for buying protection from potentially threatening political forces, such as the PLO, the Iraqis, and other restive and radical elements of the Arab population in the Middle East.

The manner in which the oil income of the Persian Gulf sheikhdoms is divided among the ruling class and the members of the tribal clan is usually a "house secret," closely guarded from the foreign press and diplomats. However, an interesting insight is provided by the sheikhdom of Qatar, a barren, flat, 4,400-square-mile peninsula that extends from the Arabian peninsula out into the Persian Gulf. Oil was discovered in Qatar in the early 1950s. This sheikhdom is inhabited by a small indigenous population of about 60,000 Qataris—excluding the 200,000 foreigners who have since flowed into this area to take up the jobs of operating the oil fields and their ancillary activities.

The Qataris had previously eked out a precarious living by raising goats and camels, plus some fishing, pearling, and conventional smuggling. They were once described as having the "leanest and meanest existence" in the whole area. Today, the bonanza of Qatar's oil revenues is allocated by "the rule of the four quarters": one-quarter to the ruling sheikh, Khalifa al-Thani; one-quarter to other lesser sheikhs; one-quarter to members of the ruling al-Thani family, numbering some 450 to 750 persons; and one-quarter for the general benefit of the 60,000 native-born Qataris. Qatar, which produces 440,000 barrels of oil per day, has an annual income of approximately $5.6 billion. For the mass of those Qataris, who have to be content with their one-quarter share of the total oil revenues, that works out to a per capita income of $23,000, a definite improvement, to say the least, on their previous earnings from breeding camels and goats, pearling, fishing, and the occasional smuggling venture.

Saudi Arabia, the richest and most productive of the oil countries, is a mirror which reflects the common problems of Persian Gulf states. Theoretically, Saudi Arabia is a "low absorber"; that is, its oil revenues are so massive and its indigenous population is so small that it just can't find ways and means to spend this money in an economic and feasible manner. In 1981 its total oil revenues were expected to top $123 billion, while its total budget was set up for expenditures of $73.5 billion. This should mean a surplus of about $50 billion. But these figures—as are those for the other Arab duchies on the Persian Gulf—are rubbery "guesstimates" of what will be received and how much will be spent and for what purposes. Foreign diplomats, bankers, and businessmen treat financial reports issued by the Arabs with the same degree of caution and skepticism that similar reports from the Soviet government are greeted with in Moscow.

The Saudi government reveals information about its bustling oil industry only in the broadest of outlines. Fiscal accountability in the peninsular sheikhdoms is something unheard-of, at least to the general public.

When the first of these billions of petrodollars began to pour into the Middle East, like a swollen Mississippi River in flood breaching its dikes, they set off a spending spree unmatched in world history. And it is still going on full blast. For the Arabs are trying to buy a place for themselves in the last quarter of the twentieth century as a modern industrial and westernized nation, but at a frightfully expensive cost. Two striking examples come to mind to illustrate the hugeness of the commitment of the Saudi Arabians to modernizing their desert land without creating a giant snafu, as well as without going bankrupt in the process. The Saudi government has let contracts to the Bechtel Corporation of San Francisco to build a mega-industrial and petro-chemical complex on the Persian Gulf at Jubail, a tiny fishing village. This once-desolate site is being transformed into a seaport the size of the giant harbor of Rotterdam, Europe's largest. The whole industrial complex would cover an area of 66 square miles with an additional 282 square miles for expansion. Jubail would be an automated industrial establishment, with refineries, petrochemical plants, steel mills, aluminum plants, processing plants, storage areas, power plants, its own road and rail transportation network, etc.

Quite apart from the Jubail industrial complex will be the construction of a brand-new city to house 170,000 workers and their families in the desert area to the north of Jubail. That, in itself, is a staggering project, because it means creating a modern city, with sewage, water, electrical, and other facilities, plus housing, roads, and all the infrastructure of any industrial municipality.

Jubail, both the city and the industrial project, is so big and so complex that no truly reliable estimates can be given as to total cost and time of completion. Initially, Jubail was estimated at $40 billion, with another $20 billion for roads, communications, and other facilities to be added.

The Bechtel Corporation of San Francisco has been given a cost-plus contract, which means it plans what is needed, constructs what it decides is required, buys the equipment, and hires the work forces; then adds it all up, plus its commission, and sends the bills to Riyadh. As David Shireff, editor of the *New East Economic Review*, commented, that means "Bechtel has a license to spend money."

But industrial megalomania is compounded further. On the west side of Saudi Arabia in the tiny fishing village of Yanbu on the Red Sea, there is a slightly smaller duplicate of Jubail under construction: another mega-industrial complex, plus a city for 150,000 workers and their families. The multibillion-dollar cost-plus contract for Yanbu was given to the Ralph M. Parsons Co. of Pasadena, California.

The basic rationale of Jubail and Yanbu is to utilize the 4 billion cubic feet of natural gas flared off each day from Saudi Arabia's rich oil wells. The gas will provide power and be transformed into petro-chemicals and other products. It would be like building the U.S. Mint next to the Homestake Mine, when it was first discovered, and trans-forming the tons of precious yellow metal that it produced into a stream of golden dollars.

In the summer of 1975, the Saudi government decided to go all-out to industrialize and modernize the desert kingdom. As *Fortune* magazine commented in a survey (July 31, 1978), this change from "optimum to maximum expenditures . . . resulted from the Saudi Arabian feeling that it must borrow as much technology from the West as rapidly as possible while the oil leverage lasted." And the other smaller oil countries on the Gulf have followed the Saudi lead as far as their revenues and circumstances permitted.

Everything being done at or to Jubail and Yanbu will be 100% new and imported. Everything that goes into these giant projects will have to be transported to these isolated construction sites. Not only the construction equipment and the material but the hundreds of thousands of items of supplies and services—water, for example, in a waterless wasteland, and food, thousands of workers, engineers, stores stocked with goods, down to the last ten-penny nail—have to be trucked in, or landed on the sandy beaches at Jubail and Yanbu. It has been a logistical nightmare. Four years after the construction work was started, costs at Jubail had skyrocketed from the original estimate of $30 billion to actual pay-out of $70 billion. And the expenses for construction and equipment are still rising steadily and inexorably. Jubail, for example, is not scheduled for completion until 1987. At the present rate of expenditure, its costs will be astronomical before it and Yanbu ever "come on stream."

The objective of Saudi Arabia is to capture about 8% of the world's petrochemical business by 1990. The Saudis are facing some stiff competition: DuPont and Dow in America, Britain's ICI, Germany's Hoechst, Leverkusen, and BASF, successors to the I. G. Farben, once the greatest chemical company in the world. The installations at Jubail and Yanbu will be as modern as money can buy. But they are going to cost the Saudis three to four times more than the same units would cost if constructed in America or Europe. And that is an extremely conservative estimate.

But even more significant is the fact that merely to maintain and to operate these and other industrial plants in the Gulf area at their expected efficiency and rate of production, once they come on-stream, "the OPEC governments must be prepared to provide annual operating costs that may amount to one-quarter to one-third of the initial establishment costs," according to an internationally recognized oil expert.[12] That means, for example, if Jubail costs $100 billion to complete—also bearing in mind that that figure is three to four times what

---

[12]Walker J. Levy in the *New York Times*, Jan. 5, 1979.

the same installation would cost in America or Europe—its management must allocate $25 billion to $33 billion each year just to get production rolling and to maintain the industrial complex. The same will be true for Yanbu. With those financial millstones around their necks, these great new automated industrial petrochemical complexes of Saudi Arabia will be pricing themselves out of the world markets before they produce their first ton of petrochemicals. Another substantial future expenditure will be required to establish worldwide sales and distribution organizations, which today are nonexistent.

Despite their technological backwardness, the Arab rulers and their advisers are not stupid men. It is now becoming obvious to them that they are boxing themselves into economically indefensible positions because of the squandering of billions upon billions on their modernization and industrialization programs. They have to find a way out of this impasse. It takes several forms. The general idea is to get the big oil companies personally involved in these programs, as a price for guaranteed supplies of crude oil for their home markets. The code words are "package deals" and "incentive oil." Mobil, Shell, and the Japanese have recently entered into agreements to participate in industrialization projects in return for "guaranteed" deliveries of oil. The Saudi Basic Industries Corporation, known as Sabic, is also negotiating with Exxon, Mobil, Shell, Dow Chemical, Mitsubishi of Japan, and the Celanese-Texas Corporation, each to construct a petrochemical plant at Jubail. There was a great deal of public interest shown by these giant corporations, as well as publicity given to these proposals in the press. But the current oil glut has destroyed the original incentive for the oil companies to cooperate in this venture.

The Americans, Japanese, and others can read the handwriting on the wall just as well as the more knowledgeable Arabs. There does not seem much likelihood that the seven sisters will let themselves get too deeply involved in bailing the Saudi government out of its costly blunders. Of course, all the European, American, and other foreign businessmen never utter a critical word publicly about these Arab industrialization and modernization programs, especially those with the lucrative cost-plus contracts. Nor is there any tendency publicly to rebut or to contest statements such as those of Sheikh Zaki al-Yamani on current developments, even if they are nonsense or mere propaganda. Finally, Saudi Arabia, Kuwait, the United Arab Emirates, Qatar, Iran, and Iraq do not permit western journalists to wander around their countries at will, gathering independent material for their reportage. All information on all aspects of the oil industry is controlled, as far as possible, by the respective Gulf governments. So it is not surprising that the western world has a distorted and magnified picture of the power and influence of the OPEC oil bloc in the Persian Gulf.

It takes an Arab to see through another Arab. King Hussein of Jordan is reported to have commented to a western journalist: "Jubail and Yanbu will be the Pyramids of the Saudis." But then Jordan has no oil fields of its own and can afford to take a more objective view of the current Gulf scene.

The Saudi Arabians, and to a lesser extent their fellow oil producers in Kuwait, Qatar, and the United Arab Emirates, as well as in Iran and Iraq if they can ever resume their prewar volume of production, are true victims of Parkinson's laws. They have expanded beyond the limits of practical and feasible planning—beyond the limits of their physical, i.e. their technical, capabilities. They have been spending their oil income or committing their future revenues to long-term capital investments that, in the final analysis, are both amateurish and illogical. A typical example of this economic self-delusion is the sheikhdom of Dubai, one of the United Arab Emirates—in reality, a piece of desert about the size of Rhode Island that is striving to act like a sovereign nation. Dubai had an annual oil income of about $2.2 billion at January 1981 prices, and a native population of about forty-thousand Dubaiians, excluding the foreign workers, who far outnumber the local citizenry. In the Persian Gulf, Dubai is considered relatively small potatoes. However, the ruler of Dubai, Sheikh Rashid bin Said al-Maktum, seventy-five years old, has been involved in Persian Gulf trading long before oil was discovered. So now he has the vaulting ambition to transform his minuscule principality into a real-life economic powerhouse. He has constructed a thirty-nine story skyscraper as an "international trade center"; it rises out of the flat desert surroundings like a giant phallic symbol. Sheikh Rashid has also contracted for construction of the biggest dry dock in the world—so huge that none of the giant supertankers afloat today can fill it. That will be the centerpiece of the new "Port Rashid." Another new and larger man-made seaport is also being constructed a few miles farther down the coast. Both of these multibillion-dollar harbors will have a berthing capacity larger than the whole of San Francisco Bay.

Sheikh Rashid is a go-for-broke entrepreneur. Others say he has been "conned by greedy European contractors . . . the Dubai ruler has grossly miscalculated the market."[13] He is also constructing a $1.4

<hr>

[13]*Economist*, Dec. 13, 1980.

billion aluminum plant, which when completed may be the largest of its kind in the world, as well as numerous other industrial installations. Finally, as a bit of whipped cream on top of this multibillion-dollar industrial program, he is constructing a $120 million sports palace, which will include the first ice-skating rink ever built on the Arabian peninsula. As of the end of 1977, Sheikh Rashid had already borrowed over $2 billion from American and European banks against his future oil revenues and at that time had to pay over $100 million a year in interest charges. So he is definitely in no position to reduce his oil output, because he needs all the petrodollars he can get.

The Persian Gulf states are gradually losing the economic and political leverage—a loss accelerated by the oil glut—which they once possessed without challenge by their rigid control of the production and pricing of crude oil through OPEC. Somewhat belatedly and ruefully they are discovering that the laws of supply and demand are still functioning and are beginning to work against their oil monopoly. The breakup of OPEC is not too far distant.

The Saudis and the other oil-producing Arabs are not going to go bankrupt in the foreseeable future. But they face a simple dilemma that at this stage seems insoluble. They have invested so much of their oil revenues in their industrialization, modernization, and urbanization programs—all at highly inflated rates—that they have to keep paying out huge sums to maintain and operate these uneconomic and unprofitable investments. And because of the lack of any fiscal planning and controls, they have to keep selling their oil. For the last few years, for example, Saudi Arabia has had to dig into its reserves to pay the budgetary deficits caused by "cost overruns," etc. Though many of the OPEC members would prefer to reduce their oil exports and raise prices, thus keeping incomes up and conserving their only resource, trying to achieve that objective is unattainable; it's a mirage on their desert horizon. As Prof. Parkinson noted sagely, expenses rise in direct proportion to income. The constant and growing need of the individual Arab oil producers for more money has irreparably broken the common price front established by OPEC.

This is the result of the economic shortsightedness that Saudi Arabia and the other oil duchies around the Persian Gulf have developed since OPEC took over full control in 1974 of the production and pricing of crude oil. This neglected theme is strongly developed by Prof. Eliyahu Kanovsky, in a special article in the new Volume 2 of the *Middle East Contemporary Review*, a standard and authoritative reference work on the economic and political developments in that area.[14] Prof. Kanovsky challenged the conventional assumption, long held and widely accepted in Washington and other world capitals, that Saudi Arabia has continued to produce oil at near-maximum capacity because of basic political considerations. The Saudis wanted to use it as a political club to keep oil prices from rising as high as some of the "hawks" wanted to charge; second, the high rate of Saudi production was a political concession to the United States. Yamani was pictured as one of the "moderates" who did not want to inflict economic damage on America, whose military services Saudi Arabia might need in the near future.

Prof. Kanovsky dismisses that as propaganda, stating flatly that "Saudi economic actions, including oil pricing and production, are determined by what it views as its vital economic, i.e., not its political, interests." And the "vital economic interests" are simply the fact that Saudi Arabia needs all the oil revenue it can lay its hands on, argues Prof. Kanovsky, because its public and private spending have always kept pace with and even exceeded its income in recent years.

This controversial and thought-provoking viewpoint, strangely enough, is confirmed by OPEC headquarters itself. In September 1980, Rene Ortiz, secretary-general of OPEC, stated: "For OPEC member countries, the price of oil determines the level of their national income and contributes substantially, if not totally, towards their budgeting. It also plays a vital role in determining living standards and the future development of their societies."

So the pressure is on, and gets stronger with every passing day, and OPEC cannot withhold its oil from the world market. The "cash-flow" needs of its members are increasing in direct proportion to the prodigal expenditures of their petrodollars, just as Parkinson's law dictates. So the once feared "oil weapon"—the threat to embargo oil exports from the Persian Gulf, which used to send shivers through the foreign ministries of the industrial nations—is also losing its power to intimidate.

The Saudis and the other oil sheikhdoms around the rim of the Persian Gulf suffer from a common disability: They seem unable to stay within their budgets. For example, for the 1981 fiscal year, the Saudi budget was set at $75 billion, but expenditures will run to almost $100 billion. In some instances, budget allocations have been exceeded by as much as 93%. Past budgeting shows the same irregularities. The five-year (1975–80) industrial development program called for total expenditures of $140 billion. Yet the Saudis grudgingly

[14]The review is published by Homes & Meier, New York; price $85.

confirmed that total spending on industrial development for this five-year period jumped to $210 billion. The new five-year plan (1980–85) calls for expenditures of $250 billion for industrial development and another $105 billion for the armed forces. That's a prediction, not a promise of what will happen.

The Saudis have total defense forces, including an army, air force, navy, and national militia, numbering about 86,000 men. With its current $105 billion budgetary allocation, which also includes the most modern weaponry that money can buy on the open market, the Saudi defense force on a per capita basis is the most expensive in the world today.[15] However, in measuring up its fighting qualities, on a man-to-man basis, it may not equal the Russians, Chinese, Americans, NATO forces or even the Khmer Rouge of Cambodia.

What makes the economic structure of the Middle East oil producers such a mind-boggling exercise in analysis are two basic elements: You can't trust the figures handed out by the Arab governments to be accurate, either as to revenues or expenditures; and, more important, there seems to be a minimum of fiscal control over revenues, planning, and spending. One is reminded of the old U.S. Army adage concerning its barracks areas: "If it doesn't move, paint it!" That seems to be what the Arabs are doing to improve their image on the world business scene.

The economic chickens are coming home to roost. The Arab sheikhs have sat around the OPEC conference tables in regular sessions from 1973 to the present. On each occasion they agreed to raise the price of crude oil. Then after each meeting the OPEC representatives would predict another price hike to be forthcoming at their next scheduled conference.

If these OPEC leaders had not been so greedy or so ignorant of the economic facts of life, their global monopoly on the vital supply of fuel and energy might have lasted many more years. But the turning point came in the first quarter of 1981. Just as the Hunt brothers of Texas had failed to corner the world's silver market, so OPEC has also demonstrated it lacked the necessary background, experience, and financial reach to make its oil cartel a permanent and vital force in the world's economy for the foreseeable future. In short, OPEC blew it.

The OPEC countries were handed their monopoly of the world's

[15]The officers' club in Riyadh, capital of Saudi Arabia, illustrates the solicitude the regime has for the morale and welfare of its officer corps. This luxurious, elegantly furnished structure cost $17.5 million. Its current membership is reportedly only 950 officers, obviously of top-drawer social levels.

supply of crude on a platter. They didn't suspect the oil riches below their sandy deserts; they didn't drill a well; they didn't spend a dime or five minutes of their time to develop the vast infrastructure of pipelines, storage tanks, refineries, harbors, and fleets of oil tankers to haul the crude oil away to the markets of the world. Then at the proper psychological moment, they expropriated the biggest and richest sector of the petroleum industry in the world, just as Drake and his fellow captains raided the Spanish galleons laden with the gold of the Incas in the times of good Queen Bess.

Now, large-scale expropriation is a common enough practice among nations, especially if they think they can get away with it at a minimum of cost to themselves. As the late Broadway *bon vivant* Wilson Mizner put it: "Everybody's got a little larceny in his heart." However, it is not very intelligent to take over somebody else's property and business if the injured party has the power and the means to take effective reprisals. That was the basic mistake of the OPEC cartel in the conduct of its oil monopoly. The OPEC members took the oil concessions of the seven sisters, but then they could not operate the cartel by themselves. They have had to employ hundreds of thousands of foreigners to operate their oil industries, as well as their governmental operations, etc. Their defenses, political as well as economic, are extremely vulnerable to internal as well as external aggression or attack.[16]

It was not the takeover of the monopoly once enjoyed by the seven sisters, the large foreign oil companies that had developed the Middle East petroleum industry, that was the major blunder of OPEC. There was an arguable case to be made on its behalf; after all, the Arabs were originally demanding only a larger slice of the huge profits the foreign oil companies were refusing to share with the owners of the rich oil fields. But what the member countries of OPEC did to the pricing structure of crude oil in the following years was an incredible miscalculation that will ultimately—and in the foreseeable future—result in the breakup of the Middle East oil monopoly.

What OPEC has done recalls the famous remark of Talleyrand about Napoleon's order to murder the Duc d'Enghien: *"C'est pire qu'un crime; c'est une bêtise!"*—"It's worse than a crime; it's stupid!" Today, that twentyfold increase in the price of oil since 1973 is the

[16]Tiny Kuwait, the third-largest oil producer in the Gulf area, which enjoys a $21 billion annual income, "could be jerked to a dead stop by a well-aimed bomb dropped on, say, its main water desalination plant," reported the London *Economist* (Dec. 13, 1980) in its survey of the current Middle East oil industry. This illustrates the vulnerability of the oil duchies, because of their large and complex infrastructure and industrial development.

bêtise that haunts the directors of OPEC, for a while the greatest and most lucrative money-making system in history.

The Arabs weren't content even with quadrupling the price of crude once they took over full control of the production and sale of their oil in 1973–74. They pigged it; in successive stages they pushed the price ever higher, until the industrial nations were fully awakened to the dangers that threatened their own economic existences. OPEC has made the whole world conscious of the need to conserve energy and determined to get out of the stranglehold that OPEC has imposed on the world supply of crude oil.

When OPEC was at the height of its ecopolitical power in the late 1970s, its members were confidently predicting that by the year 2000 the world would be consuming 40 million barrels of OPEC oil per day on a yearly basis. The price per barrel would be $50–75 and even higher, they assured each other at their frequent conferences behind closed doors. If those goals were achieved that would mean a yearly levy on the wealth of the industrial and other consuming nations of $730 billion to $1.09 trillion. They would have to accept the terms of OPEC or go without oil. But today, the estimate of OPEC production for A.D. 2000 has been drastically reduced from 40 million barrels per day to 12 million. The downward trend in exports has already set in. For example, in 1979, OPEC exported 31.6 million barrels per day out of the total world consumption of 52 million barrels by the non-Communist nations. By January 1982 total world consumption, exclusive of the Communist bloc, had dropped to 44 million barrels per day, of which only 18 million originated from OPEC. The industrial nations are reducing their oil consumption by 4–6% per year. They are also importing more oil from Mexico, Canada, Norway, Angola, and Malaysia. This is not a short-term trend, but a definite change in the world market for Persian Gulf oil. There is the possibility—it's a lively topic in high-level petroleum circles—that by A.D. 2000 or perhaps years sooner, the United States could end its dependence on Middle East oil, because of new technological advances in fuel and energy. As America has been the biggest single consumer of Saudi Arabian oil, a market loss of this magnitude is also threatening the whole economic and political future of the Persian Gulf states.

Sheikh Ahmed Zaki al-Yamani is clearly aware of this possible development and what its repercussions could mean not only for Saudi Arabia but for the whole Middle East. In autumn 1980, he made a speech to the Saudi University of Petroleum and Minerals, the key paragraph of which was excerpted by *Petroleum Intelligence Weekly* (February 1981):

If we force the western countries to invest heavily in finding alternative sources of energy, they will do so. This would take no more than seven to ten years and would result in reducing their dependence on oil as a source of energy to a point which will jeopardize Saudi Arabia's interests. Saudi Arabia will then be unable to find markets to sell enough oil to meet its financial requirements. This picture should be well understood.

Until recently, the members of OPEC were confident that they had an unbeatable ploy to defeat the attempts of the industrial nations to bring down the price of oil through effective conservation measures. No oil glut could develop on the world market because the OPEC countries would simultaneously reduce the amount of oil pumped out, while raising prices to compensate for the decreased exports. Hence, oil would remain a scarce and high-priced commodity, so they confidently rationalized. Then came the 1981–82 oil glut and the whole world floated in oil—and the best-laid plans of mice and men went out the window. The Arab sheikhs had also failed to anticipate the effects of their multibillion-dollar spending sprees in their efforts to catch up with the twentieth century. They forgot Parkinson's immutable law: A nation's expenditures always keep pace with and usually exceed its rising income. Now they all need all the money they can collect to carry on their inflated and costly commitments to modernization and industrialization.

Early in 1982, OPEC members agreed to limit their total daily output to 17.5 million barrels to keep up the price of oil. However, within weeks, OPEC unity was broken as various members began to sell oil in excess of their quotas in order to increase their revenues to meet rising expenditures. Maintenance of production quotas and prices seems no longer possible.

New and entirely unexpected economic factors have entered into the ecopolitical development of the Persian Gulf states, because though they are oil-rich, they are population-poor. And it is this anomaly that will dictate the breakup of OPEC's once almost invulnerable oil monopoly. Some of the Gulf states are beginning to question whether or not they have slipped into a quagmire from which they cannot escape without surrendering a large measure of political and economic control of their countries.

To carry out their inflationary and costly development programs, they have had to import labor, from white-collar executives to blue-collar workers, from teachers to doctors, from accountants to computer operators, from mercenary soldiers to garbage collectors—no home-trained talent is available in the general range of administrative, technological, or basic skilled and unskilled workers. By diversifying their basic oil industry into petrochemicals and a host of ancillary industries, they are creating new jobs, which for the next decade or two can be filled only by better-educated and more-experienced foreigners. And as more menial labor is increasingly needed, because of the urbanization and industrial growth, the native Arab is not available. He will not accept such work; it is demeaning to his tribal and nomadic background. Besides, the native-born Kuwaiti or Saudi or even the "leanest and meanest" of the Qataris is guaranteed better and more lucrative employment than unskilled labor by his oil-rich government. There is no incentive, nor any desire to compete in that labor market. So the labor gap has to be filled by the poor, the hungry and jobless males of the neighboring nations. These illiterate and unskilled workers are politically dangerous, because they can be influenced by the radical underground which wants to take over the sheikhdoms and their riches for its own use. These hapless and victimized men at the bottom of the social ladder have no personal stake in the oil-producing states, except their short-term employment and second-class status. They can be the pawns of political adventurers or radical groups which seek to gain power through riots and other mass demonstrations. The revolution in Iran, which toppled the shah in a matter of days, has given us a graphic demonstration of the power of mass action which can bring about swift and drastic changes in government and the social order.

Also, the problem in the Persian Gulf is being compounded daily. By importing these hundreds of thousands of foreigners, the local governments are expanding the need for increased social services, housing, food, public utilities, etc.—also requiring more foreigners to maintain this infrastructure.

It is also becoming obvious to the rulers of the Persian Gulf states that when foreigners in the basic work force in their respective areas outnumber the local natives by as much as three to one, their political and economic control of the oil sheikhdoms is increasingly insecure.

The reader may well have noticed the absence of information and commentary about political situations and developments per se in these crucial Gulf states. That is because I have concentrated on the central problem of the strength and durability of the OPEC cartel. If the cartel begins to break up—as I think inevitable—this will lead to unforeseen political rivalries and feuding among the oil-producing states. However, any changes in the present governments of the Gulf states would directly involve the interests of the superpowers, the other industrial nations, and the Third World countries. If, for example, a radical movement overthrows the present Saudi king or his successor, then the fat is truly in the fire. This could lead possibly to a Soviet-American confrontation, or the destruction of some major oil fields and equipment, as well as the complete collapse of the OPEC bloc and its monopoly. It could also be the prelude to World War III.

However, these weighty and possibly cataclysmic matters are the constant concerns of the major world governments. Fortunately for this author, such developments are well beyond the purview of this book.

Still, there is one consoling thought. The oil of the Persian Gulf loses its ecopolitical power if it is not made available to the world market. The industrial nations, including the Japanese,[17] have learned one hard lesson from the OPEC cartel. Get out of the clutches of the Middle East oil producers, whoever their rulers may be—radicals or rightists—as expeditiously as possible.

It is within the realm of possibility that those men who succeed the present OPEC leaders and will be ruling the oil-rich Gulf countries will have learned a thing or two from the blunders and miscalculations of the petroleum cartel. Mere possession of the Gulf oil fields means little unless there is a substantial market for its exports of crude—and at prices which the consuming nations of the world can afford to pay without damage to their own economies. That possibility may be one of the factors that will prevent World War III.

Prof. J. B. Kelly, a recognized English expert on the Middle East and its current economic affairs for a quarter of a century, takes a dim view of the future of the Persian Gulf area, predicting that

if the Arabs and the Persians and their partners in OPEC continue on their present reckless course, they could well bring the age of oil in world's history to a premature end. The Gulf could then revert to the backwater it has been for centuries past, its shores lined with the rusting carcasses of refineries, petrochemical complexes and gas liquefication plants, the skeletons of which may still be visible two or three millennia hence, to confound any archeologist who may stumble on them and perhaps lead him to wonder, like Shelley's traveller in an antique land, whether he is not contemplating the vestiges of a once magnificent civilization.[18]

---

[17]For example, Japan's large cement industry, a heavy consumer of energy, is shifting entirely from oil to coal for its power. Meanwhile, public utilities around the world are substituting more coal and natural gas for oil. *Wall Street Journal*, April 13, 1981.

[18]Kelly, *Arabia, the Gulf and the West.*

CHAPTER SIX

Awakening
Asia

An' the dawn comes up like thunder outer China 'crost the Bay!
—RUDYARD KIPLING, "Mandalay"

It is the culture of discipline and the postponing of immediate satisfaction
for the future—even for posterity.
—KIM KYUNG WON, cabinet secretary,
government of South Korea

All the awakening has to do with money—it doesn't have anything to do
with any new spiritual development. Money has awakened people who
have been on the margin a long time. Money has also opened their eyes to
their deficiencies.
—V.S. NAIPAUL, Indian sociologist and
author, *New York Times*, Dec. 1, 1980

O N a February morning in 1941, the S.S. *President Pierce* dropped anchor in the harbor of Hong Kong at the end of its long run across the northern Pacific from San Francisco. I was standing at the rail on the promenade deck, drinking in the sights of my first physical contact with Asia. Hong Kong is a spectacularly impressive harbor, filled with ships of all nations and all descriptions—passenger liners, coastal steamers, naval vessels, freighters, the sail-rigged Chinese junks, and hundreds of sampans darting through the crowded waters like cyclists weaving in and out of a traffic jam. The initial impression was one of intense activity, of movement of thousands of people carrying out their daily tasks. As the American liner slowed to a dead stop, numerous sampans maneuvered to get next to the ship, just under its garbage-disposal chute. Within a few minutes, the remains of the ship's breakfast came pouring out of the chute. Some of it fell into the sampans, the rest into the dirty harbor water. No matter; each particle was fished out by eager hands. Directly below me was an old crone inspecting bits of garbage passed to her by a young boy. What seemed to be edible, by sight or by smell, was popped into a stewpot resting on a bed of glowing charcoal.

Watching this spectacle with me was a British businessman, a resident of Hong Kong, who had crossed the Pacific on the *President Pierce*. I turned to him in shocked surprise. "Do they actually eat the ship's garbage? Are they as poor as that?"

"Don't worry," he replied briskly. "Hong Kong has the best garbage on the China coast, much better than Shanghai's."

As I lifted my glance to Hong Kong's waterfront, the contrast between poverty and plenty was even more apparent. Rising above the dockside was the city's biggest building, the sixteen-story, thronelike headquarters of the Hong Kong and Shanghai Banking Corporation, the citadel of British financial and commercial power in the Orient. Strung along the quayside were offices of the great trading companies: Jardine, Matheson & Co., Ltd., Butterfield & Swires, Hutchinson, and Wheelock Marden. These and many other British firms had contributed to transforming this rocky island into the Orient's business center in the freewheeling days before World War I.

Since its founding in 1862, Hong Kong has been a stronghold of capitalistic free enterprise, a 400-square-mile enclave of economic power, perched on the south China coast. The ability of this crown colony to generate wealth has never ceased to fascinate the mainland Chinese, particularly the governments in Peking in this century. Sun Yat-sen, the instigator of the 1911 revolution, which toppled the decadent Manchu Empire, was inspired to comment: "How could the foreigners do so much as they have done with this barren rock of Hong Kong within seventy or eighty years, while in four thousand years China had no place like Hong Kong?"

However, the wealth which Hong Kong produced largely for the British before World War II is quite small potatoes compared to the postwar economic growth the crown colony has experienced. At the end of 1982, Hong Kong was the "third largest financial supermarket in the world" (after New York and London) and the second biggest bullion market (*Economist*, Nov. 13, 1982). This capitalistic powerhouse is a bustling beehive of 6 million industrious, money-chasing Chinese, who are achieving one of the highest living standards of any Asiatic country. The real growth rate for Hong Kong has been 10% annually for years. Its productivity has been increasing at 8% annually since 1960. Hong Kong's 1982 per capita income was $4,673, behind Singapore's $5,123. Neighboring Red China's income is $350 per capita. In the 1980s Hong Kong is riding the crest of a boom that should have peaked out several years before. Yet this is only one of the many paradoxes that make this crown colony—the last remnant of the British Empire—the supreme anachronism of our time.

In the last decade Hong Kong has become one of the most affluent cities of the western world. It is the New York of the Pacific, complete with towering skyscrapers. The value of property in the city of Hong Kong equals and probably in many instances exceeds comparable property in midtown Manhattan. For example, a deluxe apartment in a Hong Kong high-rise rents for as much as $15,000 a month. The purchase price for an adjoining single parking space is $20,000.

Yet in the year 1997 the government of neighboring Communist China will become the legal owner of this bustling capitalistic powerhouse. That is when the ninety-nine-year lease for the "New Territories," which constitutes 90% of the crown colony, expires. The lease was extracted by the British from the moribund Manchu Empire in 1898.

Hong Kong possessed the only sheltered deepwater harbor on the China coast between Shanghai and Indochina. That was the original basis for its economic development. But what has made Hong Kong dynamic and prosperous, particularly in the years after World War II, has been the freedom which its businessmen and entrepreneurs enjoy in their operations, plus a minimum of taxes. The British colonial administration does not have the power to interfere in the affairs of business firms. Nor has the British government displayed any desire or inclination to intervene in the local economy. Even the public utilities such as gas, electricity, telephone, and public transport are provided by private companies. Only 14% of the GNP is accounted for by public spending. But every year the colonial budget shows a surplus, even though Hong Kong's taxes are among the lowest in the western world. Yet of all the major cities in south and east Asia, "Hong Kong alone got rich on laissez-faire."[1]

Hong Kong's only prewar rival was Shanghai, which declined economically after the Communist takeover of Peking in 1949. But Shanghai's loss was Hong Kong's gain. The bulk of Shanghai's Chinese business community migrated to Hong Kong, as well as other capitalist-minded Chinese after Mao Zedong decreed the new socialist order was in force. Some 3 million political refugees settled in the crown colony, and they have gradually but inexorably elbowed the British to the sidelines and have taken over the direction and management of Hong Kong's economy, with wondrous results for themselves. There are many more Chinese millionaires now living in the colony than there are British millionaires.

There are even a number of "Red millionaires," so called because they are involved in business projects initiated by the Peking government. The leader of this group is Li Ka Shing, the most prominent of the property tycoons. He has close links with Peking and is one of the directors of China's International Investment Trust and has been its partner in many of its property acquisitions in the colony. Another leader of the Chinese community is Sir Yue Kong Pao, who has been operating the biggest fleet of oil tankers and bulk cargo ships afloat on the high seas. He lives in a palatial villa and commutes to work in his

[1]*Economist*, Dec. 6, 1980.

motor yacht. Pao has been selling ships and reinvesting in Hong Kong property.

Red China has consistently refused to recognize the validity of the 1898 lease of the New Territories. Nor has it accepted as binding the earlier treaties of 1842 and 1860 by which the island of Hong Kong and the Kowloon peninsula were ceded to the British by the Manchu emperors in Peking, practically at gunpoint. While the Peking government has declared these treaties to be invalid, it has not yet taken any direct action to contest British control of its last Crown Colony. There is good reason to believe that sometime before 1997, the London and Peking governments will reach some mutually satisfactory arrangement by which Hong Kong will continue its present role as a free-wheeling, free enterprise enclave on the south China coast. The basis for this optimism is an elemental fact of life: Hong Kong produces more hard currency—$6 billion to $7 billion a year, or 35% to 40% of its foreign exchange—for Communist China the way it functions today than it would if it had to adjust its economy to Peking's Procrustean economic and political controls. It is also becoming evident that Red China has a new perspective and value judgment regarding "this efficient money-making machine," a description of the crown colony by its departing chief secretary, Sir Jack Cater. In 1980 and 1981, Deng Xiaoping, vice-chairman and the pragmatic policymaker in Peking, issued statements assuring the investors in Hong Kong, worried about its future, that they "should put their hearts at ease." It would appear that Peking does not plan to kill the goose that lays such golden eggs, worth billions in hard-currency revenues out of Hong Kong.

In fact, Peking is investing heavily in Hong Kong property. The China Resources Agency, which controls all Red China's trading operations in the colony, has built a fifty-two-story skyscraper headquarters on waterfront property. From its heights it looks down on the Jardines, the Swires, and other British enterprises. The Resources Agency is also planning to build an entire city for 500,000 in the northeastern corner of the New Territories, as a real estate investment. This development would appear to confirm reports that no drastic changes are contemplated by the Chinese government after 1997.

Hong Kong has an importance to the free world's economy that far transcends its present status as a progressive and prospering city-state of remarkable growth and stability. Hong Kong could be the hinge on which China swings slowly but inevitably away from its Marxist-Leninist ideology to its own modified form of a state-capitalism-cum-free-market system. Such a development will have far-reaching and beneficial repercussions in the United States, Western

Europe, Japan, and the Third World. Conversely it would inflict incalculable political damage to the Soviet Union and its neo-imperialistic expansion. The closer that Communist China comes to a free market system, the quicker Asia and other Third World areas will be stimulated to develop their own economic potentials. That can only benefit America, Europe, Japan, and other non-Communist countries.

Red China is being educated to the benefits and values of free-market capitalism by example and by osmosis. Right on its very doorstep it has Hong Kong, a lively example of capitalism in action. What is even more convincing to Peking's officialdom is that Hong Kong's postwar expansion is largely the work of other Chinese. It was brought about by the entrepreneurs and businessmen who were booted out of Shanghai by the Communists in the 1950s and rebuilt their lives and fortunes in Hong Kong. Hence a Communist Chinese can see at first hand how a capitalist Chinese works and prospers. Nothing succeeds like success—and this maxim is also valid for the inscrutable Oriental. Hong Kong's and Singapore's amazing postwar development have had a strong impact on Peking's thinking. In a recent visit to Singapore, China's vice-chairman, Deng Xiaoping, remarked to his hosts: "If only I just had Shanghai to work with."[2]

Peking is taking its first steps toward experimenting with free-market economics within its own borders. In 1981, China disclosed plans for the creation of a series of international trade zones within relatively short range of Hong Kong. It means that the free market system will begin to operate in a limited fashion in a number of business bridgeheads inside Communist China. Within these zones foreign firms will be able to set up manufacturing, processing, or commercial operations with their own managers. They will be permitted certain capitalistic practices, such as establishing their own wage scales, the right to hire and fire their own workers, and other procedures not yet allowed in China. The first of these trade zones will be at Shenzhen, just across the border from Hong Kong. Already it has attracted $1 billion in foreign investment, including funds from Hong Kong Chinese, involved in about eight hundred separate deals, mostly small processing or assembly plants. Also to be included are housing facilities, shopping centers, and other requisite public services. At present there will be five trade zones in Guangdong (Kwangtung) and Fujian (Fukien) provinces, with three more promised if the program proves its worth to promote industrial and commercial activity and income for the Peking government. These capitalistic ghet-

---

[2]Quoted in Anthony Sampson, *The Money Lenders* (New York: Viking, 1981).

tos in a land where Marx and Lenin are deified could be another portentous step in China's shift from ideology to pragmatism. The dragon appears to be shedding its Marxist skin bit by bit.

America's wars in Korea and Vietnam unleashed a technological revolution on the far shores of the Pacific Ocean. A large part of the billions of dollars that the U.S. government spent overseas to equip its armed forces to fight these wars helped to lay the foundations for "Tomorrow's Workshop,"[3] comprising the new industrializing nations of Asia, including Japan. America's military intervention in the Pacific theater was unsuccessful, leading to a stalemate in Korea and a defeat and withdrawal from Vietnam. Yet the Americans left behind them a whole new technology in communications, transportation, construction, health care, electronics, etc., that was to change the face of Asia after peace and stability returned.

Two decades after the Korean war, the pursuit of economic development and power has fired up the energies of this once-somnolent quarter of the globe. It released the talents of the peoples of the Orient, virtually to the exclusion of other political and military considerations. What is happening in Hong Kong is being repeated to a lesser degree elsewhere in the Far East. Asiatic countries, including the giant of them all, the Chinese People's Republic, are awakening to the *ecopolitical* age. They are becoming aware that economic growth offers them more security and stability as well as a better daily existence for the individual than any political ideology or military capability. Of course, economic development is the basic need of every country. However, today the Third World is a sad casebook of failures to achieve that goal.

The Far East is learning that true and solid economic growth can be sustained only within the framework of a free market system. It does not require a political ideology to make it work. This truism—that economics can function separately from politics—is hard for the U.S. government to understand. By contrast, Washington always seems to equate free enterprise with political democracy. Republicans and Democrats alike generally assume that these two always go together, like ham and eggs, or nuts and bolts. But in this turbulent fourth quarter of the twentieth century, with the world still reeling from the effects of the last great war, democratic governments are luxuries which only the stable and affluent nations can afford.

[3]The descriptive title for a May 1977 survey of economic trends and developments in Asia, published by the *Economist* of London.

In East Asia, the free enterprise system thrives and prospers in a political environment which is distinctly hostile to democracy. The Asians have discovered a formula leading to economic growth and wealth that seems to have escaped the attention of most other Third World nations. It is simple, yet requires a sophistication of outlook that comes only with a higher level of education.

A Third World country seeking to expand its economy must first carefully study international events and trends. It must be knowledgeable about the world economic scene, about products, trends, etc. What is new in industrial capital and consumer goods? What is becoming obsolete? What are its own economic assets and capabilities? When the answers to these and a multitude of other questions are found, then a commonsensical long-range development program can be worked out. The key objective of such planning is to realign one's national economy to the international trends and developments—and ride with it into the future. What this means in practice was best demonstrated by postwar Japan. In the span of a generation Japan rose out of the ashes of defeat and destruction to become a major economic power on the world scene by following this formula.

After the war, Japan was powerfully influenced by America's industrial development and state of technology, far advanced compared to the rest of the world. So Japanese businessmen turned away from old industries, such as textiles, and opted for high-technology products, such as the manufacturing of pocket radios, tape recorders, high-quality cameras, TV sets, and a host of other consumer goods that had an immediate sales appeal on the world markets. The Japanese continued to move into new fields. They concentrated on shipbuilding, specializing in the construction of giant oil tankers and bulk cargo carriers, to keep pace with the growing worldwide consumption of petroleum products and raw materials. Next came the mass production of small fuel-saving cars and trucks, which were soon successfully competing against General Motors, Ford, and Chrysler in the U.S. marketplace. In recent years the Japanese have made great strides in computer technology. The net effect of its intelligent market surveys and planning has been to obtain for Japan a solid and secure business bridgehead on the world economic scene. (The next chapter will concentrate in detail on Japan's amazing postwar recovery to become one of the major economic powers.)

History has a way of repeating itself—only in new forms and with differing scenarios. After Pearl Harbor, the rampaging Japanese armed forces were able to swiftly overrun the countries of Southeast Asia: Indochina, Malaya, Thailand, Burma, the Dutch East Indies, the

Philippines, and Borneo. Japan was also firmly entrenched in China and Manchuria, as well as occupying Korea and Formosa. The Tokyo government announced the formation of the "Greater East Asia Co-Prosperity Sphere." This was to be an enforced economic union of these countries, to be dominated, controlled, and operated by Imperial Japan and largely for its benefit, once victory had been attained. But that was not to be.

Four decades later there is a real-life "co-prosperity sphere" of nations in the Far East, only now it is not operating under that wartime title. Its members include Japan, South Korea, Taiwan (formerly Formosa), the city-states of Hong Kong and Singapore, the People's Republic of China, Malaya, the Philippines, and Indonesia (formerly the Dutch East Indies). Postwar Japan, which is as militant in its present industrial, commercial, and financial expansion as ever it was in its military conquests, dominates the far eastern economic scene. It has achieved, by *ecopolitical* means, expanding and prosperous markets for its goods and services, which it failed to achieve by armed force and invasion. And Japan has set an example which these other far eastern countries and city-states are following, not only successfully but enthusiastically.

For the period 1972–78, the five countries of the Association of Southeast Asian Nations (Thailand, Malaysia, Singapore, the Philippines, and Indonesia, which have a total population of 240 million) and their three neighbors (Taiwan, Hong Kong, and South Korea, with 60 million people) have averaged between a 6% and 11% annual growth rate. This now is the only group of countries which are doubling their real GNP every seven to twelve years. If this trend continues—barring accidents such as war, there is no reason why it shouldn't continue—the affluent industrial powers of the world will soon be clustered in three groups of 200–250 million people each. These will be the United States, the European Economic Community (EEC), and the Asian nations, plus Japan with a population of 100 million, which by itself is the second-ranking economic power in the world today.

In reality there are "two Asias": those countries which are stagnating or regressing in their poverty and mismanagement; and a small bloc of countries and city-states which are steadily improving their national economies and their living standards. In other words, there are nations like India and Bangladesh which are either unable or unwilling or both to work their way upward and out of their Third World status. Then in sharp contrast there are countries like South Korea and Taiwan, occupied twenty-four hours a day in developing

176

their industrial and commercial potentials. Why is there this difference between the "two Asias"? Why is one Third World country able to achieve economic growth while another cannot?

The answers to these vital questions can be found if, at the outset, one recognizes certain fundamental truths that are operative, not only in the Far East, but also in Africa and elsewhere in the Third World. One hears and reads much about "class warfare" as being the root cause of the poverty and backwardness of the Third World countries. However, one obtains a fresh perspective on reading Michael Lipton. He contends that the most important class conflict in the poor countries of the world today is not between labor and capital. Nor is it between foreign and domestic interests. Rather it arises out of the conflict between the urban and the rural classes, between town and country. The peasants are disorganized and impoverished, and lack the wherewithal to boost their economic status. The urban sectors, by contrast, are articulate and organized, and are the power bases of the local political bosses. Lipton further points out that

the urban classes have been able to win most of the rounds of the struggle with the countryside, but in so doing they have made the development process needlessly slow and unfair. Scarce land which might grow millet or bean sprouts for the hungry villagers, instead produces a trickle of costly calories from meat and milk which few except the urban rich (who have ample protein anyway) can afford. Scarce investment, instead of going into water pumps to grow rice, is wasted on urban motorways. Scarce human skills design and administer, not clean village wells and agricultural extension services, but world boxing championships in showpiece stadia.[4]

Bangladesh, formerly East Pakistan and one of the most densely populated areas in the world, is a good example of conflict between the rural and urban populations. Bangladesh encompasses one of the most fertile areas on earth, the rich alluvial delta of the Ganges and Brahmaputra rivers. Yet over 60% of its 92 million people suffer from chronic malnutrition, according to the World Bank surveys. This situation worsens as the available food supplies lag further behind the population increases each year. Today this country is the world's largest importer of food, triple the quantities of the 1960s. Despite its agricultural potential, Bangladesh produces only as much rice as Japan did in A.D. 1400, according to the *Wall Street Journal* (April 16, 1981).

The prime cause of the food crisis in Bangladesh is a rationing system inaugurated by the British during the famine in Bengal in 1943, which is still in force today. It is overweighted in favor of the

---

[4]Michael Lipton, *Why the Poor People Stay Poor* (London: Temple Smith, 1977).

urban class as a sort of permanent dole. According to the World Bank, a farmer might receive a monthly ration of 21 pounds per year while a city resident will get 320 pounds on his ration. The government of Bangladesh argues that to outlaw the ration system, which controls basic feed grains and rice, would be politically explosive. Nor does the government invest any money in agricultural reform and improvement. With unstable prices, the peasant farmers have little incentive to invest their slim resources—if any—in increasing their food output. The government controls the food supplies, including incoming foreign aid shipments.

It is somewhat of a paradox that a substantial amount of American foreign aid to Third World countries has also contributed to, rather than alleviated, the urban-rural conflict. A prime example of this is the Food for Peace program launched by President Eisenhower's administration in 1954 with passage of Public Law 480. This provided for food aid at cut-rate prices from surplus U.S. stocks. The surplus food was sold on a long-term, low-interest credit basis. The food aid program was directed at countries like India, Egypt, Pakistan, Burma, Bangladesh, and other Asiatic and African countries. These newly liberated states found themselves faced with hungry peasants, archaic agricultural systems, and a shortage of foreign exchange to buy food on the world markets to meet their deficiencies.

The governments of these countries used the U.S. food surpluses to keep down the price of food in their home marketplaces. This favored their growing urban populations, at the expense of the peasant farmers. This situation did little to encourage the farmers to increase the production of food, despite the rising population. As a result food production has been advancing at the rate of only 2.5% annually in the developing countries while at the same time the demand for food jumped at the rate of 3% per year.[5] It is now estimated that for the year 1981 the developing countries—which in prewar times were generally self-supporting in basic foodstuffs—will have to import 92 million tons of cereal grains compared to imports of 20 million tons in 1960. This is the result of government's neglect of domestic agriculture in favor of jerry-built industrial development programs. It is an economic cancer that seems to resist all therapy.

Once the dichotomy between city and countryside is clearly outlined, then problems can be properly evaluated and practical solutions can be found. No Third World country can achieve any substantial economic growth until the conflict between the rural and urban classes

[5]*Economist*, Nov. 18, 1980.

is resolved in a mutually acceptable fashion. After close study of post-war events and trends in the Far East, three successive processes required for economic growth of a Third World country have been pinpointed, which I identify as the Macrae development theory.[6] These processes have been the basis for the surprising emergence of the "little Japans" of the Far East, the bustling and booming economies of South Korea, Taiwan, Singapore, Hong Kong, Malaysia, and Indonesia, as well as Communist China's "creeping capitalism."

For a Third World country to make any progress toward economic independence and self-sufficiency, the following objectives must be reached:

1. There must be total employment of manpower in the rural areas. To achieve this requires the elimination of ceilings on wages paid to the peasants and prices paid for their produce. Such measures will give the peasants, who compose 70–80% of the population of most Third World countries, a growing reservoir of purchasing power. This will in turn create an expanding market for the consumer goods manufactured by the urban workers, and generally sustain industrial employment. To maintain their economic advantages the peasants will work harder and produce more food for the cities with their industrial populations, and, eventually, for export. In establishing the first of the 52,000 agricultural communes which now dot the Chinese countryside, the top priority was to make them economically self-sufficient. This was expedited by bringing them electricity before transport. For example, 12-horsepower "walking tractors" were introduced into the communes. This is an all-purpose piece of machinery, adaptable for earthmoving, plowing, pumping water for irrigation, moving heavy loads, and generating electricity. It is a portable power source, a sort of miniature public utility system for each commune. A variety of community services were also developed: the shoemaker, the weaver, the roofer, the carpenter, the grocery store, the medical clinic, etc. The commune became a self-contained economic unit, giving work to every able-bodied person, male and female, as well as providing jobs for the young and the elderly. The net result was to increase the annual income of those families living in the communes to $350 and upward,[7] as well as providing a rising standard of living for the once downtrod-

[6]Norman Macrae, deputy editor of the London *Economist*, is a one-man think tank concerning the far eastern economic scene. Back in 1962 he was the first to recognize and call attention to the amazing economic renaissance of Japan and its implications for the western world at large. I am indebted to Mr. Macrae for his long-term guidance and have borrowed freely from his storehouse of economic facts and figures.

[7]From "China's Creeping Capitalism," *Fortune*, Dec. 28, 1981.

den coolie. (By comparison the average annual income of the peasant farmer in India is $190.)

2. An industrial development program must involve a cost-conscious technology and (more important) a mechanism for constantly upgrading it. A Third World country which has largely existed on its agricultural output and other native resources must not plunge into a time-consuming and costly heavy industrial project, such as the construction and operation of steel mills. It must tailor its industrial development to fit its own resources and capabilities. For example, Hong Kong and Singapore specialize in light industry, handled by thousands of small factories and workshops. The industrial development must also be flexible enough to adjust to changes in the world export markets, to shift manufacturing from one product to another at a minimum of expense.

3. Big business must be made both respectable and acceptable, and government controls and interference must be kept to a minimum. Postwar Japan is a prime example of this process in action. Since the end of the U.S. occupation, the Liberal Democrats, the political instrument of big business, have governed Japan. The policy-making of the government has dovetailed with the objectives of the great corporations. One English observer commented that Japan has no foreign policy; instead it has an export policy and that is largely determined by the great trading companies—Mitsui, Mitsubishi, Sumitomo, and other corporate giants. It is axiomatic that private enterprise has the motivation and the mechanism to stimulate economic growth, which a government cannot provide, even with the best will in the world.

Chung Ju Yung was thirty-two years old and owner of a small garage in Seoul when World War II ended. As South Korea began flexing its muscles in the first days of freedom after almost four decades of harsh Japanese rule, Chung also expanded into the construction field. He hit his stride in 1950, when the American armies entered South Korea to repel the North Korean takeover of the whole country. Chung began building air strips and other military installations for the U.S. armed forces. Soon he was the No. 1 contractor for the Americans in Korea, because he took his construction crews right into the combat areas. Chung was fascinated by the giant bulldozers, excavators, and other modern construction equipment which the Americans brought in with their tanks, planes, and guns. He had found his niche in the world of business. When the shooting stopped in Korea, Chung had plenty to do rebuilding his war-shattered South Korea. He also resumed work for the Americans, handling military construction projects for them in Vietnam and Thailand. From then he began to expand on a global basis, in Alaska, Australia, and the Middle East. In Saudi Arabia he has garnered construction contracts totaling over $2 billion for his Hyundai ("Modern") conglomerate. Chung's companies build the heavy machinery and equipment used for construction and for cement, pulp, and paper manufacturing, textiles, automobiles, air conditioners, etc. Hyundai has also entered the automotive field, producing a small car. Chung's research team combs the world for the most cost-effective machinery to use in its worldwide operations, and quickly discards old technology when it is surpassed by the new.

Chung Ju Yung, the former hod carrier turned millionaire, is only one of the successful breed of entrepreneurs who have given South Korea "the fastest export-led economic growth ever known by anybody," including Japan. South Korea, a nation of 31 million people, has been developing at a phenomenal rate, averaging 7–8% growth since 1961. That year its GNP was about $3 billion, or an average of $85 a year for each South Korean. In 1982 it was running about $65 billion, or $1,680 per capita.

Another of the successful entrepreneurs is Cha Kyung Koo, chairman of a multibillion-dollar industrial and commercial empire, which is actually named "the Lucky Group." It describes its corporate mission in life as "Transforming Dreams into Reality." It translates this into action in a varied field of business enterprises: electronic equipment, computers, chemicals, construction and engineering services, insurance and securities. The Lucky Group had a gross income of $4.9 billion in 1980, a spectacular record for a firm in business for less than a decade. Mr. Cha explains: "We are headed for markets outside of Korea; that's for sure! We have the most joint ventures with foreign partners, mainly the Americans, Germans, and Japanese."

Apparently it's not just luck that accounts for South Korea's emergence as a dynamic new industrial power on the Asiatic scene. Firms like Hyundai, the Lucky Group, Daewoo, and other large industrial combines are very aggressive in going after business around the world. They now operate in thirty-one countries. To the surprise and consternation of American and European firms, the South Koreans have underbid them on a large percentage of the multibillion-dollar construction projects in Saudi Arabia and elsewhere in the Persian Gulf area. In 1978, they won $9 billion worth of contracts. They bring their own equipment and manpower with them from distant Korea. There are now more than 100,000 Koreans at work in the Middle East, including crews of skilled and unskilled laborers, and engineers and other technical and executive personnel. South Korea is one of the very few countries in the world which enjoys a balance of payments surplus with the OPEC countries, selling more goods and services to the Persian Gulf nations than it pays them for the Middle East oil it imports. As a result of the swift global expansion in the construction field, four Korean firms are listed among the twenty largest firms in the world in this category.

In 1920, when Korea was a Japanese colony, Paek Il Gyu, a fervent nationalist, published *The Economic History of Korea*. It was more of a blueprint for the future than a history of the past. Paek emphasized the need "to foster an education in economics which may prove to be the key to the economic independence of Korea. And economic independence will accelerate political independence."

That line of *ecopolitical* philosophy must have had its effect. One factor which explains the surprising economic strength of South Korea is the high level of literacy. After the bloody fratricidal war with invading North Korea ended in 1953, the South Korean government gave top priority to expansion and improvement of the education of young Koreans. Money was spent on schools and teachers, rather than on industry, which came later. Now more than 80% of South Korean boys and girls continue into secondary schools, even though their parents have to pay for it from the age of fourteen onward. The number finishing their university studies has quadrupled in the last decade. Thousands of young Koreans have completed their education in U.S. colleges, and return equipped with technological training in a variety of fields. They are now staffing the ranks of the industrial conglomerates which are able to operate competitively on a global basis.

On the international scene, South Korea is a relative newcomer to the world markets. For most of the twentieth century it existed in the shadow of Japan, its conqueror and colonizer. After World War II, Korea was divided at the 38th longitudinal parallel into halves—a North Korea dominated by Soviet Russia and in the south the Republic of Korea, existing as a protectorate of the United States. North Korea, with a population of 17 million, was the industrially developed half of the truncated nation, possessing 55% of the arable land, 90% of the electrical power, 70% of the mineral production, and most of the heavy manufacturing installations. South Korea, with 36 million people, had a much greater problem in becoming self-supporting. Then in addition, in the years after the Korean War (1950–53), the government in Seoul was hamstrung by political strife. This was ended abruptly in 1961, when a military junta, headed by General Park Chung Hee, took over and established a dictatorship which lasted unchallenged until Park's assassination in 1979.

Park's rule was politically repressive. Open dissent and criticism were not tolerated. But from an economic standpoint, South Korea was transformed into an oasis of free enterprise capitalism on the Asian continent. South Korea has been a new spawning ground for the entrepreneur on the far side of the Pacific Ocean. Under Park's direction, the country has adhered to the Macrae theory of industrial development, perhaps not by design but rather by instinct. The three essential conditions for solid economic growth were amply fulfilled: total rural employment so as to stimulate a healthy and profitable agriculture; introduction of cost-conscious technology, plus the mechanism to change or retool as events and circumstances required; and a friendly and favorable climate for big business to grow and to profit.

As the son of a poor peasant, General Park was aware of the need to put South Korea's agriculture on a sound basis. He lifted wage and price controls, giving the farmers greater freedom over their own operations. This made farming economically attractive. Industrial corporations were encouraged and assisted to buy or to license as much of the latest technology as was affordable, particularly in the field of construction and electronic equipment. Finally, big business had few problems with the Park government; no harassment, few controls, and a general laissez-faire attitude prevailed in the crucial years of early development.

Perhaps the ghost of Paek Il Gyu returned to inspire the leaders of government and the business community. For with a sure touch, they aligned the economy of South Korea with international trends and developments, such as large-scale construction and industrial development projects, electronics and computers, etc.—and they are profitably riding them into the future.

Malaysia is a Third World country that is determined not to repeat the mistakes committed by other developing nations. It has learned from the experiences of neighboring states that real economic growth cannot be achieved under military rule or a "socialist" regime that is also hostile to capitalism and the free market system. Instead Malaysia is finding its way to prosperity and political stability by practicing free enterprise capitalism in a democratic framework.

Malaysia is a federation of small kingdoms, which formerly were British colonies. Half of it is a long peninsula which extends southward out of the continent of Asia. The other half is the northern quarter of the island of Borneo, 700 miles to the east across the South

China Sea. Peninsular Malaya was a colony of little value until the British introduced natural rubber, which had been smuggled out of Brazil at the turn of the century. Today Malaya produces more than a third of the world's natural rubber. Other major commodities are palm oil, tin, pepper, and hardwoods, all of which were developed under British or Chinese ownership and operation. Malaya was once Somerset Maugham country, the land of the plantation-owning white "sahib," with brigades of Malays at his beck and call. Full independence came in 1957, but only after a savage guerrilla war with Chinese Communists had played havoc with the production of rubber. The hostilities began in 1948, and by 1954 the British forces had broken the back of the Communist guerrilla movement.

One of the more compelling reasons why Malaysia avoided becoming a socialist-oriented "people's republic"—a course taken by so many other Third World countries on attaining their independence—was the six years of guerrilla warfare which wracked the country and virtually wrecked its economy. An equally persuasive motive for electing free enterprise over socialism was a simple matter of common sense. Malaysia's economy was dependent on selling five major commodities—rubber, tin, palm oil, hardwoods, and pepper—on the highly competitive world markets. Of necessity, this involved collaboration with foreign companies and commercial reciprocity. It meant opening the door to foreign investments, as well as goods and services from overseas. Hence, a free market economy must be allowed to function without government interference or controls.

The Malaysians have little cause to regret their choice of free enterprise capitalism. The economic growth rate has been a steady 7% a year. The per capita income jumped from $370 in 1970 to $1,660 by 1980, while in the same period, the national GNP rose from $3.9 billion to $22.8 billion. Exports climbed from $1.8 billion to $12.6 billion annually by 1980. Malaysia is one of the few Third World countries which does not have to import food; in fact, it has an export surplus. The natives have fish, rice, coconuts, and bananas in abundance, their native foods for generations past. While the rural population has increased tenfold in this century, only about half of the arable land is under cultivation. But there is ample capacity as well as productivity, not only to feed the farm and urban populations but also for export. Finally, life in the rural villages is steadily improving. There are new roads for transport and communications. Safe water is available, and medical clinics have improved the general health of the Malaysians.

However, there is one serpent in this facsimile Garden of Eden—

racial conflict. Of the 13 million people in this federation, 54% are Malays, 35% Chinese, and 10% Indian. The Malays control the government and the national parliament, and they provide the manpower for the security forces. The Chinese have dominated the business community from top to bottom, with the Indians also serving as traders, storekeepers, artisans, etc. For all practical purposes, the Malays have little say in the economic life of Malaysia. And the Malay government wants to remedy this situation thereby reducing the present economic advantages of the Chinese and Indians.

However, before going further into this racially explosive situation, it is useful first to consider the special role which the Chinese play in Southeast Asia.

The first Chinese traders migrated from the Fukien and Kwantung provinces of their homeland into the Southeast Asian territories about A.D. 200. In the intervening centuries these overseas Chinese established themselves in what is known today as Malaysia, Singapore, Indonesia, Burma, Thailand, Cambodia, Vietnam, Laos, Borneo, the Philippines, etc. Other Chinese followed them, seeking their fortunes away from the "middle kingdom." The Chinese multiplied, and today they number about 16 million. Though they may be generations removed from their ancestral homes, they have maintained their own ethnic identity, their culture and mores; they are aloof, reserved, and separate from the natives among whom they reside. Every city in Southeast Asia has its own "Chinatown," which does not impinge on the consciousness of the stranger unless he seeks it out for a visit. These overseas Chinese have been called "the Jews of the Orient"; it is part tribute and part racial slur. For though these overseas Chinese are racial minorities in the countries where they live, they dominate the economic life in Southeast Asia, except in Communist-controlled Vietnam, Cambodia, and Laos. Elsewhere they have become the traders and merchants, the bankers and entrepreneurs, the shopkeepers and artisans. The leaders of the Chinese communities operate on an international basis through a network of family and ethnic connections that is both effective and baffling. As an *Economist* survey reported (Dec. 22, 1979):

The Chinese are industrious, enterprising, given to gambling, great feasts, hungry for money. In Malaysia, as throughout Southeast Asia, most of the petty trade is in Chinese hands and a lot of the large scale trade too. The Chinese in the countryside own small rubber plantations, pineapple gardens, vegetable plots, sawmills. In the towns they own taxis, buses, food shops, cinemas. On a larger scale they own banks, deal in gold, trade in rice and urban land, dominate the stock exchange. Together with the Indians they provide the top technical people for public service. They are, in other words, indispensable to the country's commercial and economic life.

The dominance of the Chinese is abetted because a large percentage of them reside in the cities, where they constitute 56% of the urban population. The Malays are unchallenged in the countryside, where they are the peasant farmers. In the eternal contest of town versus countryside in Malaysia, and elsewhere in Southeast Asia, the urban Chinese wield the levers of power.

This economic imbalance has stirred up resentment in Malaysia—as well as in neighboring Indonesia for the same reasons—and serious rioting has taken place in the 1960s. Chinese civilians were killed and their properties ravaged by the angry Malays. Since 1971 the Malaysian government has been trying to change the pattern of ownership of local companies along racial lines. The objective to be reached by 1990 is 30% share of all companies to be allocated to the *bumiputras* ("sons of the soil"), the political label for native Malays; 40% to be in the hands of Malaysian residents of other races (i.e., the local Chinese as well as the Indians); and 30% to be owned by foreign residents. However, as of 1982, a solution to this complex problem of racial desegregation of corporate ownership has still eluded the authorities. For one thing, the Malays do not have either the available capital or the business background and experience to step forward. For example, many new business ventures which are financed by the Chinese will be headed by a Malay appointee. These corporate "straw men" are known as "Ali Babas." Behind the facade, it's business as usual with the Chinese entrepreneur controlling and directing the enterprise. While the Chinese try to keep a low profile on the economic scene, their presence and power are hard to conceal. For example, in a 1981 special advertising supplement in *Fortune* magazine, twelve of the thirteen prominent Malaysian businessmen interviewed were Chinese. The thirteenth was a member of the Indian community. This situation is one more endorsement of the classic description of the "sons of Han" as "the world's most businesslike people."

The most accurate yardstick of Malaysia's commitment to the free enterprise system can be found in Sime Darby, the only multinational company that has grown out of a jungle. This former British corporation, now owned by Asians, is the commercial flagship of the Malaysian economic policy. Sime Darby exemplifies the aggressive capitalism that the government of Malaysia supports and encourages. Sime Darby was founded in 1910 by three Scotsmen, two Sime brothers and H. M. Darby, to grow rubber for export to the Western world. Today it is the biggest conglomerate in Asia, involved in more than two hundred enterprises in twenty-three countries. As its Chinese chairman, Tun Tan Siew Sin, commented dryly: "About the only thing we don't own is a brothel."

However, more important than Sime Darby's present size and scope was the postwar transformation of this relict of British colonialism into a modern and dynamic Asian business conglomerate without any government pressure or interference. In this changeover, the Malaysian government showed that it would not repeat the mistakes that other Third World countries made on attaining their independence. In these ex-colonies, the big foreign-owned properties, such as mines, plantations, industrial plants, etc., were nationalized. Their European owners received only a fraction of their true value as compensation for their loss. In addition, their European managers and directors were also ousted. They were replaced by natives, generally without the requisite training or experience to continue the profitable operations of these properties. Native incompetence replaced European expertise, to the ultimate deterioration of the expropriated firms and loss of income for all concerned.

As the biggest single corporation in Malaysia, Sime Darby did not suffer the same dismal fate. British ownership and management remained unaffected until a crash on the Hong Kong and Singapore stock markets in 1973 brought an end to a feverish bull market in the shares of Sime Darby and other Southeast Asian firms. The Malaysian government went into the depressed market and bought up 30% of the Sime Darby shares. This encouraged Chinese and other non-European investors also to buy these shares. Control of the firm passed from London to Kuala Lumpur, capital of Malaysia. The government also refrained from naming its own directors of the board and kept the European managers in their place. Tun Tan Siew Sin ("Tun" is Malay for the title "Sir"), formerly finance minister and later banker and chairman of nine private companies, became chairman of Sime Darby. He recruited James Scott, a Scotsman from the Dunlop Rubber Company, to be the chief executive of Sime Darby, which continues to operate along orthodox business lines to carry out the pragmatic economic policies of the federation.

Chairman Tan reportedly endorses the American business philosophy: "Expand or perish." With that end in view, Sime Darby has acquired a varied portfolio in recent years: the Pepsi-Cola bottling plant in Hong Kong, the BMW auto franchise in Singapore, an automobile assembly plant in China, part ownership of a bank with American Express as a partner, a paper carton factory in distant Dubai on the Persian Gulf, a company producing detergents in Australia, a new 10,000-acre cocoa plantation in Borneo, etc., all controlled from a $32 million skyscraper headquarters in Kuala Lumpur.

At the southern tip of the Malaysian peninsula lies the island of Singapore. This 240-square-mile city-state is a pulsating, booming economic powerhouse. Today, Singapore is one of the dynamic NICs—newly industrialized countries—which give the world a fore-taste of what Asia's teeming millions can achieve if directed by intel-ligent and imaginative leaders, following sound policies of self-inter-est. Singapore is an *ecopolitical* success story. Twenty years ago (1960) this once great British naval base and trading center was teetering on the verge of ruin, about to fall under the control of Communists. Two decades later Singapore is a major world banking center and a beehive of electronic production as well as a producer of other light and heavy industrial goods. Its 2.3 million residents enjoy a per capita income of $5,023, the highest in all Asia after Japan.

The secret of Singapore's renaissance appears to be a contradic-tion in terms. It has created a free market economy designed to achieve precise political goals. The Singapore government, which is virulently anti-Communist, has harnessed the capitalistic system to serve socialistic objectives. These are, basically, fair distribution of incomes through wage controls and graduated income taxes, and equal opportunities for employment, housing, medical care, and education. All this is carried out under the rigorous supervision and control of a puritanically minded, corruption-free government that watches over its flock with the diligence of a KGB block warden and the solicitude that a Tammany Hall precinct captain once practiced. As the London *Economist* remarked editorially: "Nobody before has tried to bring off this special trick and there are no orthodox terms to describe it. Let us call it for the time being a well-policed, welfare capitalism, laced with Chinese *chutzpah*."[8]

Anthony Sampson, international economic journalist, gave it an-other perspective: "Singapore combined international capitalism with domestic socialism. . . . To most Singaporeans it was the triumph of pragmatism over an out-dated ideology; and that was the emphatic view of their durable Prime Minister, Lee Kuan Yew."[9]

The unquestionable end result is positive. By giving its workers an escalating standard of living, Singapore's industrial productivity

[8]"Survey of Singapore," *Economist*, Dec. 29, 1979.
[9]Sampson, *The Money Lenders*.

and technology have dramatically increased. This in turn enhances this city-state's competitive position on the world markets.

Sir Stamford Raffles, an imaginative empire-builder, was the founder of Singapore. While seeking to expand the trading operations of the East India Company, he acquired the island of Singapore in 1819 from the sultan of Johore. This commercial outpost was sited at the southern opening of the Strait of Malacca, then as now a major trade route and a shortcut between the South China Sea and the Indian Ocean. Raffles was a man of vision. He saw the possibilities of this island as a base for British expansion into the rich Orient. In succeeding years Singapore developed into a linchpin of the British Empire. It was a refueling station for its growing merchant marine and navy, a military garrison, and a major commercial center which sucked in the wealth of the Orient and pumped it onto the banks in distant London.

After World War II, Singapore's role on the world stage steadily diminished, as the dissolution of the British Empire set in like a terminal case of cancer. The once-great trading entrepôt stagnated and unemployment rose, while Singapore's slums expanded to equal the worst in Asia. A single brewery in operation constituted 75% of the island's gross national production. Meanwhile the Communists seriously threatened Singapore's political stability. In 1959 elections were held to take over the crown colony. At this juncture, a modern-day Stamford Raffles emerged, who was to become the architect of new postwar Singapore that under his direction would once again be a major economic power center in the Orient.

He was Lee Kuan Yew, then thirty-six years old, son of well-to-do Chinese parents, an honors graduate of Cambridge University, where he had acquired an enthusiasm for socialism. On his return to Singapore, Lee founded his own People's Action Party (PAP) and threw his hat into the political ring. With Communist support, he was elected the first prime minister of the city-state of Singapore. Once installed in office and faced with the grim realities of economic survival of the new city-state with its 2 million inhabitants, Lee quickly realized that a political ideology could not solve Singapore's pressing needs. He broke with the Communists and has been their implacable opponent ever since. He rationalized that economic growth must be the city-state's primary objective. Hence, to achieve this objective, Singapore must align its economic development with the leading industrial nations of the world. It must produce what is saleable in their markets; it must offer services which encourage foreign investments in Singapore's industrial development. *Ipso facto*, Singapore must choose capitalism and not socialism to mesh its postwar economy with the world's leading industrial nations.

Singapore is 76% Chinese with a high level of literacy; Malays number 15%, Indians 7%, and the rest are Europeans and Eurasians. The city-state had an abundance of cheap skilled labor to offer foreign manufacturers, and also liberal tax incentives to encourage them to establish industrial plants in Singapore. The rush to Singapore began in 1968, and since that time over $7 billion has been invested in this small island, including about $1 billion from U.S. companies. Mainly light industry was attracted, but of high technology level, such as manufacturers of precision optical equipment, aerospace components, electronic equipment, and scientific and medical instruments.

There is also developing heavy industry, connected with ship-building and repair and construction of oil-drilling equipment. Brian Chang, a forty-three-year-old engineer, started working as a coolie laborer. Today he owns and operates a 55-acre shipyard which has a $250 million backlog of orders for construction work, including harbors in the Persian Gulf, and for oil rigs.

Finally, Singapore has become the financial center for Southeast Asia. Fifty of the world's leading banks have established offices in the mushrooming cluster of skyscrapers that dominate the Singapore landscape. The *Wall Street Journal* also publishes its far eastern edition in Singapore.

Lee Kuan Yew is still prime minister, uninterrupted in his tenure of office for twenty-two years. More than any other person, he is responsible for Singapore's rebirth as a bustling prosperous economic power center. The results of his policies have been startling. Since 1973 the growth of the domestic product has averaged 11.5% annually. The overall economic growth rate is projected to continue at its present 8% well into the 1980s. Except for Japan, Singapore enjoys the highest living standards of any Asian country. Over 60% of its 2.3 million people live in modern and attractive public housing developments, complete with swimming pools, shopping centers, schools, and health clinics. Medical care and education are free. A self-supporting social security system permits a Singapore resident to retire comfortably at the age of fifty-five. The city's streets are swept daily. No beggars or prostitutes are permitted to operate or loiter in public places. There are many new parks and green belts to beautify the inner city and provide recreational space. Crime and unemployment are at a bare minimum. In fact, about ten thousand "guest workers" from Malaysia and India have been imported to handle the menial jobs, such as garbage disposal and street sweeping.

But there is a price to be paid. The government permits no opposition, either political or social. Nor is there a free press. Dissent or criticism of government and its actions is punished. Nor can labor unions function freely. Yet to the mass of Chinese residents in Singapore this situation is not so onerous as it appears at first glance. Lee himself explains that his continuing unchallenged rule of the city is due to a Confucian ethic which governs their thinking. "They do not believe that sending in an opposition to throw darts at the government is going to help them," he told Henry Kamm of the *New York Times* (Sept. 24, 1980). Another government minister further commented: "The whole of Chinese history knows no opposition, only good government and bad government. They accept it if the government is good for them. They are not attuned to western democracy."

If, judged by western standards, Lee Kuan Yew's government is politically backward, on the economic side it has recently embarked on what is "perhaps the bravest industrial experiment of the developing world."[10] Singapore is deliberately seeking to become a center of high-technology production in Southeast Asia. In so doing, it will be following the footsteps made by Japan in the last decade. Of course, Singapore cannot seriously threaten Japan's preeminence in the field of high technology. But if Singapore can carry out this program to upgrade its industrial potential, on the basis of its own educated engineers and technicians, the implications of this experiment for the long-range economic development of the Far East—where half of the world's population resides—are portentous to the highest degree.

Regulating the workers' wages is the principal tool to carry out this New Economic Policy, launched in 1979. Since 1978 the Singapore government has forced wages up by more than 60% in a succession of moves. The purpose is to weed out labor-intensive industries—originally attracted to Singapore by the availability of cheap labor—and to stimulate the growth of the fledgling high-technology sector. For example, some textile and electronics firms are moving out because of rising labor costs, but this is acceptable as part of the New Economic Policy to streamline the labor force. The economic strategy involves three related developments: successive wage increases, low-interest loans to attract high-technology industries to settle in Singapore, and a major training program for workers designed to raise their skills and productivity. There are also other incentives, such as income tax reductions for industrial firms, proportionate to the number of better-paid skilled native workers they employ.

[10]*Economist*, Jan. 17, 1981.

Whether Singapore can pull off this industrial transformation is subject to some questioning. There are criticisms from foreign businessmen that Singapore is in too much of a hurry. But this view is not voiced in Singapore's official circles. Patrick Yeoh, of the Singapore Development Bank, commented: "By 1990 we should be where Japan is today."

Singapore's unique economic growth, with its accompanying political stability, is an important event in the short and turbulent history of the Third World. This bustling city-state has blazed a trail for other less developed nations to follow in their efforts to achieve the same objectives. Lee Kuan Yew spelled it out in a 1978 address to the International Chamber of Commerce in these words:

Our developments would not have been possible if we had not been able to plug into the world grid of industrial powerhouses in America, Europe and Japan. Other developing countries should be encouraged and helped to do the same thing. How soon and how effectively they can tap into this world grid depends on them, upon how realistic and pragmatic their governments are in their policies, so as to strike a bargain with those who have capital, management and technology.

The Singapore formula for success is relatively simple, at least as applied to Southeast Asian countries. The developing country must:

1. Establish and maintain a completely free market economy.

2. Exploit rather than suppress the unique entrepreneurial capabilities of the overseas Chinese.

3. Establish quality controls on all production.

4. Avoid industrial development projects which take a long time before they are operational and revenue-producing, such as a steel mill.

5. Subsidize farmers, so there are incentives to produce more and hold their labor on the land.

6. Reject foreign aid, because it will shift public spending into projects which essentially do not benefit the economic growth and which, of themselves, encourage graft and corruption.

In short, the inexorable lesson that must be learned by the Third World bloc is that taking the capitalistic road offers the best chance of achieving their national goals: true political independence and stability, together with economic growth and a rising standard of living for their peoples. That is what has been amply demonstrated around the world, both negatively, as in black Africa, and positively, as in Southeast Asia.

CHAPTER SEVEN

Silk Cocoons to Silicon Chips

. . . the real question is when and to what extent Japan will choose to
have a foreign policy that is more than an export policy.
> —The *Economist*, March 31, 1973

. . . as far as Japan is concerned, international strategy has to be built
around economics rather than politics.
> —PETER F. DRUCKER, in *Fortune* magazine,
> Nov. 3, 1980

Japan encourages its strong industries; the United States protects its
weak ones.
> —U.S. Comptroller General's report
> to U.S. Senate, 1979

The Japanese aren't a nation; they are a very large tribe.
> —A senior U.S. executive
> stationed in Japan

Japanese society . . . has been shaped by history and geography to be
austere and adaptable.
> —KYONOSUKE IBE, chairman of the
> Sumitomo Bank, Tokyo

IN 1953, Akio Morita, a twenty-nine-year-old Japanese engineer, made his first trip to the United States, a trip that was to have window-rattling repercussions in the international business world years later. Morita was interested in a new American invention, the transistor. Invented by Bell Laboratories, the transistor was to usher in the age of electronics. The Japanese engineer was convinced that with this little device, hardly larger than a common housefly, he could produce a pocket-size radio. So he paid $25,000 for a license to manufacture transistors in Japan.

This act, coupled with its speedy implementation, is now one of the economic milestones of the twentieth century. Morita's introduction of the pocket-size transistor radio marks the beginning of Japan's rise out of the ashes of defeat and destruction to become the second-greatest industrial power in the world, close on the heels of the United States. The amazing success of this small radio on the world markets paved the way for a flood of other innovative consumer goods that quickly followed: TV sets, stereo equipment, pocket calculators, cameras, etc. These best-selling and money-making exports in turn financed the revival and modernization of Japan's industrial machine. Within a comparatively short time, the 110 million Japanese were providing a wide range of capital and consumer goods and services, from tiny and complex silicon chips to 500,000-ton oil tankers, from construction of chemical plants to factories manned by robots. As the 1980s began, Japan was producing more cars than Detroit, more steel and cameras than West Germany, more watches than Switzerland, and more ships than Scotland and Scandinavia together, just to list a few of the noteworthy records set by the bustling Japanese.

195

Modern Japan is something unique in the world today. It is an amalgam of government, business management, and labor, all working together harmoniously to achieve a common objective: the creation of the world's first *ecopolitical* superpower. As an island nation, Japan is aware that its continued survival depends on imports of food and vital raw materials to sustain its people and its industrial economy. World War II taught the Japanese a profound truth: Wars of conquest cannot guarantee economic security. Only peace offers that possibility. So in the last three decades, they have devoted their energies and their talents to rebuilding and then expanding their national economy. In so doing they have come in sight of their objective.

This resurgent Japan is the archetype of a functioning ecopolitical state, a nation which gives top priority to the growth and modernization of its economy above other political and defense considerations. The Japanese operate on the principle that expanding industrial capacity, coupled with a high level of technology, is the best guarantee for their continuing security and prosperity in a hostile and competitive world. The state of world affairs in the 1980s seems to confirm the wisdom of this Japanese policy line. The belligerent superpowers are stalemated in a rough parity as far as their military capabilities are concerned. At the same time their positions of dominance have been eroded. The United States is no longer the unchallenged leader on the world stage. The Soviet Union has just about stripped its economic cupboard bare to beef up its armed forces at the expense of lowered living standards for the Russian people. Alone of all the major powers, Japan is enjoying prosperity and stability, as its exports continue to sell on the world markets. After several abortive starts in the past, Japan's day on the world stage appears to have dawned. Shaped by its history and traditions, a born-again Japan has been a child of fortune of the postwar era. It has literally leaped from poverty to riches, from weakness to strength, in the span of a single generation.

However, what is more significant is that Japan has raised the curtain on the "Pacific Century." Historians will identify the postwar emergence of Japan as the beginning of the shift of economic power away from the Atlantic to the Pacific community of nations. The industrialization of the Far East is well underway, not only in Japan but also in South Korea, Taiwan, Singapore, Hong Kong, and Malaysia. Giant Red China with its billion-plus population is already stirring to the economic "pragmatism" of its post-Mao government, seeking to unlock the country's industrial potential fettered for decades by traditions and ideology. The *Economist* of London (May 7, 1977) coined an apt phrase, "Tomorrow's Workshop," to signal the growing importance of these nations in economic affairs. The Pacific Century will become a reality because it is the world's newest economic frontier. It has something to offer everyone. For the merchant there are vast new markets for goods and services, from the simplest of agricultural tools to sophisticated electronic computers. For the industrialist there are new manufacturing bases where he can improve his competitive position on the world markets, because of a glut of cheap and skilled labor available. And for the banker there is a whole new horizon of opportunities to finance as commerce expands and industry opens up. The Pacific Century is not a mirage, not just an entrepreneur's dream. It has already begun in Japan and Southeast Asia. The world of business has also taken note of the fact that Siberian Russia is becoming more important to European Russia. And in the United States, public interest is quickening concerning new business opportunities in the Far East.[1]

Herman Kahn's Hudson Institute, which has been closely following the postwar evolution of the Far East, points out that the foundations are already in place for its expanding economic development. Kahn explains that the Pacific Basin should be regarded in terms of cities rather than countries. A few examples are Singapore, Manila, Taipei, Tokyo, Sydney, Hong Kong, Los Angeles, Vancouver, Guadalajara, Lima-Callao, and San Francisco. The mushrooming growth of Singapore and Hong Kong demonstrates that in the Far East, coastal cities can become Tomorrow's Workshops virtually on their own resources if the business climate is favorable and the incentives sufficiently attractive. Populated centers usually have the cheap labor available and the infrastructure, and can contribute to economic growth independent of the adjacent countryside. China's program to create semiautonomous international trade zones, in which foreign companies can manufacture and sell under their own management, is another confirmation of this thesis.

To find the key to Japan and its amazing postwar resurgence, one must delve into its history. There are patterns of social behavior, traditions, work ethic, and conduct that have their origins in the dim and distant past. For example, the special character of the national economy today, such as the close, almost incestuous, relationship between big business and the government, stems directly from the alliance between the merchant class and the samurai, or warrior class, whose mutual interests became apparent several centuries ago. The loyalty

[1]The establishment of a separate Asian edition of the *Wall Street Journal*, published daily in Singapore, is confirmation of the growing American commitment to the Pacific Basin, the eastern rim of which is the United States.

and unquestioning obedience that the Japanese peasant gave to his feudal lord and protector in medieval times is mirrored today in the relationship between the worker and his "contemporary feudal lord,"[2] the plant manager of an industrial firm, in return for guaranteed lifetime employment. In no other industrial nation does the past so impinge on and influence the present as it does in Japan today.

Japan was and still is a hierarchical society. The people recognize and accept this state of affairs. The Japanese are comfortable in knowing that every person has his or her "proper place": in the home, in the office or factory or at the marketplace. This is acknowledged in the ceremonial politeness. When two Japanese meet, they bow to each other. The degree of inclination or the depth of the bow subtly discloses which of the two is socially superior and which is inferior. This carries over into the family circle itself. The children bow to their parents, the wife to her husband. The head of the family, or the office boss, bows in return, but not so deeply as his inferiors bow to him.

In all of its recorded history, Japan has never been subjected to a revolution, political or social. There have been civil wars and intense factional conflicts throughout Japan's early history, but never was an emperor overthrown by a revolution, cloistered and impotent as emperors were throughout much of their reigns. There were assassinations and poisonings, but a dead emperor was quickly replaced by a live one. The sociopolitical structure remained intact. For the emperor was the symbol of sovereignty in the past, as he is today. The governing of the nation has been in the hands of men who were independent of the emperor but exercised power in his name. Nor did the constant territorial warfare between the various clans in feudal times change or reform the rigid structure of society and its conduct and way of life. That is another carryover from the past to the present.

Prior to World War II, Japan had never been invaded by a foreign army throughout its recorded history. In 1281, a Mongol army of 200,000 led by Kublai Khan, grandson of Genghis Khan, attempted an invasion. His invasion fleet was repulsed and scattered by a typhoon of great intensity, which the Japanese historians described as a *kamikaze*, a "divine wind." In 1945, in an effort to repulse the threatened invasion of American forces, the Japanese air force launched its *kamikaze* bombing strikes on U.S. warships. The pilots dive-bombed their planes in suicidal attacks on American naval vessels, with great but not decisive destruction.

Largely because of its history and traditions, there has always

---

[2]As categorized by Kenichi Omae, a management consultant in Tokyo, in the *Wall Street Journal*, Jan. 18, 1982.

been and still exists a strong strain of xenophobia in the Japanese national character. This is not uncommon in an island people, who resent intruders and wish to insulate or isolate themselves from the influences of the foreigners. This xenophobic element has given the Japanese a deep-seated conviction that they are innately superior to foreigners, who, from the earliest days on, were categorized as "barbarians." The Japanese have looked down their collective noses at those races and nationalities who do not possess the Spartan character and austere attitude toward life which the Japanese have displayed throughout their known history. The fact that Japan had never been conquered or colonized, until World War II, was a source of pride and distinction. One of the earliest missionaries, the Jesuit Francis Xavier, took note of this national quality in a report to his superiors in Rome: "The people we have met so far are the best who have yet been discovered and it seems to me that we shall never find among the heathens another race equal to the Japanese."[3]

In 1603, Ieyasu, one of the great figures in Japanese history, became shogun (the title translates literally as "barbarian-repelling generalissimo"), to unite and to rule Japan in the name of the emperor, who was a shadowy figurehead in those times. Fearful that foreign influences, particularly the Christian missionaries, would adversely affect the Japanese way of life, Ieyasu and his successors of the Tokugawa Shogunate closed off Japan from the outside world for 250 years. He established a hierarchical society in which every man, woman, and child had his or her "proper place." It involved a rigid caste system. On top were the emperor and the court nobility. Just below them were the samurai, the warrior class who were the enforcers of the shogun's rule. The samurai occupied a place in feudal society similar to that of the Prussian Junker army officer in Kaiser Wilhelm's Germany. In descending order next came the farmers, and the artisans, followed by the merchants. Beyond the pale were the *Eta*, the pariahs of society, who performed all the menial tasks such as street sweeping and garbage collecting and who were not even counted as part of the population. The merchants had a low social status because they handled money, the most disruptive element in a feudal society.[4]

---

[3]From William H. Forbis, *Japan Today* (New York: Harper & Row, 1975).

[4]The Tokugawa shoguns (1602–1868) recognized the inherent menace that money power held for the social structure of their oligarchy. So they created a safety valve by allowing the establishment of an entertainment quarter in their capital. This was an area devoted to the pleasures of the flesh, including the notorious Yoshiwara brothels, geisha girls, restaurants, baths, pornography shops, and a variety of theatrical performances, to occupy the minds and the appetites of the merchants and artisans. The famed Ginza, the Broadway of modern Tokyo, can trace its origins back to this nightlife sector of ancient Edo, the original name of the Japanese capital.

Only the samurai, as guardians and warriors, were armed with their fearsome slashing swords. They were forbidden to work for money. Instead they received a small monthly stipend from their feudal lord. But in times of peace it was never enough to sustain their superior status and pretensions. On the other hand, the merchants had the money and wanted to climb up the social ladder. Hence their daughters, provided with substantial dowries, began to marry into the impoverished samurai caste. It became a two-way traffic. Members of the samurai began joining the merchants in business enterprises, giving the latter group contacts and status hitherto denied them. In fact the Mitsui Company, the senior of Japan's great industrial and trading conglomerates, was founded by a member of the samurai in 1606. This was the beginning of the unexpected alliance between the sword and the cashbox. It has survived to this day in somewhat revised form in the close relationship between the government and the industrialists that is such a potent factor in Japan's economic development.

However, despite all their nationalistic pride and chauvinism, the Japanese are the world's greatest copiers—or to use a more polite word, adapters. Undoubtedly the source of Japan's power and growth lies in its genius for copying or adapting somebody else's inventions or ideas and improving on the originals. For example, Japan's first national industry, weaving of silk, was stolen from the Chinese, who had originally discovered how to produce silk. About A.D. 300, Japan sent a team of Koreans to China to acquire the closely guarded secret of transforming cocoon fibers into silken thread. The Koreans returned with four Chinese girls, who taught the art of weaving to the Japanese. A shrine to commemorate this event was later erected near Osaka.

In fact, in the seventh and eighth centuries Japan began to acquire the lineaments of her civilization from the Chinese. Japan had no written language, so she took over the Chinese ideographs and used them to write her own totally different language. Japan had a religion which involved some forty-thousand gods, so in the seventh century she adapted China's Buddhism as a religion "excellent for protecting the state." As part of the package Japan also borrowed Chinese architecture for the Buddhist temples, monasteries, and other public works. Chinese art and ceremonial tea-drinking were other cultural imports. The Chinese calendar and the philosophy of Confucius also crossed the China Sea to add to the intellectual development of the brash and culturally deprived Japanese. "It is difficult to find anywhere in the world any other such successfully planned importation of a civilization by a sovereign nation," writes Ruth Benedict in her penetrating study of the patterns of Japanese culture.[5]

The Achilles heel of this economic colossus of the western Pacific arises from the fact that Japan is an island nation and its people have an island mentality. They have a knowledge of the world, but not world experience, such as the British—another island people—or the French and even the Americans have garnered in the nineteenth and twentieth centuries. At the beginning of the seventeenth century, when Shakespeare was writing his masterpieces, when Captain John Smith had just established the first English settlement on the American continent, the Japanese chose to cut themselves off from the outside world, and they remained cut off for two and a half centuries. They were confident that they could adequately fend for themselves. They were sustained in this self-imposed exile from world society by their mythology. They believed themselves to be descendants of Izanami and Izanagi, the gods who formed the earth and its first inhabitants, the Japanese. Then in 1853 Commodore Perry had to break down the door and drag the reluctant Japanese into the realities of the nineteenth century.

The Japanese are strangers to the outside world, and the world is strange to them. Since their nation is now prosperous, thousands of Japanese are seeing the world for the first time. They travel abroad in small groups, like schoolchildren visiting a museum under the guidance of their teacher. The Japanese who have to live overseas are diplomats or businessmen on foreign service assignments for their government or their firms. In general they hive together in small colonies like busy bees. They take over hotels and restaurants, form their own clubs, and "Japanize" their surroundings as far as possible. They never seem to explore foreign lands, except to carry out market surveys to ascertain what countries might be likely export markets for Japanese goods.

Japan has forged ahead by harvesting the ideas, inventions, and innovations of other lands, adapting them to fit its purposes and needs. Japan's own contributions to world civilization are scarce: to mention a few, Hiroshige prints, the tea ceremony, rock gardens, geisha girls, the shrines at Kyoto, silk and the kimono, floral arrangements, and the *Tale of the Genji* by Lady Murasaki, written about A.D. 1010 and probably the first realistic novel that has survived down through the ages.

---

[5]Ruth Benedict, *The Chrysanthemum and the Sword* (New York: World, 1967).

Japan's self-imposed isolation from the outside world was rudely ended in 1853 by Commodore Matthew C. Perry and four warships of the U.S. Navy which sailed uninvited into Tokyo Bay. The American government wanted the right of a port-of-call for its U.S. ships plying the Pacific, as well as the freedom to trade with Japan. The threatening appearance of Perry's flotilla, bristling with cannon, rang down the curtain on the country's feudal past. The Japanese reluctantly entered the nineteenth century to join the rest of the world. The eyes of its more enlightened officials were opened to an uncertain future. They quickly grasped the reality that Japan was very deficient regarding its national defense. They had nothing to protect the country against an attack by a foreign navy, such as Perry's menacing "four black ships." They did not want to allow the Americans, British, Dutch, or Portuguese to gain a foothold on Japanese territory, as they had succeeded in doing in China and elsewhere in the Far East. To remedy this situation they had to buy modern armaments from Europe and America. They had to trade with the world. To do so effectively required creation of an industrial economy[6] to produce goods and process raw materials. Thus the industrialization of this lone-wolf nation was quickly launched in the early days of the Meiji Restoration. The Emperor Meiji emerged from behind the confines that had made him a myth and mystery to the Japanese people, to take his "proper place" openly as the head of the nation.

The Emperor Meiji, who proved to be a strong man in his own right, sought a modernization of Japan that was something more than just an imitation of England, America, or Germany. He and his advisers wanted those features of Western civilization that would renovate Japan but not change the fundamental character or values of the Japanese people. A mission was dispatched to Europe and America to survey what they had to offer. As a result the Japanese government began "to shop the world for expertise and technology. Importing thousands of advisers, the country learned about universities, medicine and the civil service from the Germans; government, armies and the law from the French; agriculture, post offices, lower schools and diplomacy from the Americans; railroads, telegraphs and navies from the British; techniques of painting and sculpture from the Italians."[7]

A high degree of native intelligence was applied to the industrial-

[6]Among the gifts which Commodore Perry brought for the emperor was a small steam train, built to one-fourth scale, and a circular track. Who could have predicted then that 111 years later, in 1964, the Japanese National Railroad would begin operating the first super-speed (125 mph) "bullet train," the fastest rail transportation in the world?

[7]Forbis, *Japan Today*, 1975.

ization of Japan under the reign of Emperor Meiji. The country was essentially a feudal state, supported by its own peasantry and fishermen. It was transformed into an industrial economy within a few decades according to a master plan drawn up by the small coterie of nobles and samurai officers who were the emperor's executive staff. First, they decided what industries were needed to achieve the twin objectives: national defense and economic growth. Then the government formed its own agency to build and operate these industries, such as textiles, mining, shipbuilding, glassmaking, etc. The state also financed their construction and operation through a postal savings system which the government had organized to raise money from the public. Loans could have been obtained from foreign banks, but the Tokyo government preferred to get its funding from Japanese sources. Meanwhile, foreign technicians and specialists were imported to run the new industries until Japanese executives obtained sufficient experience and know-how and could take over the industrial management. Hundreds of young Japanese were sent abroad to America and Europe to learn at first hand how modern industries operated. Once these new industries were established the government sold them at bargain prices to the leaders of *zaibatsu*, the business oligarchy that was to dominate the Japanese economy ever since. The Mitsui and Mitsubishi clans were the chief beneficiaries of this subsidization of industry.

As Ruth Benedict points out:

> Her statesmen judged that industrial development was too important to Japan to be entrusted to the laws of supply and demand or to free enterprise. But this policy was in no way due to socialistic dogma; it was precisely the *zaibatsu* who reaped the advantages. What Japan accomplished was that with a minimum of fumbling and wastage, the industries she deemed necessary were established.[8]

By this action the foundations were laid for the close working relationship between big business and the government that still exists today and that gives the Japanese such a formidable competitive advantage on the world markets. And also today the savings of the Japanese people still provide the greatest share of the financing for the daily needs of industry and commerce.

Thus it can be seen that Japan has recognized the top priority of economic growth; that its government acquired an *ecopolitical* outlook from the Meiji Restoration onward. Only later when the national econ-

---

[8]Benedict, *The Chrysanthemum and the Sword.*

omy was on firm ground did basic priorities begin to be ignored, particularly by the new national army and navy of the emperor, at great cost to the relatively young nation.

The Japanese wanted no foreign intervention in their economic or political affairs, especially in the adolescent years before the nation reached its maturity. But as its industry developed—able to build warships for its navy[9] and guns for its army—the Japanese began to flex their own acquisitive muscles. Before the turn of the century they had wrested Korea and Taiwan (Formosa) from the Chinese. To the astonishment of the major world powers, Japan decisively defeated Russia in a Pacific war in 1904–1905, destroying the Russian navy in Tsushima Straits and capturing Port Arthur against superior Russian armies. World War I brought Japan a major port of Tsingtao on the mainland of China, plus other bits of territory including Germany's former island possessions in the Pacific, the Caroline, Marshall, and Mariana groups.

However, the growing eagerness of the Japanese to acquire their own colonial territories was to prove to be a very costly mistake. The Japanese began to succumb to the delusion that has plagued so many other rising young nations—that conquest of somebody's else's territory is the path to prosperity and power. With the clearer perspective that hindsight gives, one can see that Japan embarked on the conquest of an empire in 1937 with the invasion of Manchuria. This was the first step in a war of aggression that was to lead to Pearl Harbor and ultimately to Japan's surrender to General Douglas MacArthur on the battleship U.S.S. *Missouri* in Tokyo Bay, Aug. 14, 1945. As Eliot Janeway has so cogently written:

Before World War II, Japan's colonial empire had been a parasitic growth on her economy. Colonies spawned more colonies and loaded new burdens on the productive portion of her society. So long as materialist dreams kept Japan bogged down on the continent of Asia and diverted from the rich markets

[9]Skepticism about Japan's ability to produce heavy industrial goods capable of meeting American or European standards, coupled with the fact that the Japanese are adept at copying but not at inventing, has given rise to some hoary and inaccurate stories. In the Army and Navy Club in Manila in 1941 just before Pearl Harbor, I first heard this one: The British intelligence in London had discovered that the Japanese naval attaché had orders to obtain the blueprints for a new type of destroyer for the Royal Navy. British naval engineers then "doctored" a set of plans, redesigning the ballast so as to make the warship unseaworthy when it was put in service. It was then arranged that the plans were surreptitiously handed over to the Japanese without arousing their suspicions. In due course the new destroyer was built in a Kure shipyard. Without any fanfare it was launched in the Inland Sea, and promptly turned turtle and sank with all hands on board. The U.S. naval officers, who regaled me with this and other stories denigrating the combat capabilities of the Japanese, were supremely confident they would be victorious over "the Nips" if war started. That was before Pearl Harbor opened our eyes to a new reality.

awaiting her in the Americas and in Europe, she traveled a one-way street to disaster. But after defeat in World War II freed the Japanese economy from the delusions of imperialist grandeur, Japan promptly developed the most dynamic growth rate in the world. Her productivity, released from the distractions of empire-building and from the burden of armaments required to support it, began to pay national dividends big enough to finance lower export prices and to attract foreign capital. By the mid-1950s Japan's invasion of the American market was fully launched.[10]

At the close of World War II, the U.S. armed forces took over the administration of defeated Japan. In his new assignment as supreme commander of the Allied powers, General Douglas MacArthur in effect became a postwar shogun of defeated Japan. As in the pre-Meiji times, the strongest military man became the shogun, ruling the nation in the name of the politically impotent emperor. MacArthur's orders and decrees became the overriding law of the land for the Japanese. Meanwhile Emperor Hirohito remained secluded in his moat-encircled palace in his capacity as the powerless "symbol of the state and of the unity of the people."

The U.S. Joint Chiefs of Staff in Washington had formulated a master policy directive for MacArthur as a basic guideline in dealing with the defeated Japanese, which stated in part: "You will not assume any responsibility for the economic rehabilitation of Japan or the strengthening of the Japanese economy. You will make clear to the Japanese people that: (a) You will assume no obligation to maintain or have maintained, any particular standard of living in Japan . . ."

General MacArthur initiated a program of social and economic changes designed to break up the traditional close relationship between the government and big business. Its ultimate objective was to drastically reduce Japan's economic power and growth potential. Among the many measures of reform and change put into effect was the dismantling of the huge and powerful industrial and commercial conglomerates, such as Mitsui, Mitsubishi, Sumitomo, and other zaibatsu (translated as "money club") organizations. Owners of large blocks of their shares were divested of their holdings. The top-level executives in industry and finance were removed from their executive suites, as well as high-ranking officers of the armed forces. Finally, a large reparations bill was presented to the Japanese which would have meant the transfer of ownership of most of Japan's heavy industry to the victims of its military aggression, if it had been carried out.

Saner counsels began to prevail in Washington and Tokyo, as the

[10]Eliot Janeway, *The Economics of Crisis* (New York: Weybright & Talley, 1968).

consequences of these punitive measures began to be weighed. The cold war with Russia, over the spheres of influence of the two superpowers, was mounting in intensity. In Germany and Japan, the United States could not permit the virus of Communism to infect the surviving populations of these two defeated and war-damaged former enemy states. MacArthur quietly applied the brakes to the "economic reforms" and changes. America's reparations bill of $670 million was also subsequently withdrawn, while the U.S. government contributed over $2 billion in food supplies to prevent mass starvation among the Japanese people. The *zaibatsu* could be put back together again; the deconcentration had only been skin-deep to date. A new second generation of executives was in place to reorganize and revitalize the war-stricken economy. With the signing of the 1951 peace treaty in San Francisco, Japan was master of its own house again, in control of its domestic and foreign affairs. The way was cleared for the economic renaissance to begin.

But in the immediate postwar years, Japan's prospects were grim. Japan had emptied its cupboards to fight the war. It had spent its industrial capital. It was bankrupt and indigent. In addition, its major cities had been extensively firebombed; its industrial centers had been left in disarray. Its domestic food production was also crippled, largely because of acute labor shortage on the farms and what remained of the nation's fishing fleets. The farmers and the fishermen had been drafted into the armed forces; if not casualties, the survivors were scattered in China, in Southeast Asia, and on the islands in the Pacific where the Japanese had been fighting. Japan was on the ropes. Edwin O. Reischauer, who later served as U.S. Ambassador in Tokyo, was then working with the U.S. forces in Japan, and wrote at that time: "The economic situation in Japan may be so fundamentally unsound that no policies can save her from slow economic starvation."[11]

Japan's economic revival began with the Korean War, 1950–53. Lying only 112 miles from Korea across the Tsushima Straits, Japan was an ideal staging area for the American and United Nations forces during the war. But more important to the Japanese, the United States spent over $4 billion in military procurement in Japan. The American money helped to finance Japanese production of ships, trucks, and other industrial equipment. It served to stimulate the moribund economy, just as a blood transfusion saves the life of a dying patient.

The second generation of managers, who replaced those purged

---

[11]By Edwin O. Reischauer, *The United States and Japan* (Cambridge, Mass: Harvard University Press, 1965).

by the Americans for their part in Japan's past military aggression, was a hardheaded and imaginative group. Before they reached any conclusions as to what they would produce, for what markets and in what quantity, they carried out a survey of world economic conditions. They studied the present and projected the future. They analyzed industrial and technological trends and developments to determine what fields of industry showed promise of growth and what areas would probably decline. Out of this intense study and research, the top-level Japanese—businessmen, bankers, and government officials—came to several basic conclusions. They would gradually cut loose from traditional industries, such as textiles, which every other industrial nation was trying to protect against Japanese exports. Instead they would direct their efforts and their resources in areas which showed growth possibilities, such as high-technology consumer goods: cameras, radios, TV sets, optical goods, recorders, stereos, etc. Their surveys also showed new opportunities in traditional industries such as steel and shipbuilding, where new technology would give them a decisive competitive advantage. They reacted to the old Oriental maxim that "a poor man can smell food quicker than a rich man."

Largely because they have to import virtually all the raw materials to sustain their industrial economy, the Japanese planners realized sooner than their counterparts in other countries that Middle East crude oil was becoming the prime source of fuel and energy in the developed nations, and also that the worldwide demand for basic raw commodities—grain, iron ore, copper, coking coal, wood, etc.—would rise sharply. Hence there would be an increasing need for larger oil tankers and bulk cargo ships to provide faster and cheaper maritime transportation. So the Japanese modernized their shipyards and their construction methods. The engineers introduced labor-saving shortcuts by automating the cutting and welding operations in shipbuilding, which has always been a labor-intensive industry. The Japanese also copied the assembly-line construction methods developed during World War II by Henry Kaiser to mass-produce the ubiquitous 10,000-ton Liberty ships. Soon the Japanese shipyards were awash with construction orders. At the height of the shipbuilding boom, the Japanese were launching 50% of all new ship construction in the world.

Insofar as steel production was concerned, the wholesale bombing of Japan's steel mills was to prove to be a blessing in disguise. The managers and engineers were not saddled with old or obsolete equipment; they could rebuild their steel mills and install the latest innovations in a very competitive industry. They bought a license for the new oxygen-jet process perfected by VOEST in Austria, which produced a better-quality steel at lower costs than the Siemens-Martin and Thomas process used in America and in Europe. Soon the Japanese were selling their oxygen-jet steel at 30% below what Pittsburgh and the Ruhr were quoting, despite the fact they had to import all the raw materials. For 80% of Japan's postwar output of steel has been produced with the oxygen-jet process. Shigeo Nagano, chairman of Nippon Steel, captured the rationale of the Japanese industrialists with this comment: "So long as we had to start from nothing, we wanted the most modern plant and equipment. We selected the cream of the world's technology. We learned from America, Germany, Austria and the Soviet Union and we have adapted their methods in our own way."[12]

Beginning in 1955, after the adaptation of the American transistor into a global best-seller pocket radio, the Japanese sent thousands of their engineers to the United States and Europe to buy up the latest technology that other nations had developed. In the 1950s and 1960s the Japanese government spent over $3 billion for patents and manufacturing licenses covering foreign technology in a wide range of capital and consumer products. It is ironic that the Japanese acquired this technology very cheaply. The American and European companies which sold the patents and licenses did not foresee that they were creating a competitor who would give them sleepless nights in the coming years. And for the Japanese, their investment in new technology has paid off in a fashion that has few equals in the whole history of modern business.

However, the Japanese not only bought or borrowed foreign technology; they improved on it and found new uses for it. The electronics industry provides us with an example of Japanese progress in a field of high technology in which the Americans had played a pioneering role. As Toshio Takai of the Electronics Industries Association of Japan explains: "In the late 1950s, the European and the American electronics industries were paying more attention to military and industrial electronics than to consumer electronics. So that was what we decided to concentrate on."[13] The Japanese companies in this field had bought the U.S. licenses to manufacture silicon chips and other components. They were ten to fifteen years behind the United States in electronic technology and in its application in the industrial sector. However, the field was wide open for them in consumer electronics—

[12]Quoted in *Time*, May 10, 1971.
[13]Quoted in *Business Week*, Dec. 14, 1981.

that is, in the manufacturing of electronically operated consumer goods, such as TV sets, radios, cameras, etc. Among the first of the Japanese products in this field was the pocket calculator, which proved to be a best-selling export not only in the United States but around the world. Japan today is the world's largest manufacturer of consumer electronics. As a result, Japan is now the only serious competitor of the U.S. electronics firms in the strategically important computer industry, which holds the keys to economic growth in the decades ahead.

In fact, the Japanese are seeking to be world leaders in new fields of technology arising out of their heavy research and development in electronics. The Ministry of International Trade and Industry (MITI), which has been sponsoring R&D in these fast-moving technologies, has stated: "Possession of her own technology will help Japan to maintain and to develop her industries' international superiority."

Yet the question is raised: Can Japan ever be the equal of America or Europe in technological development? Dr. Leo Esaki, now the only survivor of Japan's four Nobel Prize winners, said bluntly: "Japan never has accumulated enough intellectual capital. . . . The Japanese never challenge the unknown. There is a lack of the spirit of exploration. . . . Eventually you come down to a lack of individualism."

Other scientists have complained about Japan's regimented educational system and the "stifling hierarchy" of the university laboratories which suppress new ideas. Dr. Tadatsuga Taniguchi, the first to isolate the interferon gene, explained, "It is often very difficult to get educated in such a laboratory and you come to lose your own creativity." The "consensus mentality," which governs decision-making in technology as well as in basic business affairs, is another brake on scientific progress in Japan. It serves to limit independent research in favor of group action. In the field of education, the Japanese universities graduate over eighty thousand engineers every year, compared to sixty thousand plus in the United States, with twice the population. But "unlike the U.S. schools which long ago moved away from the classical approach [to engineering] to emphasize hands-on training, the Japanese still concentrate on abstract science and rote learning of fundamental principles. As a result Japanese engineering students gain little or no practical laboratory experience," according to *Business Week* (Dec. 14, 1981).

Japan's scientists have made no more than a handful of major breakthroughs in scientific theory in the past fifty years. The Japanese preference for adapting and improving technology already developed elsewhere has worked thus far. But what happens when western technology becomes more expensive and more difficult to adopt? Japanese products will face stiffer competition on the world markets in the foreseeable future.

There are many reasons to explain why Japan was able to rise out of the defeat and destruction of World War II to become No. 3 in the global listing of economic powers. However, their common denominator is simple and clear: The Japanese are not only more productive than the Americans and Europeans on a per capita basis, they also have a greater collective commitment to their work. Why should this be so? The answer is to be found rooted in the nature of Japanese society.

A most important and revealing psychological study of how the Japanese society works, its structure and mechanism, is provided by Chie Nakane's postwar book *The Japanese Society*.[14] Ms. Nakane is a Japanese sociologist and anthropologist who has spent many years abroad in America, Britain, and India. Thus she has a background to support her findings about why Japan is so different from other western industrial nations.

In most other countries, she writes, people feel a sense of community with others who are like them, have common interests, or are in the same type of work or social organizations, or are members of the same social class. Workers associate with workers, those in the middle class with their own kind, etc. In other words, society outside of Japan is organized in horizontal layers; people associate with others of their own social level. However, the Japanese society, in general, is organized vertically, Ms. Nakane explains. The Japanese come together in groups, for example, or "in frames," which will include those who live in the same village or neighborhood, or who work for the same company. Many Japanese think of their jobs as an extension of their family life. A worker when referring to his *ie* (household) may be talking about his employer, as well as his own family. Because the "group" or "household" concept governs Japanese thinking, it is natural, for example, for an electrician employed in a Hitachi factory to feel closer to *all* of his co-workers at Hitachi than he does to other electricians working for other Japanese companies. However, what motivates the worker to give not only his loyalty but also a social commitment to his modern "feudal lord" is the security of lifetime employment, if he qualifies for the job. But there is much more than that to create a strong bond between the worker and management. Almost two-thirds of all workers for the big companies and their many

---

[14]Chie Nakane, *The Japanese Society* (London: Weidenfeld & Nicolson, 1970).

subsidiaries live in company-owned houses or flats. Almost all public transport costs to and from their places of work are reimbursed to them. All hospital services are free. Cheap meals are served in the works canteens. Company-owned supermarkets provide almost all household goods at low prices. A worker can play tennis on a company-owned court, have his hair cut at the company-owned hairdresser, have a beer at the company-owned social club, and go to a swimming pool which is also owned by the firm. On a weekend he can take his family and stay overnight at a company-owned recreation center in the mountains.

It is not surprising that the unique labor-management relations have been described by some as "corporate socialism." For, in effect, the big companies in Japan take on a large share of the social welfare work which in other countries is handled by state or private agencies. However, these benefits when piled on top of lifetime employment are not altruistic gestures on the part of Japanese big business. Rather they represent enlightened self-interest of the highest order. As a direct result, Japan has the highest productivity rate of any industrial nation. Also because of the enlightened labor policies, coupled with the security of lifetime employment, the workers have not opposed the introduction of labor-saving machinery or practices in industrial operations. If a robot replaces a worker, the latter is assigned a new task at the same pay and benefits he previously enjoyed. The Japanese have been less plagued by strikes than any other industrial nation in the postwar period. Japanese goods are more competitive because the workers produce more at lower costs and exercise much greater quality control than their counterparts in America or Europe.[15] In the automotive field, the productivity of a Japanese worker is seven times higher than that of the man on a Detroit assembly line (*Time* magazine, March 30, 1981).

Japanese firms take great pains to engender the group spirit of their white-collar and blue-collar employees. Most firms have their distinctive work uniforms. Symptomatic of psychological practices to keep the employees "company-minded" is the company song, to be chorused by all when starting work each day. Here is the anthem sung

---

[15]Between the two world wars the reputation of Japanese goods suffered on the world markets because of the poor quality of the merchandise. The concept of quality control is a postwar development, and was initiated by an American efficiency expert, W. Edwards Deming. In 1950 he lectured industrialists in Tokyo on the need to rehabilitate the reputation of "made-in-Japan" goods if they expected to have any sales impact on the world markets. He recommended strict quality control of all phases of manufacturing operations, from raw materials to finished products. Today, there is an annual Deming quality control award, one of the most coveted prizes for industrial production.

by the workers and office employees of Matsushita Electric Co. as the company began to expand rapidly in the 1960s:

> For the building of a new Japan
> Let us put our strength and mind together,
> Doing our best to promote production,
> Sending our goods to the people of the earth,
> Endlessly and continuously,
> Like water gushing from a fountain.
> Grow, industry, grow, grow, grow!
> Harmony and sincerity!
> Matsushita Electric![16]

In such a self-centered nation as Japan, with its homogenized population, history has a way of repeating itself with some variations. What was done in the days of the Meiji Restoration to launch the industrialization of Japan was repeated after World War II to reindustrialize the bombed-out and bankrupt nation. The initial funding to get the economic recovery started—apart from the $4 billion of U.S. procurement expenditures during the Korean War—came from the postal savings of Japanese workers. The Japanese today manage to save about 18% of their incomes for a total of $42.3 billion in 1981, still the highest rate of savings in the world today. Postal savings together with welfare pension funds have provided a pool of capital funds to finance large and small business ventures and for the purchase and development of new technology.[17] These funds are also allocated for loans as well as equity investments by the Japan Development Bank, the government agency to utilize this people's capital. In 1981, the

---

[16]When prosperity came and Matsushita was firmly established in the world's markets, the lyrics of the company's anthem were rewritten to match the more euphoric mood of the 1970s and 1980s:

> A bright heart overflowing
> with life linked together,
> Matsushita Electric!
> Time goes by but as it moves along
> Each day brings a new spring.
> Let us bind together
> A world of blooming flowers
> And a verdant land
> In Love, Light and a Dream.

Other big industrial firms also have their company anthems and other promotional practices to keep the old company spirit alive and kicking.

[17]As an example of the government's financial support of new technology, it provided the funds for the successful commercial development of Sony's Trinitron tube for color TV, and the Wankel engine for cars. The Japanese government gets involved right down to the marketplace in projects which it thinks have good sales potentials.

government had a total of $92.7 billion to disperse for the overall growth and improvement of the Japanese national economy.[18]

Direct government intervention is mainly concerned with the financing of small businesses ($25 billion in 1981) as well as major technology projects. The big industrial firms and conglomerates usually get their financial needs served by the big banks. They draw 70–80% of their working capital from the commercial banks and only 20–30% from their own shareholders. This means that for practical purposes the stockholders are in a minority. The Japanese firm creates its own working capital by borrowing most of it from the banks. Hence the president of a Japanese firm is far more receptive to any suggestions from his banker about how to manage his firm than to suggestions from his stockholders.

Japan's banking and credit structure—"a very unorthodox system run by very orthodox men"[19]—has been able to provide a continuous flow of money into the industrial and commercial operations of private business. The banks are prepared to take what appear to be greater risks in loans or credits than American or European banks would underwrite. However, behind the banks stands the central Bank of Japan, which will quickly come to the rescue of any financial institution which has extended too much credit. And behind the Bank of Japan stands the Ministry of Finance, which will make the necessary funding commitments to keep the national economy afloat in the stormiest of seas.

By comparison with the United States and Europe, there is a close familial relationship between the Japanese government and the business world. It is not cast in the same mold as the "military-industrial complex," which President Eisenhower warned about and which has now developed in America. Rather what exists in Japan is more a partnership that is familial in character. This government-business collaboration was a creature born of necessity. It came into being after World War II when this island nation was faced with the acute problem of survival in a hostile and politically divisive world. It harked back to the Meiji Restoration when the samurai and merchants joined forces to begin the industrialization of a feudal land.

The United States had decisively defeated Japan in the Pacific war. In the months and years following the surrender to General MacArthur in Tokyo Bay, the Japanese have successfully masked their feelings about this national humiliation. There have never been out-

---

[18]Figures from *Business Week*, Dec. 14, 1981.
[19]Norman Macrae in the *Economist*, May 27, 1967.

cries for revenge. The atomic bombs on Hiroshima and Nagasaki convinced them that military power was excess baggage if they wanted to rebuild and revitalize their nation. History, tradition, and national pride combined to set their sights high. The Japanese did not want to survive as a third- or fourth-rate power, a producer of cheap toys and trinkets. Their leaders saw clearly that the way back to the front ranks on the world stage was through economic growth and strength. Never for one minute would an educated Japanese doubt that his country merited a place among the world's major powers. Thus, the example for postwar Japan to follow was the United States, then the leader on the international scene.

The ambitious second generation of managers who now occupied the top jobs in industry and finance, together with the new postwar mandarins of the Tokyo government, came to a rough agreement on the required course of action. This called for pooling of resources and submission of all to a centralized direction and control of the economy, at least until life returned to a semblance of prewar normalcy. The principal instrument to carry out this program was the Ministry of International Trade and Industry (MITI), formed in the late 1940s. Somewhat in the role of a big brother, MITI worked directly with the leaders of the business world and with the government's central Bank of Japan. Since the day it first opened its doors, MITI has attracted the top graduates of Tokyo University, which is the most prestigious educational institution in the country. MITI, now housed in a giant new skyscraper which dominates the Tokyo skyline, has become the country's think tank for economic affairs, both nationally and internationally.

Prof. Ezra F. Vogel of Harvard, a leading American expert on contemporary Japan, finds MITI's big-brother role in the supervision and direction of Japan's business world somewhat analogous to the way America's National Basketball Association operates. In sports like basketball, says Prof. Vogel, "the league officials establish regulations about the size of the team, the recruitment of players, the rules of play that result in relatively equally matched teams of great competitive abilities. They do not interfere with the internal team activity to tell the coach how to run his team, although they do try to provide information that should enable the coach to improve." Prof. Vogel points out that MITI operates in the same fashion. Similar to America's NBA, "many decisions made by MITI might be more properly viewed . . . as a consensus among the most significant actors."[20]

[20]Prof. Vogel's analogy was reported and endorsed by the London *Economist* in its survey of Japan, Feb. 23, 1980.

Despite MITI's wide range of controls and general direction of the national economy, the end result has not been a "planned economy" in the classic pattern of European socialism. Rather what developed has been described as a "government-guided capitalism." For example, there is stiff competition encouraged by the government between firms in each industrial sector. There are five large Japanese firms now competing fiercely to dominate the domestic computer market. The ultimate winner will then have the government's support to take on IBM on the international market. The overseers at MITI have long regarded the domestic market as a proving ground to winnow out the weak from the strong before facing the rigors of the international marketplaces. Finally, Japanese companies can ignore governmental recommendations if they can get away with it. For example, MITI recommended against development of a postwar automotive industry. At one point when the new industry was still in its embryonic phase, the Ministry of Finance—the second most important agency—advised the car manufacturers to collaborate to produce a single small car model along the lines of the popular German Volkswagen. This too was rejected by the industry, whose collective merchandising expertise was vindicated in the world marketplaces. In 1981 over 10 million Toyotas, Hondas, Datsuns, Subarus, and Mazdas were sold, compared to Detroit's total of 6 million cars.

As the U.S. Comptroller General's Office has already noted, "Japan supports its strong industries." It also discourages the weak ones. MITI takes steps to weed out those firms or industries which are not succeeding in the export field, or which are facing increasing competition from other countries, such as textiles from South Korea or Taiwan. The purging is discreet and low-key. MITI informs the Bank of Japan, which in turn informs the commercial banks which firms or industrial sectors are no longer considered to be creditworthy. When next the money market tightens up, their loan applications are sidetracked indefinitely. They cannot exist long without their regular tranfusions of bank credits.

Big business has dutifully followed, with relatively few exceptions, MITI's *gyosei shido*, "administrative guidelines," as they reached the executive suites. Noncompliance with MITI's requests or directives was virtually unthinkable in the first decades of the economic revival, for this government agency had unchallengeable money power. It could arrange to cut off the credit or loans of commercial banks to large and small business firms. The commercial banks are themselves always in debt to the central Bank of Japan for funds which they in turn loaned out to Japanese companies. Bank of Japan collaborated closely with MITI. It could request the central bank to intervene in the money market to tighten or loosen credit to individual firms. MITI also controlled the purchasing of foreign patents or licenses by Japanese firms. Hence it could open up or shut off foreign technology to its Japanese clients. This could make or break an individual Japanese manufacturer.

Japanese businessmen were not without reciprocal powers. The big corporations through the *Keidranren*, the Federation of Economic Organizations—Japan's equivalent of the U.S. National Association of Manufacturers—fed their political contributions to the leaders of the Liberal Democratic Party (LDP), which has been ruling the country since Japan regained its independence in 1951. Incidentally, the main politicking in postwar Japan has been carried out within the LDP between the five principal factions struggling for control of the party. However, whoever becomes the prime minister ensures that his government's controls and regulations do not rest too heavily on the shoulders of the businessmen. By comparison to America or to Europe, businessmen in Japan enjoy an unparalleled freedom of operations. They are really constrained only by their own "consensus agreements" with their colleagues in other firms, which involve cartel arrangements, price-fixing, market allocations, and other practices dear to the heart of a corporation executive. Hence one can say without fear of contradiction that the relationship between the government and the corporate world is friendly and mutually accommodating. It could hardly be otherwise, considering that Japan has "an economy explicitly designed to pump out large amounts of well-made exports in whatever field of industrial production the government machine and the business community between them decide Japan ought to be dismaying its competitors with next."[21]

In 1950, when their future was only an improbable dream, the Japanese enjoyed an annual per capita income of $380. By 1980 it had risen to $8,940, compared to $10,040 per capita income for the United States. (In 1982, the GDP was $9,700 per capita.) Then in 1981, as the Europeans and the Americans got bogged down in recession, the Economic Council of Japan, an advisory body serving the Tokyo government, predicted that by the year 2000, Japan will have the highest per capita income of any nation in the world.[22] The council put this figure at $21,150 compared to an estimated $17,600 for the United States. If this prediction comes true, Japan will have become the first economic superpower in the world.

[21]*Economist*, March 31, 1973.
[22]*New York Times*, Jan. 19, 1982.

The spectacular economic growth of Japan in the last few years, coupled with the economic decline of the United States, has been a heady elixir for the Japanese. They are becoming convinced that they alone have mastered the art of economic growth; that Europe and America—once the models they emulated—have become weak and inefficient, no longer masters of their own destinies; that the Japanese alone have the patience and the long-range plans to achieve economic superpower status by the year 2000.[23]

That is a moot point. For all their long-range planning, the Japanese are being surprisingly short-sighted in their international policies and practices. They are facing serious problems, largely of their own making. For example, the Japanese want free access to the world markets for all of their products, from desk computers to agricultural machinery. Yet the Japanese seek to exclude, or at least keep down to a minimum, their imports from other industrial nations. This is accomplished by a number of strategems, such as nit-picking inspection of foreign imports by customs officials, discriminatory tariffs, so-called "safety regulations to protect the Japanese consumer" which can bar a foreign product, and the purposely complicated distribution systems which make it difficult for foreign products to reach the Japanese customer. From the first days of their economic recovery, the Japanese have supplied a rationale for their closed-market system: "Japan is a poor island nation without natural resources. It has to import raw materials and export manufactured goods in order to live. It cannot afford to import foreign goods that compete with domestic products made for the Japanese consumers."

However, this falls far short of the truth. The main reason why the Liberal Democratic government maintains its restrictions is to satisfy the demands of its broad political constituency, ranging from the farmers to the industrialists. For example, the farmers are heavily subsidized, about $20 billion a year, for their output of rice, vegetables, and fruits. Due to the electoral districting system, the farmers enjoy a three-to-one advantage over the urban voters in parliamentary representation. This margin assures that the LDP will stay in power, as it has done for thirty-five uninterrupted years, so long as the food subsidies continue. However, if present restrictions on imports on American rice, flour, meat, fruit juices, and other items were lifted,

---

[23]A note of condescension has crept in. For example, in the Tokyo press there have been stories that major aircraft producers like Boeing and Europe's Airbus consortium are now being considered "as candidates" to participate with Japanese firms in the development of the next generation of airliners. This news was not greeted with any noticeable interest in the Seattle headquarters of the Boeing company, already at work on this project.

they could be sold for about a fifth of the prices which the Japanese housewife now has to pay to feed her household. But that development would greatly anger the farmers and probably cost the LDP its control of the government. And if similar trade restrictions on other U.S. products were lifted, this would cause another backlash from industrial circles, also the financial supporters of the LDP.

This big-exports, few-imports policy has enabled Japan to pile up excessive favorable trade balances. In 1981, it extracted over $18 billion more from the United States than it paid out for imports from America. For the same period, Japan's favorable trade balance with the European Common Market was $13 billion plus. To explain this away, the Japanese have begun voicing criticisms and expressing their doubts about the declining economic capabilities of their major competitors. The United States, West Germany, Great Britain, etc., are all suffering from the "developed-nation disease." They have lost their will to work hard, to sacrifice as the Japanese have been doing. "Japan's economic miracle has begotten a swelling self-confidence that has the Japanese believing their own press clippings—and the West's own bad reviews. . . . Japan has become a model—even to itself."[24]

However, if the Americans and Europeans have their economic weak spots, so too have the Japanese, only they seem to be unaware of them. Their "island mentality" blinds them to the hostility which their aggressive, no-holds-barred export offensive has aroused abroad, particularly in the United States and Europe. In some categories, Japan's exports have driven competitors to the wall, creating blocs of unemployment. For example, in Britain imports of Japanese motorcycles have put the once-thriving British producers out of business. The once-famed German Leica has gone down before the onslaughts of Nikon and Canon. Ford, GM, and Chrysler, as well as the United Auto Workers, have lost hundreds of millions of dollars in car sales and tens of thousands of jobs because of stiff Japanese competition. These are only a few of the hundreds of examples of economic damages sustained in Europe and America. In reply the Japanese can state their case: They are producing better and cheaper goods than are the aggrieved American and European manufacturers. But they still keep up the walls to protect their domestic markets from the foreign exporter. International trade to them is still big-exports, few-imports policy. If this situation is not drastically changed, the Japanese will face reprisals from Europe and the United States, in the form of

[24]*Wall Street Journal*, dispatch from Tokyo, Jan. 25, 1982.

higher tariffs, import quotas on Japanese goods, and other restrictive measures. To forestall this development, the Japanese must export industries instead of products, by establishing manufacturing plants in their overseas markets. Already they are grudgingly taking this inevitable step. However, the Japanese industrialists are reluctant to embark on this course. They fear they will lose a large measure of the tight control of the manufacturing operations to foreigners, whose ideas and motivations are different. Can the manager of the new Honda plant at Marysville, Ohio, maintain the same high quality control that is the norm of Honda's assembly-line operations in Nagasaki? Can the Japanese export the same group loyalty and company mystique—that "Grow! Grow! Matsushita!" *esprit de corps*—that make manufacturing in Japan so efficient and profitable? That is the challenge that faces Japan as it stands on the threshold of becoming an economic superpower.

Japan has something to say to the world at large. Ecopolitics works; it has proved itself in the postwar rise of defeated and devastated Japan to the ranks of the major powers in a generation's time. Japan has demonstrated that intelligent concentration on economic growth, coupled with high technology, can promote the security and prosperity of a country more effectively and at far less cost than fighting and winning a war. Prior to World War II, a nightmare haunted the generals and admirals who then controlled the Japanese government. They feared the day when the United States and its allies might cut off Japan from its oil supplies in Indonesia and Burma, so they stockpiled some 19 million barrels of crude oil to fuel their armed forces. Then they launched their air force at Pearl Harbor, the beginning of their conquest of Southeast Asia and the oil fields of Burma and Indonesia. But General Tojo and Admiral Yamamoto could not snatch victory in this war, which came to an end in the surrender in Tokyo Bay four years after Pearl Harbor.

Geopolitics brought nationalistic and militaristic Japan to the brink of ruin; *ecopolitics* revived the stricken nation and gave it security and prosperity beyond the dreams of the most sanguine of the Nipponese war lords. General Tojo's 1941 stockpile of 19 million barrels of crude oil would provide fuel and energy for only three days at Japan's 1982 rate of consumption. The nation is no longer dependent on one or two sources to meet its fuel and energy needs. Japan is equipped adequately to handle its own affairs. There is no real fear of being deprived of vital raw materials, for Japan has goods, high technology, and services urgently needed by those Third World nations which possess oil and other commodities.

It is quite surprising how elastic the supply systems have become since the postwar development of world markets and global economies.

CHAPTER EIGHT

Victory Out of Defeat

For some years now, our economic policy has simultaneously been our foreign policy.

—CHANCELLOR HELMUT SCHMIDT, interview in
Finanz und Wirtschaft, March 1975

Geography is the mother of history. The central European plain stretching from the Bay of Biscay without a break to the Urals, and inhabited by many different states, is a standing invitation to strife.

—G. P. GOOCH, *Germany*
(London: Ernest Benn Ltd., 1926)

CHANCELLOR Otto von Bismarck thought he had created a durable German empire but was only setting the stage for World War I and the end of his own creation, the reborn *Kaiserreich*. Kaiser Wilhelm II schemed for "a place in the sun," but his thoughtless warmaking led to defeat, the impoverishment of Germany, and the end of the Hohenzollern monarchy. Adolf Hitler, who demanded *Lebensraum*—"living space"—for his aggressive legions at the expense of Europe and Russia, started World War II, which ended in the collapse of his "thousand-year Reich" in the twelfth year of its murderous existence. Then several years after the shooting stopped, an obscure but prescient economics professor imposed an *ecopolitical* system on the embryonic West German state and thereby created the famed *Wirtschaftswunder*—"economic miracle." Thanks to a fortuitous combination of time, circumstances, and personalities, the Federal Republic of (West) Germany was transformed into the economic superpower of postwar Europe.

West Germany was Europe's first ecopolitical state, the first state in which economic objectives took priority over political or defense considerations. This new philosophy of government matched the needs and aspirations of the dazed and demoralized survivors of World War II. Being on the losing side in two global conflicts in the short span of a generation brought home the lesson that warmaking can be a very costly way of making a living, especially for the defeated. Not since the Thirty Years' War of the seventeenth century, which devastated feudal Germany and killed a third of its population, had the

Germans suffered such losses of life and possessions, such destruction of their cities and towns, coupled with the collapse of the social structure.

For the first three years of the global conflict, it was *Deutschland über Alles*. The Nazi swastika flew unchallenged from the Bay of Biscay across Europe to the Volga River deep inside the Soviet Union. Then in swift succession came major defeats at Stalingrad, Kursk, and El Alamein and the Allied invasions of Italy and France, culminating in unconditional surrender in June 1945. The war left Germany in ruins; its cities and industrial centers were burned-out shells. Hitler had proclaimed a "total war"; it ended with *Götterdämmerung*—the "twilight of the gods"—in the total disintegration of the state and its society.

The millions of survivors were hungry, homeless, and jobless, except for the rural population. The Germans were in a collective state of shock, unable to comprehend the sudden and sharp reversal of their fortunes, and the deprivations visited on them. They had inflicted war and devastation throughout Europe; now it was their turn to suffer. Life became an unending series of daily crises—scrounging a few potatoes or bread for the evening meal, or a bucket of coal to provide some heat; devising some shelter for the homeless, whether it meant a few square feet of space in a crowded airraid shelter or sharing a room with three or four other homeless people; trying to get a job in a paralyzed economy. Out of this traumatic passage, which lasted about three years, came a repudiation of Germany's militaristic and nationalistic history. Germans shut the door on the past. Imbued with the resolution *Niemals wieder!* (Never again!), the West Germans groped for new standards and values by which to govern what they could salvage of their war-torn lives for the uncertain future that lay ahead.

The survivors had no stomach for—or even interest in—political action as a means to restore some semblance of normalcy in their substandard existence. Hitler had taken them on a geopolitical roller-coaster ride, and they could see what it had done for them. They had lost their homes and work places in Allied bombing raids, as well as their family possessions; their savings and pensions evaporated in the postwar inflation, as their money became valueless. They were reduced to a bare-bones existence; the cupboard, not so long ago filled with the loot of Europe, was now empty. They had virtually no control over their individual destinies. They couldn't even pack up and leave Germany. That required an Allied exit permit, which was very hard to get. In this "darkest hour in German history"[1] the Germans became obsessed with a collective hunger for *Sicherheit*—"security"—in their disordered and purposeless lives. This craving for *Sicherheit* encompassed the whole range of their needs: steady employment, food on the table, a roof that didn't leak, medical care, school for the children, a currency that maintained its buying power, and above all, a restoration of *Ordnung*—"law and order"—in public and private affairs. It is a word dear to the heart and mind of a German. When there is *Ordnung* in the land, he knows where he stands and what he must do. Life has meaning and purpose. This postwar hunger for security was to sink deeper into the Teutonic psyche than any of the past enthusiasms for *Deutschland über Alles* and Adolf Hitler's calamitous Third Reich. It was to supply the energy that enabled the Germans to rise out of the depths of defeat and devastation to become the strongest economic power in postwar Europe. It still is a potent force in determining the German reaction to world affairs. International and domestic economic and political developments are still largely evaluated in terms of whether they promote or threaten the basic security of the Federal Republic and the individual German.

At the end of the war, Germany was divided into four military zones, Russian, American, British, and French. An Allied Control Council (ACC) was set up in Berlin to govern the defeated enemy state in the name of the four victorious powers until a peace treaty could be signed. But this was not to be; the cold war intervened. The differing and irreconcilable political and economic objectives of the Russians, Americans, British, and French made a unified Allied governance of Germany impossible. What the Russians wanted to achieve in postwar Germany was completely unacceptable to the Americans, and vice versa. The Allied Control Council was unable to function, because its directives and orders required unanimous consent of the four occupying powers. Meanwhile Germany had become the political combat zone of the cold war. Defeated Germany itself was the supreme prize of the war which Josef Stalin wished to add to his list of captive nations. Germany is *Mitteleuropa*, the meeting place and point of balance between East and West. Whoever controls Germany can then dictate the political and economic patterns of Europe. Straddling the

---

[1] In its last communiqué of the war, announcing the unconditional surrender of the German armed forces, on May 9, 1945, the *Oberkommando der Wehrmacht* (the Armed Forces high command) described this moment as "the darkest hour in German history." For once the OKW communiqué was accurate.

continent from the Baltic and North Seas to the Alps, Germany holds the key to Europe's future.[2]

The cold war reached a climax in June 1948, when the Russians imposed a ground blockade of Berlin, the seat of the Allied Control Council. All the road, rail, and water transportation between the city, which lies deep inside the Russian zone, and the American, British, and French zones in West Germany was halted by Russian soldiers. The Soviet objective was twofold: by severing their supply lines, to force the Allied garrisons in the beleaguered city to beat an ignominious retreat, and to quell the 2 million Berliners into political submission by threat of starvation. The only alternative was for the Allies to take military action, to fight their way back into Berlin. The Russians thought this was unlikely, because they enjoyed definite superiority in East Germany. However, the Russians miscalculated. The Americans, together with the British, defeated the Soviet blockade with an unexpected application of western technology to handle the political-military problem. The American and British air forces organized the *Luftbrücke* (air bridge), a 24-hour daily airlift of cargo planes, transporting food, coal, gasoline, and other necessities for the Allied garrisons and two million civilians blockaded in West Berlin. The airlift was to last ten months and three weeks and reached daily cargo volume of 14,000 tons. Finally the Russians admitted defeat by ending the ground blockade.

Even before the blockade the Iron Curtain had descended on Germany, marking the division of Europe into Communist and non-Communist halves. This development forced the Americans to revise their policies and plans concerning the defeated nation. It was now recognized that the four contentious occupation powers could not govern the country as originally proposed. Yet it was imperative to find a way out of this dilemma. The complete collapse of Hitler's Third Reich and the unconditional surrender of its armed forces had created a power vacuum. In East Germany, the Russians filled it with their own hand-picked Communist government, supported by their army of occupation. In West Germany the Americans, British, and French had differing ideas about the future of the defeated enemy. But something clearly had to be done. West Germany could not be left an economic and political wasteland. The Germans had to be given the chance to

---

[2]Sir Halford Mackinder (1861–1947), dean of British geographers, was the founder of the school of geopolitics. He formulated the famous geopolitical thesis that if ever Germany and Russia could be joined together or if one nation controlled the other, this combination would dominate "the heartland," the Eurasian landmass. This in turn could lead to world domination. Adolf Hitler and Josef Stalin adhered to the Mackinder school of geopolitics.

work their passage back into the family of nations and to rebuild their own lives. Otherwise political chaos would follow, the Allied powers reasoned, and the ultimate beneficiary of this neglect would be the expanding Soviet Union.

General Lucius D. Clay, U.S. military governor, proposed a merger of the American and British occupation zones as the first step to create a pro-Western democratic West German Republic. At the outset the Germans would be given the responsibility of managing their own economic affairs, so as to stimulate the lagging food production and to rebuild the war-battered industrial sector. The immediate objective was self-sufficiency in the foreseeable future. By 1948, General Clay was handing out $750 million a year in grants of food and other necessities to forestall mass starvation, epidemics, and a complete breakdown of West Germany's moribund economy. But there was scant sympathy in the U.S. Congress for the postwar plight of the defeated Germans and little urge to vote more money for their support. Creating a half-state out of the American and British occupation zones was at least a start back on the long road to normalcy.

In February 1948, the new ersatz state of "Bizonia"—as it was described in the press—made its debut on the European scene. Bizonia had a reasonable facsimile of a government: an executive branch, headed by an economic director, and six quasi-ministries for agriculture, finance, transportation, communications, civil service, and planning; an economic council of fifty members serving as a quasi-legislative body; and a judiciary system to enforce and adjudicate the decisions of the Bizonal economic administration.

Heading the Bizonal administration was Prof. Ludwig Erhard, a relatively unknown Bavarian economist, one of the few available politicians without a Nazi background. He was housed in an old army barracks in a Frankfurt suburb. The Economic Council shared space in the bombed-out Frankfurt Stock Exchange with a local theatrical company. The various ministries were located in other cities in West Germany. In the early stages Bizonia had little real substantive power, because the American and British military governors retained overriding authority to accept or reject any of the Bizonal policies and practices. But power was to come shortly to Erhard and his colleagues, virtually at the same time as the beginning of the Berlin blockade.

On June 22, 1948, without any advance notice to the public, currency reform (*Währungsreform*) was introduced at the instigation of the American and British military governments. The abrupt changeover in currencies involved drastic fiscal surgery on the West German economy, later described by a British M.P. as "one of the harshest acts of confiscation imposed on a people by their conquerors. Yet it saved Germany."[3] The Germans received one new Deutschemark for ten old and hopelessly inflated and discredited Reichsmarks. However, the per capita exchange was limited to the redemption of only six hundred Reichsmarks for sixty new Deutschemarks. This new currency, incidentally, had been printed by the U.S. Mint at Denver, Colorado, and bore a resemblance to the American dollar bill in its engraving and texture. In West Germany, it was estimated that about 93% of the "paper wealth" of Germans—that is, securities, stocks and bonds, savings accounts, etc.—was wiped out in this currency reform. However, debts were also scaled down to the same ratio: one DM paid off obligations worth ten RMs, for individuals and businesses alike. In addition, prewar German bonds and other financial commitments of the Nazi government—except those held by the Allied governments— were also wiped out.

At first glance currency reform seemed to be a ruthless and confiscatory operation imposed on the hapless Germans by the victorious occupying powers. But in reality it was just the reverse. The West Germans suffered little economic damage due to currency reform. The old Reichsmark had already lost its value in the eyes of the Germans. On the eve of currency reform the inflated RM was quoted on the black market at RM 23,000 to U.S.$1. American and British cigarettes had replaced the RM as a yardstick to measure the value of commodities and consumer goods. A package or carton of Lucky Strikes had an immediate buying power on the black market. One cigarette was worth about $1 in all transactions. It could command goods or services which the Reichsmark could not. Currency reform was analogous to the amputation of a gangrenous leg. Without the operation the patient would soon die from the spreading poison of gangrene. With the drastic surgery his life would be saved.

The new Deutschemark was a fiat currency, with no gold or silver backing or government guarantee of value whatsoever. Yet it was quickly accepted as a money with value. In the first few days it was quoted on the black market at DM 10 to $1, and it rose to DM 6 to $1 by the following year. Finally when the West German economy began to gain momentum in the mid-1950s it was pegged at DM 4.20 to $1 and had become one of the "hardest" of European currencies.

Currency reform triggered the start of economic recovery that was to transform this segment of bankrupt and devastated Germany into the second-ranking trading nation in the world after the United

[3]Aidan Crawley, M.P., *The Rise of West Germany* (London: Collins, 1973).

States. But this metamorphosis would not have been possible without another related development: the abolition of all rationing as well as all price and wage controls by Prof. Erhard. It was a totally unexpected action, courageously taken on his own initiative against the advice of his own German colleagues and in the face of probable Allied disapproval. But he managed to convince General Clay of the soundness of his rationale and received somewhat reluctant American approval of the new *Soziale Marktwirtschaft*, the "socially responsive free market system."

The introduction of the *Soziale Marktwirtschaft*, a doctrine of ever-expanding industrial productivity, exposed the Germans to the uncontrollable laws of supply and demand in a free market system. After twelve years of Nazi totalitarian control of all aspects of economic affairs, the West German economy was, in effect, "denazified" by Erhard to make it work again. And it was a painful shock for the Germans to face up to the grim postwar realities: no more aid for the unemployed, no assurance of food through a rationing system, and no more price ceilings on food and other essential consumer goods. The individual German had to work hard or face starvation, produce or fall by the wayside. There was no cushion of social security to support the weak and incompetent. But Erhard promised his fellow Germans a bright new day would dawn for them if they all worked hard and accepted today's Spartan existence as a down payment for tomorrow's rewards. He held up to their eyes the vision of the United States of America; of how one nation had become the richest and most powerful in all the world by concentrating its talents and its energies on its own economic development. In his constant exhortations, he told the Germans, especially the workers who were inclined to socialism, "Free enterprise has given the American citizen a living standard and a chance for self-expression that is unparalleled in the rest of the world."

Replacing the discredited Reichsmark with a new Deutschemark, coupled with the ending of rationing and price and wage controls, quickly restored the West German economy to the rigors and disciplines of the marketplace. Any economy, if it is to achieve stability and prosperity, must undergo this baptism of fire. West Germany survived, because the goods that had been hoarded suddenly came to the marketplace. Store windows and shelves blossomed with merchandise. The new Deutschemark was accepted in payment for these goods, thereby strengthening its credibility. The black market withered on the vine; the *Zigarettenwirtschaft*—"cigarette economy"— went out of business almost overnight.

The currency reform and the end of rationing and wage and price controls by themselves could not have produced the *Wirtschafts-wunder*—the economic miracle of the 1950s and 1960s. What strengthened Erhard's free market system in its initial stages was the Marshall Plan. West Germany received almost $4 billion from the U.S. government in grants of dollars, foods, and raw materials. This assistance primed the pump at a time when West Germany's resources were spread very thin indeed. The U.S. foreign aid gave the Erhard program a big push at a crucial period, and it never lost that momentum in the years ahead.

In a ruthless coup d'état, the Communist Party seized control of the government of neighboring Czechoslovakia in February 1948. This event was a clear signal that the Russians were trying to extend their power and influence as deep into Central and Western Europe as possible. This sudden takeover strengthened the resolve of the Allied powers to create an independent West German state, comprising the American, British, and French zones of occupation. As a result the new Federal Republic of (West) Germany began with the official convening of the new federal parliament (Bundestag) on September 17, 1949. The first chancellor was Dr. Konrad Adenauer, a veteran Rhineland politician and mayor of Cologne for seventeen years until ousted by the Nazis in 1933. His economics minister was Prof. Erhard. The Adenauer-Erhard team was a unique sort of two-tier government; Adenauer handled all political affairs, domestic and foreign, while Erhard had full responsibility for economic growth and development. The combination worked well; the voters gave them four consecutive four-year terms in office. Under Erhard's administration his *Soziale Markt-wirtschaft* now became official government policy and set the tone and character of the West German economy.

The main concern of the new government was the economic recovery of West Germany—the repair and reconstruction of homes, factories, public utilities, transportation, and communications. That was largely Erhard's responsibility. He was the architect of the new postwar West Germany that would arise from the ashes of World War II to enter upon a new existence. Yet Erhard was a strong critic of government interference and controls in the economic affairs of the state, which he labeled *Dirigissmus*. Erhard laid down the basic guidelines: The government was to assist the private sector but not dictate to it how to run its business affairs; the government's role must be to create a favorable environment and climate that encouraged the growth of industry and commerce. He set forth his basic philosophy in these words: "Only when the German can freely choose what work he will do and can freely decide what goods he will consume, will our people be able to play an active role in the life of our country." In other words, a free market system was a prerequisite for a politically stable and progressive society.

Ludwig Erhard was a nonconformist in a society that had long lived with the conformity demanded in a totalitarian state. He was a lonely outcast in the Nazi years, forced to live by his wits as a market researcher. But he was a student of economic history and he had studied Germany's past carefully. He was confident that he had the program that would enable a defeated Germany to make a successful economic recovery. Against the advice of all but a few close collaborators, he launched his big gamble on the future of the war-ravaged country.

He gambled that the instruments to achieve his objective would be financial and economic orthodoxy. He ignored the heavy political pressures and panaceas involving socialism and "planned economy" in all its manifold aspects. He bet on the free market system. He also gambled on human nature: that men were primarily motivated by their never-sleeping appetite for material gain, coupled with their deep-seated instincts for survival in hard times. In short, they acted and reacted according to the dictates of their search for security in a troubled world.

Erhard also operated on the assumption that man seldom is motivated by love or charity for his fellow man. But he was convinced that the average individual had sufficient measure of intelligence and initiative to acquire as much financial security for himself and his family as his talents and circumstances permitted. And if thousands upon thousands of West Germans were given the freedom and the incentive to chase after material gain, their collective efforts would be a powerful stimulus to achieve economic recovery. Erhard did not think that any government was by itself capable of providing security on a permanent basis for its citizens through any political ideology or economic formula. Man, not his government, is ultimately responsible for his own fate. That was the essence of Erhard's credo.

Erhard was a convert to the views of Adam Smith (1723–90), the father of capitalism, who laid down the principle that man "by pursuing his own interests frequently promotes the interests of society more effectively than when he really intends to promote it." Erhard's admonition to his fellow Germans and to the Allied authorities—"turn the money and the people loose and they will make the nation strong"—

was not so pedantic as Smith's dictum but it carried the same message: Only freedom and incentives could produce solid and sustained economic growth and prosperity.

So Erhard gave top priority to West Germany's *Wiederaufbau*—"rebuilding." He channeled the talents and the energies of his compatriots into the repair and reconstruction of homes and factories, transportation and public utilities, *bierstuben* and breweries—the whole infrastructure of a modern industrial state. But businessmen and individuals were given complete freedom to carry out their own projects in rebuilding their lives and careers. Erhard operated on the common-sense principle that the greater the activity, the more it contributed to the improvement of the national economy. The money earned was quickly cycled back into commerce and industry for more goods and into banks which provided more credit for the *Wiederaufbau*. Erhard used the fiscal powers of the government—like a conductor directing a symphony orchestra—to stimulate the activity of West Germany. Tax exemptions played a major role.

When the Allied Control Council took over the administration of defeated Germany, it promulgated a stiff new income tax, designed to siphon off the billions of inflated Reichsmarks then in circulation. This tax code was described as "in outward appearance the stiffest piece of income taxation ever inflicted on a western country."[4] When West Germany became an independent political entity, this same tax schedule was retained. For example, an unmarried male earning DM 3,000 a year (then equivalent to $714) paid a tax of DM 285 ($67). As income increased the tax escalated until in the top brackets it took 95% of income, the highest levy in the world.

However, Erhard offered every German a way to reduce income tax liabilities. He laid down a basic principle that income or profits which were plowed back in the physical repair, reconstruction, and modernization of any business enterprise were tax-free. Also money deposited in certain banks, such as *Bausparkassen*, which financed construction of new housing, or in other government-designated industries, such as steelmaking or shipbuilding, was also tax-exempt. The outstanding aspect of Erhard's program was the wide range of incentives it offered, not only to the businessmen, but to the general public as well. The general idea was to draw on the total financial resources of the nation, right down to the *Hausfrau*'s piggy bank, and put this wealth to work rebuilding the national economy.

[4]Henry Wallich, *The Mainsprings of German Revival* (New Haven: Yale University Press, 1955). At this writing Mr. Wallich is a member of the U.S. Federal Reserve Board.

Erhard launched his incentive program on the conviction that the war-battered German industries could, in effect, pull themselves up by their own bootstraps. In large measure, they could finance the reconstruction and modernization of their bomb-damaged industrial plants if sufficient tax exemptions were authorized. Erhard was right on target. During 1953–54, for example, DM 2 billion was raised to begin the repair and reconstruction of the great Ruhr steel mills. Of this amount DM 1.3 billion came from tax-exempt profits of the steel firms, which were resuming operations as fast as money became available. German businessmen were reacting enthusiastically to the incentive program. For one thing, it was just about the quickest way to get rich. By plowing tax-exempt profits back into the reconstruction and modernization of an industrial plant, this increased the value of the industrial installation. So did its ability to borrow ever-larger amounts of cash to finance its expanding operations. And as the value of the shares of industrial firms climbed on the Düsseldorf and Frankfurt stock exchanges, so did the portfolios of their owners. In those early years of the *Wiederaufbau*, there were very few if any "income millionaires" but a surprising number of "shareholder millionaires," as a result of this development.

Erhard was an independent-minded and unconventional thinker, going well beyond the views held by both the surviving German officials and the Allied authorities. He had looked down the long corridors of German history and grasped an essential truth that had long escaped the consciousness of the German people and their leaders since Bismarck's time. Germany's struggle to be a major world power could have best been achieved and preserved by unrestricted economic growth and technology rather than by concentration on military and political measures. The true strength of Germany since Bismarck's time has been its industrial capabilities, coupled with its technical expertise. For example, German scientists practically invented the chemical industry. And Erhard was convinced that the Germans must be reeducated to their economic rather than their political potential.

Based on conditions in postwar Germany, Erhard envisioned, perhaps dimly at the outset, the great opportunities that were looming ahead for the Germans. If the Ruhr, once the "machine shop of Europe," as well as its other industrial sectors, could be reactivated, West Germany would be in a favorable position to produce the goods and services for which there was a worldwide demand. The tremendous scale of physical damage sustained during the five years of global warfare, and also the squandering of the wealth of nations as they continued to fight to the war's bitter end, resulted in global shortages of capital goods and equipment: trucks, motors, machinery, railway engines and rolling stock, cars, construction equipment, tractors, cement works, chemical plants, steel mills, farming machinery, electrical equipment, etc. There was also a world hunger for consumer goods. West Germany was well positioned to produce what other European nations needed: the tools and machinery to reconstruct their own industrial plants and to replenish their own depleted inventories of capital and consumer goods. The war had stripped Europe of much of its industrial wealth and productivity. A fresh start had to be made. West Germany was able to provide it. For example, in two years, 1952 and 1953, 50% of West Germany's exports were capital goods: machinery, machine tools, motors, engineering products, electrical equipment, railway cars and locomotives, ships, vehicles, instruments, optical goods, etc.

America was too busy retooling her own industrial machinery to become greatly concerned about postwar foreign markets. Besides, U.S. goods were priced too high, compared to what Germany had to offer. Though severely battered in World War II, West Germany still possessed substantial productive capacity if repaired and modernized. Equally important, the new state had the biggest pool of cheap skilled labor at hand of any of the industrial nations, which included some 8 million impoverished German refugees from the other side of the Iron Curtain.

It is somewhat ironic that West Germany sold the Japanese the machinery and the tools with which they reconstructed and modernized their own postwar industry. For example, the firm of Demag of Duisburg, which has fabricated 10% of the world's steel mills in operation today, including in the Communist bloc, rebuilt the Japanese steel industry. Today Nippon Steel is the world's largest steelmaker. Then the tide turned and Japanese cameras, pocket radios, electronic goods, calculators, TV sets, and many other goods began to compete successfully with their German counterparts on the world markets.

At this early stage of its postwar recovery, Germany needed an upsurge in world trade, particularly in heavy industrial goods and equipment, so as to reactivate its latent productive capacities. Then, as the *Economist* pointed out (Dec. 30, 1962): "Just at the right time, the miracle happened. In June, 1950, the Korean War boom burst across the trading world." With the onset of hostilities in the Far East, a flood of orders poured in for German machinery, tools, steel, heavy industrial equipment, and related products. This unexpected development marked a sharp upturn in West Germany's uncertain progress to solvency and stability. Fortunately, West Germany's concentration on heavy industrial products—huge presses, forgings, generators, motors, etc.—and the ability to produce them faster and cheaper than its foreign competitors served to float its exports off on the rising tide of world demand.

Erhard had not counted on a war to give such lift to his economic program. But he and the German industrialists were fully able to cope with this sudden stimulus to a young and flexible economy. Another factor greatly contributing to the revival of West German commerce and industry was its old-fashioned, high-collar, orthodox fiscal policies, promulgated in concert by Finance Minister Fritz Schaeffer and Central Bank president Wilhelm Vocke. Their twin objectives were to transform the Deutschemark, a fiat currency, into one readily convertible into dollars or gold, just like the Swiss franc, and to keep inflation completely at bay. By holding down prices and costs, such as the cost of labor, the Germans kept their goods and services for export very competitive on world markets. For example, after the start of the Korean War the orders for steel placed with the Ruhr firms jumped from 1 million to 8 million tons practically overnight. To cope with this demand, the Ruhr steelmakers began to borrow heavily to expand their production capacities. To the surprise and anger of the Ruhr business community, Vocke took steps to restrict credit, such as by raising the discount rate. He was heavily criticized on the grounds that he was hindering industrial recovery. What Vocke actually accomplished was quite different. He kept West Germany's export prices down, while those in other industrial countries, such as England and France, rose by as much as 35%. As the Central Bank reported after the boom was over: "Germany acquired a favorable competitive position in 1952 and 1953. Whereas the upward price spiral inspired by the Korean War continued in some of the most important countries, the level of prices in the Federal Republic fell considerably."

German export prices were also effectively braked by other anti-inflation measures, such as low tariffs. When Erhard advocated a free market system, he meant what he said. He reduced tariffs to permit more imports and thus force German manufacturers to be more competitive at home and abroad. In 1952 for the first time West Germany enjoyed a favorable trade balance, and it was to remain on the plus side for the next quarter century. Fritz Schaeffer began to accumulate a tidy nest egg of gold and dollar foreign exchange reserves. By 1958, the Bonn government had a credit balance of $7.3 billion. At that point the Deutschemark was made freely convertible on the world's money market. It quickly joined the U.S. dollar and the Swiss franc as one of the "hardest" currencies in the world.

Erhard never had to look back; the future had opened its doors to the West Germans.

As an uneasy peace settled on postwar Europe, West Germany faced the choice of having a free or a planned economy, as did the other nations outside the Iron Curtain. To many of its adherents and ideologues, it seemed that socialism's day—or the "welfare state"—had dawned, and so it was widely proclaimed. Exemplifying this trend, the British voters ousted Prime Minister Winston Churchill from 10 Downing Street and replaced him with Clement Atlee, head of the socialist British Labor Party. Another of the new "verities" gaining acceptance was the thesis that survival in these turbulent times required that a nation's economy be directed and controlled by the government. However, under Erhard's constant prodding, the West German government went its own way, opting for a sort of "survival-of-the-fittest" orthodoxy. This involved a minimum of regulation and interference in the world of business, a balanced budget, a stable currency, and complete freedom of trade. It also meant living within one's income, husbanding of national wealth and resources, and plowing back earnings into the complete reconstruction and modernization of the nation's industrial machine. Production would be increased and unemployment decreased by improving and streamlining the economy itself—and not by "throwing money at it," as they say in Washington.

In those early days, the Bonn government was not "welfare-minded"—that was to come later when economic recovery was assured. Erhard, Schaeffer, and Vocke had little money for social security. Spartan thinking and measures were required. The Social Democrat opposition began to complain that the Adenauer-Erhard government favored the businessman at the expense of the worker, similar to the criticisms leveled at President Reagan in 1981–82. For the outstanding feature of the government's economic policy was the wide range of incentives offered to the businessman, banker, and industrialist. The system indeed favored the rich and the powerful; it was hard on the poor and the weak. It gave freedom of action to the strong. There was scant pretense of equal economic treatment for all sectors of society. But as Henry Wallich set forth in his study of the early postwar years:

It was a harsh system but in keeping with the situation. The war had ended in a crushing defeat and there was no illusion that peace would be enjoyable. "Fair shares for all" (as advocated by the British Socialists) might have over-burdened the strong and all might have sunk together. By being able to save their own skins, the strong were put in the position where they could pull the rest after them. The rapid advance of the economy helped everybody. . . . The rapid rise in income took the place of distribution of wealth. In this sense the *Soziale Marktwirtschaft* produced socially positive results.[5]

Thus, the Adenauer-Erhard administration was able to govern the country for sixteen uninterrupted years, 1949 to 1965, winning four national elections. The strength and staying power of this government was due to its understanding of the "security syndrome"—the almost paranoid fixation of most adult Germans on achieving a sense of security in their lives. World War II, which had begun so auspiciously for the Germans with brilliant military victories, ended in catastrophe, compounded of defeat and humiliation, millions of casualties, wholesale losses of personal and real property, a disastrous drop in living standards, and a future that looked bleak and despairing.

Security was a composite of the daily needs of life: food, shelter, heat, clothing, medical care, steady employment, protected savings and pensions, a currency with real purchasing power, etc. Security dominated the daily thought processes, the decision-making, the job, the endless searching for food and other scarce staples, and marriages, the whole livelong day from morning to night. Only a dreamless sleep provided a few hours of respite from this daily obsession.

And when times got better, the memories of the traumatic 1945–48 period—"three years of utter economic hell," as the *Economist* described this passage—stayed with and continued to influence the outlook and attitudes of the Germans for years to come. The postwar surviving adults were largely indifferent to political ideologies and slogans. The respective programs and promises of democracy, socialism, and Communism evoked little positive response. The average German was deeply skeptical that the world of politics could better his standard of living. He saw a glimmer of hope if economic life could be improved. At election time his choice was dictated by *Magenpolitik*—"stomach politics." And that attitude was widely prevalent in West Germany.

Adenauer, a superb politician, and Erhard exploited this mood of uneasiness and distrust, to the benefit of their Christian Democratic coalition government. For example, when the opposition Socialists compaigned for nationalization of heavy industry and the big banks, the Adenauer-Erhard election slogan was more relevant to the public mood: "At Peace, Our Daily Bread." So this concentration on general economic improvement and individual security shaped the character

[5]Ibid.

and the structure of the new Federal Republic of Germany in those early formative years. It was such a decisive factor that when the Social Democrats finally came to power in 1969, they could not alter the pattern. They had to jettison their Marxian inheritance and modify their philosophy of government to what the German press labeled "consumer socialism." The *Soziale Marktwirtschaft* of Ludwig Erhard remained unchanged as the basic *Realpolitik* of the Federal Republic.

West Germany's rise out of the abyss of defeat to become the major economic power of Europe was considered a miracle because it was so unexpected. Not surprisingly, this new state was to develop in a somewhat lopsided fashion, compared with other European countries. West Germany grew up like a horse with blinders on; it could see and move in only one direction. Its life was focused on economic growth. It operated by a different set of rules than the other European states. The Federal Republic of Germany accepted as a primary principle that its economic strength and resources must be the true measure of its power and influence on the international scene. Economic affairs took priority over other political and military considerations, generally speaking.

Chancellor Helmut Schmidt put it simply and explicitly in a 1975 interview with the Swiss journal *Finanz und Wirtschaft*, when he stated: "For some years now our economic policy has simultaneously been our *foreign* policy."

The international press had taken note of the peculiar character of the Bundesrepublik. In 1961, *Fortune* magazine described it as "an economy which had not become a full-fledged state." As late as 1975 the *New York Times* repeated an observation voiced by other journals that West Germany was "economically a giant but politically a dwarf." But in reality the Federal Republic was not some sort of a mongoloid body politic because of its swift growth into an economic powerhouse. Rather it was formed and conditioned by the circumstances of its rebirth. It had become Europe's first *ecopolitical* state.

Essentially West Germany was able to capitalize on its ability to resume its role as the machine shop of Europe and to pour out the industrial goods and equipment that the world needed. The Federal Republic's latent productive capacities served to promote and protect its legitimate national self-interests more effectively than the possession of a fleet of bombers or an arsenal of modern weapons. In the short span of a generation the postwar Germans finally achieved the *Lebensraum* for their restless energies and talents, which they had failed to achieve in the aggressive Second and Third Reichs of Kaiser

Wilhelm II and Adolf Hitler. With its millions of Volkswagens and Mercedes, machine tools, heavy-duty engineering equipment, machinery, and motors, as well as consumer goods, the Federal Republic has established business bridgeheads around the world more lasting and secure than ever conquered by Hitler's armies in World War II.

Erhard's *Soziale Marktwirtschaft* changed the face of postwar West Germany and was to make it the richest country in Europe. (As of Sept. 30, 1979, the Bundesrepublik's gold and dollar reserves amounted to $52.7 billion. The United States' reserves by comparison were only $20 billion.) The Adenauer-Erhard government stayed in office for sixteen years without interruption. This period saw the completion of the repair and reconstruction of West Germany. The scars of war were erased. The ugly acres of broken burned-out buildings and piles of rubble that marked the centers of German cities were replaced by new office buildings and apartment complexes. The first of many skyscrapers began to rear above the urban landscapes. The streets were crowded and their shiny new store windows gleamed with merchandise of all descriptions. The skies above the Ruhr were again black with smoke belching from thousands of factory chimneys, steel mills and power plants all humming with activity. Unemployment had been reduced to zero, except for the war cripples. West Germany was recruiting thousands of foreign *Gastarbeiter*, the Turks, Greeks, Yugoslavs, Italians, and Spaniards—even several hundred Englishmen—to meet the expanding manpower needs of German industry. Production reached and then outstripped prewar levels; Germany was becoming more prosperous and stable than ever before in its history.

The rising tide of prosperity brought with it a gradual buildup of a social security system to meet the demands of the West Germans for greater *Sicherheit* in their lives. The new program, designed to cover their needs on a womb-to-tomb basis, would be the most comprehensive and costly welfare scheme in the world. By the late 1970s its yearly expenditures would amount to almost 30% of the GNP. For example, the 1978 program involved a total outlay of about $125 billion for a nation of only 62 million people. That amounts to $2,016 for every man, woman, and child in the Bundesrepublik.

Symptomatic of the "security syndrome" was the postwar metamorphosis of organized labor in West Germany from politically to economically oriented trade unions. Until Hitler came to power in 1933, German trade unions had a long tradition of political activity. The first Workers Association was founded in 1863 by Ferdinand Lassalle as a close political ally of the struggling and hard-pressed Socialist Party. The labor leaders in the nineteenth and early twentieth centuries were convinced that the objectives of the workers could be achieved only through political power. The Hohenzollern monarchs from Bismarck's time until the end of World War I were basically antilabor—trade unions were equated with socialism—in their policies and practices, except for a few short deviations from this tradition. The Weimar Republic brought the Socialists and organized labor to power. But they were unable to prevent the massive inflation of 1922–23 which wiped out the savings and pensions of the workers and the middle class. Nor were the trade unions, in conjunction with the Socialists, able to prevent Hitler's takeover of the government in 1933. Hitler then destroyed the free trade unions, arrested their leaders, and confiscated the assets of the labor organizations. The Nazi Labor Front took over the emasculated trade unions and required all workers to join. This captive organization collapsed with the defeat and surrender of Germany in May 1945. When World War II ended, German workers were without any organization whatsoever; they were powerless, politically and economically.

In October 1949, a new postwar trade union federation (the Deutscher Gewerkschaftsbund, or DGB) was launched under the forceful and reforming leadership of Hans Boeckler. As a known anti-Nazi he had been posted for arrest by the Gestapo but managed to escape by hiding out in the Bavarian mountains. Boeckler was determined that the postwar trade unions would learn from the mistakes of the past. Henceforth the DGB would seek to promote the security and living standards of its members through economic rather than political action. It was abandoning a partisan attitude and would adopt a neutral posture toward political parties. Boeckler also proposed a revolutionary new concept in labor-management relations. The trade unions demanded the right to have equal representation with the regular managers in the executive suites of all industrial firms. Boeckler successfully argued that the most practical and expeditious way to ensure that wages and working conditions for labor could be guaranteed on a permanent basis was for the trade unions to share in the day-to-day management of industrial establishments. From an ideological or Marxian standpoint, it meant that organized labor was abandoning its traditional—and socialistic—demand for "nationalization of industry." Boeckler's proposal was a more practical and cheaper way to achieve virtually the same objective, and without the disruption and costs to the taxpayers of nationalizing, for example, the steel and coal industries. And Boeckler's arguments convinced the conservative government of Adenauer and Erhard to put through legislation making

Mitbestimmung—"co-determination"—the law of the land. And organized labor achieved about 90% of what it asked for.

At first the "Ruhr barons," the acknowledged leaders of German industry, were strongly opposed to *Mitbestimmung*, as gross interference in their managerial prerogatives. But second thoughts disclosed that this co-determination scheme had a positive side as well. For example, giving the trade unions a voice in the corporate rights and responsibilities made their representatives "management-minded" for the first time in their careers. They became more sympathetic to and understanding of the problems of ownership when they shared desks in the executive suites. And as these trade-union representatives received the same salaries, fees, and bonuses and enjoyed the same "perks," including chauffeur-driven cars and lavish expense accounts, as the regular directors, they were also more receptive to and influenced by suggestions from the owner's side of the board. Finally, trade unions would have to shoulder their share of the criticism and blame if a factory failed to prosper under *Mitbestimmung* and had to lay off workers. The trade unions now had a stake in the industrial establishment; the fortunes of organized labor would now rise or fall with the success or failure of private industry. This was something they had not quite envisioned when *Mitbestimmung* was first introduced.

Another measure of the economic pragmatism of the trade-union leadership was its opposition to the postwar anti-cartel legislation introduced by Erhard. Germany was the fatherland of the *Kartell*, which flourished with little restraint from the mid-nineteenth century until the end of World War II. Hence it was only natural for big business to revive the cartel system as an integral part of its postwar reorganization and as a defense against foreign competition. As an advocate of a complete free market economy, Erhard was determined to outlaw the *Kartell*, principally as an obstacle to the free workings of the laws of supply and demand.

However, from the earliest times, the trade unions and Socialists were never opponents of the cartel system. They rationalized that if they ever came to power it would be easier to nationalize an industry dominated by a few cartels than to take into state ownership an industry comprising a large number of relatively small firms. And in March 1954, the Federation of Trade Unions notified the Bonn government that it "supported the recartelization of industry. . . . Cartels are a fact in Germany's economic life and should be recognized as such." This postwar attitude was logical and understandable. The trade unionists were no longer interested in the nationalization of industry. However, they were sincerely convinced that in postwar Germany the cartel system provided greater job security for the workers, even at the expense of higher costs for consumer goods, than a free market system which outlawed cartels. In effect, the DGB took the line that what was good for big business was also good for organized labor and for the Bundesrepublik as well.

The worker in West Germany has lost his original *proletarian* identity and has been moving upward into the middle classes of society. The menial jobs in society have been taken over by the hundreds of thousands of *Gastarbeiter*—("foreign workers")—for most of the last two decades. The standard of living for the German worker has risen far beyond what his parents and grandparents enjoyed in their time. Proof of this is found in the fact that the Germans have become a nation of tourists. For example, in 1980, the Germans spent $9.5 billion traveling *outside* the Bundesrepublik. This was twice the amount Americans spent traveling abroad.

Once the bicycle was the worker's personal means of transport; now he can afford the Volkswagen.[6] The farmers too have advanced far above their former status as peasants. Their living standards are high because they are beneficiaries of the lavish farm subsidy program of the West German government. They too are edging into the lower levels of the middle class in their appetites and outlook.

Hans Boeckler had established the basic principle that organized labor must pursue economic rather than political power in order to best accomplish its objectives in the chaotic postwar world. He did not live to see the day when West Germany's surging recovery would give the trade unions more economic power and influence than he had ever dreamed possible. The DGB has become big business itself. It owns and operates West Germany's biggest business conglomerate, the Beteiligungsschaft für Gemeinwirtschaft AG (BGAG), which in 1979 had total assets of approximately $25 billion and net earnings of $2.2 billion. The largest unit of the conglomerate is the trade unions' Bank für Gemeinwirtschaft (BfG), with assets of over $23 billion. The DGB also owns West Germany's second-largest retail chain, Co-op Zentrale, comprising five thousand food and furniture stores, nine department

---

[6]In 1938 with great propaganda fanfare, Hitler announced that the Volkswagen, the "people's car," would soon be produced to provide a cheap auto for the masses. However, World War II intervened, and not until 1948 was production of the famous "Beetle" model begun. Before the last car of this series came off the assembly line, over 20 million had been manufactured, the greatest production record for any single automobile in history. Henry Ford's Model T record was 15 million by comparison.

stores, fifty-two supermarkets, and thirty factories. In addition the DGB controls a major life insurance company, a printing firm, an advertising agency, and Europe's largest housing-development company, which itself owns 230,000 housing units. The money which created all this came originally from the union membership dues of some 6 million workers. Because West Germany was virtually strike-free during its early years, the DGB was able to build up large cash reserves, which it invested in the variety of business enterprises listed above. It is something of a paradox that the German trade unions, originally formed to fight against the repressive working conditions imposed on the masses of labor by the Ruhr coal and steel barons of the nineteenth century, have become big business themselves in the last half of the twentieth century. Organized labor has a $25 billion plus financial stake in national economy. Despite their ideological bloodlines going back directly to Karl Marx, the trade unions of today have invested their wealth and their future as well in the healthy functioning of a capitalistic free market system. Big labor has become ecopolitical too.

A few months after he had been reelected to a new four-year term as chancellor of West Germany, Helmut Schmidt was being subjected to a drumfire of criticism and complaint. His policies and decisions were being attacked by the politicians and the press, as West Germany began to slide into a deep recession. Then, in January 1981, Schmidt gave a lecture on Immanuel Kant, one of Germany's and Europe's greatest philosophers. At first glance this lecture, "Kant in Our Time," was a strange, almost forbidding intellectual exercise, especially for a politician. However, closer study revealed Schmidt's rationale. In essence, he was using Kantian philosophy to make an appeal for more understanding of the difficulties facing a politician in making up his mind and then acting on his decision in these querulous times. It was certainly a rare event for the head of a government to employ metaphysical concepts and terminology in explaining the problems he encountered in office. But then as Goethe once remarked: "The Germans make everything difficult, both for themselves and for everyone else."

Chancellor Schmidt's search for a solution, albeit temporary, for his decision-making problems also mirrors the uncertainties and doubts of his compatriots. The West Germans have gone far past their initial objective of achieving a modicum of security in their daily lives. They have become prosperous beyond all expectations. But the old problems have been replaced by new and more worrisome difficulties.

For West Germans have become half-breeds in the family of nations. They are not "Germans" today in the same sense that the French are still "French" or the English are still "British" in mind and heart. The West Germans are undergoing an identity crisis. Who are they? Certainly they are not the Germans of old; they are no longer militaristic or nationalistic. In fact, nationalism is a sputtering flame in the German picture. Germany is divided by the Iron Curtain. The western two-thirds is capitalistic, democratic, and affluent, the leading economic power in Europe. The other one-third is, on paper, a Communist totalitarian police state with a planned economy and an imprisoned population. And neither East nor West Germany is content with its present state of affairs.

The West Germans want to be reunited with their kinfolk on the other side of the Iron Curtain, who are ethnically as German as they are. But if that were possible, what sort of Germany would result? Could the capitalist and Communist halves be reconciled? What would be its fusion of their separate aspirations toward the West and the East? What would be their compromise between Washington and Moscow?

The *New York Times* (Sept. 21, 1980) echoes the finding made by other observers of the postwar German scene: "The West Germans, and Schmidt foremost among them, have never really made up their minds about how strong they are, and this makes it very difficult for both to define what they can and want to do." Prof. Karl Jaspers, the leading postwar German philosopher until his death in 1969, chided his compatriots for chasing a mirage in their "immoderate desire for security." It has also been counterproductive. "We still have neither the roots, nor an ideal in politics; no sense of where we came from or where we were going."[7]

The Germans can't revert to their past character and identification, with its theme of *Deutschland über Alles*, even if they wanted to. Europe would not permit it, while Moscow and Washington would certainly make known their opposition to such a reversion. The Germans have become political eunuchs; they have expended so much time and energy on economic growth that they have become politically retarded, both on the home front and internationally. They are unable or unwilling to make strong commitments, either to the right or to the left. Politically, they hug the middle of the road.

For the period 1949–82, eight of the nine administrations holding office in Bonn have been coalition governments, either slightly left or

[7]Karl Jaspers, *Germany's Future* (Basel: Reiche, 1969).

slightly right of center. With one exception, the centrist Free Democratic Party (FDP) has been the junior partner in all the coalitions. The one exception was the "grand coalition," a government formed by the two major parties of conservatives and the Socialists. The FDP, which holds the center between the conservatives and Socialists, was cast in the anomalous role as opposition party to the grand coalition of the right and left wings in the Bundestag. However, in any event, no one party dominates. Throughout the postwar years, the conservative Christian Democratic bloc has averaged about 45% of the vote, the Social Democrats 40%, and the Free Democrats (liberal centrists and pro-business) about 10%. The West Germans have shown a decided preference for a judicious blending of conservative orthodoxy with sufficient "consumer socialism"[8] to be palatable to the middle and working classes. The Germans who survived World War II have made it plain that they wanted economic security first, and political stability second.

Among the West Germans there is a serious "consensus gap" about the ultimate nature and character of their truncated country, which explains in large measure the doubts and conflicts that beset the national mood and outlook. And this is further exacerbated by "an almost neurotic sensitivity to the signs of economic trouble"[9] that loom up on the horizon. Having concentrated their time and talents ever since the currency reform of 1948 on achieving financial security, the Germans are afraid that rising tension between the superpowers will cost them all that they have gained with their amazing economic recovery.

There are two basic forces at work on the West German mentality as the world moves into the turbulent 1980s. Both of these stem from that hardy perennial the security syndrome, which is probably the

---

[8]In 1959 the Social Democrats [SPD] took the unprecedented step of drastically revising the party's Marxian ideology. The Socialists were aware that the *Magenpolitik*—"stomach politics," or the betterment of living standards—had a greater appeal to the West German voter than what socialism had been promising. In other words, the Socialists finally recognized that economic affairs in West Germany took priority over political ideology. In the 1959 Bad Godesberg party congress, the SPD jettisoned much of its Marxian baggage. Henceforth the SPD would no longer be the party of just the working classes; it would also be the champion of the middle classes. As a member of the party's executive board stated: "The Social Democrats are moving out of the realm of ideological thinking. They realize that only practical programs will win votes today." The West German press labeled the new SPD *Realpolitik* as "consumer socialism." In the 1969 election the Socialists finally took control of the Bonn government in coalition with the Free Democrats, and capitalism and the free market system still reign supreme in the Federal Republic of Germany.

[9]Gordon A. Craig, *The Germans* (New York: Putnam, 1981).

most pervasive influence in the lives of the West Germans. Both of these forces bring the Germans into conflict with the erratic policies of the United States government, as set forth by the Carter and Reagan administrations. The first is a highly emotional conviction: the fear that the growing tension between Washington and Moscow will escalate into a real war with West Germany becoming the principal battlefield. This view is widely held in political and civilian circles. As Karsten Voight, the foreign affairs spokesman for the Social Democratic Party, told an audience in New York, his compatriots believe that "war between the East and the West means the end of our existence." The memories of World War II and the "three years of utter economic hell" that followed are still vivid in the minds of older Germans. They can recall clearly the bombs and the casualties, the destruction of their worldly goods, the poverty and hunger that followed. A strong antiwar feeling lies just below the surface, and it verges on a "peace-at-any-price" frame of mind. The younger generations—those born after the war ended—have no such memories, but their idealism shows itself in the demonstrations protesting the introduction of American nuclear weaponry into the Bundesrepublik as part of the NATO program against Russian aggression. In fact, this growing anti-Americanism, based on the implicit belief that Washington will "fight to the last German," occasioned an unprecedented diplomatic warning to the Germans. U.S. Ambassador Arthur F. Burns told the German press in November 1981 that if U.S. forces are not wanted to defend the Bundesrepublik, the Americans are prepared to return home.

The loss of two world wars, with the catastrophic consequences of millions of casualties, immeasurable losses of wealth, and inestimable social, cultural, and moral damage inflicted on the survivors, has taken something out of the Teutonic psyche. The postwar Germans have shown clearly that they are in no mood for any political or economic adventuring. The pulse of nationalism which once beat so vigorously through German veins is now slowed to a murmur. The appeal of patriotism is also stilled because it was thoroughly discredited by Adolf Hitler. Unique among the nations of the western world, the Bundesrepublik lies wallowing in stormy seas, unable to set sail on a course that meets with the approval of all the passengers on board.

The second force that impinges on German consciousness is essentially economic. It concerns West Germany's relations with the Communist bloc on the other side of the Iron Curtain. Since the last quarter of the nineteenth century, Germany has been an industrial nation. It had its own basic sources of fuel and energy: the great Ruhr coal mines, and the large brown coal (lignite) deposits in Silesia and the Rhineland. But Germany had to import much of the raw materials that it processed into manufactured goods, as well as a substantial percentage of its food supplies. The *Kaiserreich* built up export markets in Russia and Eastern Europe, the Balkans, and the Middle East. These were areas little developed industrially compared with Western Europe in the years before and after World War I. For example, though the French provided the financing, the Germans supplied the steel and rolling stock to build the railroads in czarist Russia. The slogan that captured the imagination of the Ruhr industrialists, and the general public too, was *Drang nach Osten*, the "push to the East," to markets that were almost exclusively German and free of European competitors.

However, after World War II these traditional markets, now behind the Iron Curtain, were closed off to West Germany. Then in 1969 when Willy Brandt became the first Social Democratic chancellor, he inaugurated the new foreign policy line of *Ostpolitik*. It meant an attempt to open up relations with Russia and the satellite countries of the Communist bloc, so as to improve trade and cultural and political relations between East and West. On the Soviet side, Premier Alexei Kosygin pushed for détente, which in the loose formulation of international politics was another version of *Ostpolitik*. These developments coincided with the Kremlin's decision to acquire as much of western technology as possible, with purchases largely financed by new credits from western banks to the Soviet Union and the satellite countries. When détente was launched the Communist bloc was in debt to western nations for about $12 billion; today that debt has climbed to $80 billion. And there are increasing doubts that the Warsaw Pact bloc can ever repay these debts, as the inability of Poland and Romania to meet their installments on interest and principal have shown.

But the old myth of *Drang nach Osten* has been revived and still has its power to rekindle the hopes of West German politicians and industrialists. The Soviet Union and its satellites are the natural markets for German goods and services. Russia has vast economic potentials in the development of oil and gas deposits and its wealth of minerals, much of which are buried under the frozen tundra of remote Siberia. What is needed is the latest technology to exploit these resources in a viable manner. The proposed new $15–25 billion 3,500-mile gas pipeline from Siberia is an example of Russo-German industrial collaboration that could be expanded to include other sizable industrial development projects. This conviction is strengthened by the fact that West Germany can become *Russia's* biggest trading partner because it has the heavy industrial equipment and technical know-how which the Soviet Union needs. All the pressure and protests from Washington to block the construction of the pipeline have thus far failed.

The Germans are aware of the risks of trading with the Communist bloc. But the Germans are supremely confident they know how to do business profitably with the Russians better than the other Europeans. This is a conceit largely compounded by geography and history. The Germans have had a long and contentious relationship with the Slavic peoples to the east of the Oder river, dating back to the thirteenth century when the Teutonic Knights dominated parts of Russia and Poland. And down through the intervening centuries when the episodic warfare between the Teuton and the Slav came to a temporary halt, the German merchants resumed their goods traffic with their Russian markets. *Drang nach Osten* has been an economic reality for a long time.

CHAPTER NINE

The Electronic Age

I am not a Marxist but I understand one thing: You can't get your politics
in order if your economics are not in order.
　　　　　　　—CHANCELLOR HELMUT SCHMIDT

THE world has changed greatly for U.S. business on the world scene. In the 1960s American corporations became "multinational." They began to expand abroad in an explosive fashion. The new multinationals had found rich and developing markets for their goods and services, particularly for U.S. technology in Western Europe. The list of American corporations with manufacturing subsidiaries abroad was long and prestigious. In 1967 the French editor Jean-Jacques Servan-Schreiber wrote a European best-seller, titled *The American Challenge (Le Défi Américain)*. He predicted that the foreign operations of the U.S. multinationals "would become the third industrial power in the world" after the United States and Russia. The London *Daily Mail* commented on this burgeoning U.S. invasion of Europe in a 1966 editorial:

The Americans with their stuffed briefcases and businesslike gleam in their eyes are crossing the Atlantic daily. They are the modern invaders of Europe, the cheque-book conquistadores, moving in from the New World to correct the balance books of the Old. The Germans welcome them, the French tolerate them. But both countries share the same uneasy thought: how far can the dollar invasion be allowed to go without getting out of hand?

But the growth of a "third industrial power" was to be denied the U.S. multinationals abroad. The *Défi Américain* was to be curbed—though not by foreign governments acting to protect their own domestic markets from the influx of U.S. goods and services. Rather the U.S. Congress passed legislation which had a crippling effect on the growth of American corporations abroad. The U.S. laws hit hard at

251

several sectors. They increased the personal and corporate income taxes on the overseas operations of American companies. There were new laws prohibiting bribery, a standard practice to conclude a profitable business deal in foreign markets; an anti-boycott law which favored the State of Israel against the oil-rich Arab countries; and other trade restrictions, political in character, involving countries deemed to be violating human rights, as well as the imposition of domestic health, safety, and environmental regulations on the foreign operations of U.S. firms. Perhaps the most damaging was the imposition by Congress in 1969 of an increase in the capital gains tax from 25% to 49%. Then in 1976, Congress wiped out personal tax deductions for overseas living expenses for U.S. businessmen working abroad. These measures effectively dampened the enthusiasm of U.S. firms to expand their overseas operations. In short a large dosage of moralistic and anti–big business legislation forced American multinationals to retreat to the boats instead of advancing out of their overseas business bridgeheads to a point that was critically detrimental to the continued expansion of the U.S. economy abroad.

For example, as reported by *Business Week* (March 12, 1979), the Carter administration's effort to limit exports of plutonium processing plants and to link export financing by the Export-Import Bank to the human-rights issues lost Westinghouse Electric $1.5 billion in atomic reactor sales in South Africa, Argentina, and Brazil, though the American firm was out in front as the low bidder. Thus if the United States is to regain its overseas business bridgeheads, most of these trade-restrictive laws, including antitrust regulations, must be drastically revised or wiped off the statute book. The European and Japanese governments do not handicap their own industrial exporters with such politically and morally motivated rules and regulations. While the overseas development of U.S. corporations faltered and then declined, the Japanese stepped in to take over markets which the Americans could not adequately or profitably serve. And the Tokyo government, through its powerful Ministry of International Trade and Industry (MITI) and the Japanese Export Trade Organization (JETRO), which operated in foreign countries, spent hundreds of millions of dollars to subsidize, promote, and expand Japan's overseas trade. As a result Japan has secure and expanding business bridgeheads throughout the western hemisphere, Europe, and the Middle East—in fact, everywhere in the free world where there are markets for Dai Nippon's goods and services. *Le Défi Japonais* has replaced *Le Défi Américain* on the world markets.

With the invention of the transistor in the Bell Laboratories of the

A. T. & T. system in 1948, the electronic age was born. At the time scant public attention was paid to this newcomer on the industrial scene. Few realized that this tiny device would be the foundation of a whole new industry of electronics, generating billions of dollars of new high-technology products, employing millions of people, and giving the United States an economic asset as valuable in its way as the Middle East oil fields are to the OPEC oil cartel. Just as the invention of the steam engine launched the industrial revolution for Britain, Europe, and the United States in the nineteenth century, so the electronic computer in its manifold forms and uses is opening the curtains on another industrial revolution. It is transforming the economies of the United States and other industrially developed nations, and it will have profound repercussions in the nations of the Third World.

Incidentally, it is hardly an exaggeration to state that modern-day "Japan Inc.," the new Pacific *Wirtschaftswunder*, is virtually the creation of America's Bell Laboratories, the $2-billion-a-year research and development giant. Since it was founded over fifty years ago, Bell Laboratories has been awarded nineteen thousand patents for inventions and techniques, and seven Nobel Prizes. Among its outstanding developments were radio telephony and the vacuum-tube amplifiers in the 1910s, the co-axial cable and television in the 1920s, early digital computers and radar in the 1930s, point contact transistors in the 1940s, silicon chips and laser beams in the 1950s, bubble memories and LEDs in the 1960s, optical fibers and E-beams in the 1970s. Bell inventions are the cornerstones of postwar Japanese high technology.

The electronic age marks the emergence of high technology as a decisive factor in the whole spectrum of international relations. Those few nations which enjoy competence in this esoteric field of human endeavor will reap great rewards for their long and difficult apprenticeship. High technology is power, because it is, in effect, a secure bridgehead in the economic struggle for dominance in the future. High technology translates into power because it is an extension of man's intelligence to the machine. The electronic age creates a new dimension for industry. For example, the computer has been developed from what was originally a super-fast calculating machine into an "artificial intelligence"—known as AI—that can mimic human thought processes. This new electronic brain, whose "cells" are tiny silicon chips with their incredibly complex electronic designs, can diagnose some illnesses, locate mineral deposits, direct oil drilling, and operate manufacturing plants, shouldering the duties and responsibilities of factory managers and assembly-line foremen. The AI also is being considered for military use. The Rand Corporation, a California think tank, has developed an experimental prototype called TATR, which after being fed the requisite information can lay out a plan of attack of enemy positions, just as the U.S. Army G-3 staff officer does in actual combat. This opens up the startling possibilities of future wars directed and fought by computers and robots. Could that be considered human progress?

At this writing, the second year of the Reagan presidency, American morale and confidence have been shaken by the deepening recession. It is hard to grasp the fact that the economic slump is in large part the result of this transition process that is constantly evolving. For example, the emergence of Japan as a major industrial competitor of the United States—so forceful as to cause panic in America's giant automotive industry—is one aspect of the technological revolution that is now well under way. While the United States is the prime instigator of this new electronic age, the American business and political circles are just awakening to the harsh reality that they are engaged in "a whole new ball game." The casualties that are being tallied in each day's newspapers—the bankruptcies, the growing army of unemployed, the shutdown of industrial plants—are the prices being paid for failure to read the handwriting on the wall.

Barring the accident of a third world war, the United States can remain the No. 1 economic superpower if it can adjust both to the demands and to the opportunities of the expanding electronic age. The only serious challenger on the horizon is Japan. The resurgent Japanese have made some impressive gains in electronic technology. They have taken the lead away from the United States and Germany in the field of industrial automation, also described as CAM, or computer-aided manufacturing. They employ more robots on their assembly lines than does any other nation at this writing. With their resulting high productivity and low costs, by comparison with the United States, it seemed several years ago that the Japanese manufacturers would dominate not only international trade but also a growing number of America's domestic markets. In the field of consumer goods, for example, such as audio equipment, calculators, cameras, watches and office equipment, Japan suddenly became a nightmare to U.S. manufacturers.

However, the Americans are reacting strongly. "The Japanese have awakened a sleeping tiger," proclaims Frank T. Curtin, vice-president of Cincinnati Milacron, a leading U.S. machine-tool producer. "We are not going to roll over and play dead any longer."[1]

---

[1] Quoted in *Business Week*, Aug. 3, 1981.

In electronic technology, America is far ahead of Japan and Germany in two absolutely vital areas: computer software and computer-aided design (CAD). In fact, some 90% of the CAD systems sold in Japan in 1980 were U.S. exports, and sales are increasing at a fast rate every year.

The difference between CAD and CAM is analogous to the difference between an adult and an adolescent. CAD involves the highly sophisticated technique of utilizing the computer to plan the *complete* electronic operation of an entire manufacturing entity, whether it makes automobiles, television sets, or washing machines. CAD gives the businessman or industrialist a "package solution" for a completely computer-operated manufacturing project—what machine tools should be used, what raw materials are needed and in what amounts, scheduling of production runs, distribution of the finished product, etc. On the other hand, CAM is concerned with the computer-controlled automation of specific phases of the manufacturing process, such as processing of raw materials, cutting and welding, and the actual assembly of the finished product.

"This leadership [in CAD systems] is the cornerstone of America's thrust into automation. . . . With this edge, U.S. companies are on the verge of achieving a dream: manufacturing enterprises where push-button factories and executive suites, no matter how physically remote, become parts of the same integrated computerized entity," *Business Week* reported (Aug. 3, 1981).

In any competition with Japan involving high technology, especially in electronic goods, two developments stand out. The Japanese have perfected electronic manufacturing operations, such as a robot-controlled assembly line, that at present are superior to what the Americans have to offer. However, in invention and innovation involving electronic products and services, the Americans are further ahead of the Japanese and Germans.[2] As the *Economist* pointed out (Dec. 27, 1980), the Americans, being members of a nonhierarchical society, "have a culture finest fitted to bring about an explosion of inventiveness and enterprise in the small profit centers and small towns,[3] where people in the information society will find it most profitable fun to

---

[2]Since the first Nobel Prizes were given for outstanding accomplishments in the field of science (physics, chemistry, physiology, and medicine), the Americans have won 103 awards in these categories; the Japanese have won only four.

[3]A great part of the initial research and high technology in the United States in the electronic field has been carried out in a suburban belt ringing Boston and later in "Silicon Valley," a grouping of microprocessing firms in California's Santa Clara County, south of San Francisco.

work and live. The grandfathers of white Americans came across [the Atlantic] to build entrepreneurship while the northern Europeans' ancestors stayed behind to maintain or to resent the established class system."

This new electronic era is transforming the nature and character of the ways that Americans work and live. The changes are taking place every day in U.S. industry and business; the whole American economy is being slowly restructured in a manner that will drastically affect our lives and those of our children and grandchildren. But the process is so imperceptible that the average American is unaware of its far-reaching implications. And what is happening in the United States is, to a lesser degree, also taking place in other industrial countries, especially Japan. And it is all caused by international competition operating within the framework of the old and reliable laws of supply and demand.

The *Economist* of London (Dec. 27, 1980) commented on this development: "America is moving rapidly but quietly from an industrial society (which means capitalist, bossed-about, partly horny-handed) to an information society (which should be much more expansive, entrepreneurial and more fun)."

To further clarify this fuzzy outline of the future, Peter F. Drucker is more specific:

> To maintain the competitive strength and leadership in manufacturing, whether in competition with Germany and Japan, or with the rapidly industrializing countries of the Third World, therefore requires a country like America to gear manufacturing technology to the available supply of *knowledge workers* rather than to the dwindling supply of blue-collar workers. It requires shifting manufacturing work from operating machines to programming machines and indeed to programming plants and processes rather than individual machines or lines.[4]

The new language of the electronic age sometimes leads to abstract concepts, such as "information society" or "knowledge workers." But when translated into the language of the industrial plant, it means ever-increasing utilization of the electronic computer in all its varied forms. The computer is programmed with various "inputs" of "information," fed into it by the "knowledge worker," that are required to perform its allocated task.

Every day and virtually everywhere in the United States—if not in person then through the ubiquitous medium of television—we are confronted with the "information society" in action. It is a marriage of

[4]*Wall Street Journal*, Feb. 13, 1980.

modern telecommunications with the computer to cope with the rising tide of "information" generated, processed, and distributed by millions of white-collar employees, including virtually all office workers, teachers, clerks, accountants, bankers, lawyers, executives, plant managers, ad infinitum. The tools are at hand. The latest in electronic software is the word processor, hooked up to a computer. With its fluorescent screen and typewriter keyboard it can send and receive information such as pictorial material, designs, statistical tables, textual material, and news reports. It produces the new literature of the electronic age. It can even play games with children or chess with experts. And the word processors and the various types of computers are aided and abetted by the revolution in telecommunications. Information-relaying satellites 23,000 miles above the planet provide instantaneous personal and group communications on a global basis. For example, businessmen in Manila, London, New York, and Rio de Janeiro can hold a group conference without any of the participants ever leaving his own desk.

In the final analysis what this portends is the foreseeable shift from blue-collar manual labor to white-coated technicians through the increasing automation and computerization of all phases of the industrial production in the United States.

The first phase of the electronic revolution is already under way. The United States is engaged in the replacement of workers with robots—computers in steel overalls—on the assembly lines in major manufacturing sectors, a replacement that will be as fast and as far-reaching as present resources permit. This is CAM, computer-aided manufacturing, Japanese-style. Japan has pioneered in adapting the robot to industrial production. At the end of 1981, Japan had an estimated fourteen thousand robots in operation, mainly in loading machines and on the assembly lines. The United States had an estimated four thousand robots at work, while West Germany had about fourteen hundred in action.

However, the United States seeks to make a quantum jump in this key sector of high technology. The Robot Institute of America reports that sales figures of robots in the United States are steadily rising, from $100 million in 1980 to an expected $2.5 billion by 1990. Governor William G. Milliken of Michigan, a state which has the highest unemployment rate in the nation, wants to make Detroit the robot capital for world industry. The city has already attracted eighteen manufacturers as the nucleus of a robot-production industry. Detroit has the skilled technicians and technological know-how to mass-produce robots on a grander scale, covering a wider range of industrial utilization, than Japan can offer. Governor Milliken and his experts have carefully studied the devastating effects of Japanese exports in the American marketplace, especially in the U.S. automotive industry, centered in Detroit. The effective way to challenge Japan and Germany is to apply a greater degree of high technology to heavy industry. The robot is one of the solutions to Japanese and other international competition. Businessmen are becoming aware of these harsh economic facts of life. There is a vast new market opening up, not only in the United States but also in Europe. Ford Motor Co. will spend $250 million in 1982 to expand its use of robots by 30%. General Motors plans to have fourteen thousand robots in action by 1990, and other major industrial companies will follow its lead. If this first phase of industrial restructuring is not carried out, the Detroit car manufacturer or the Schenectady household appliance producer will be forced out of business by competitors in Japan or Mexico, Taiwan or South Korea. Labor is more plentiful and production costs are much lower outside the United States. For example, including fringe benefits and health care, a blue-collar worker at GM averages $19 per hour, while in Japan, the same worker earns an average of $11 an hour as of April 1982. So the lesson is loud and clear: Automate or stagnate and then gradually disappear from the world markets.

The second phase of the electronic revolution of industry—which has been erroneously described as the "reindustrialization of America"—carries transformation of the U.S. industry to its ultimate and logical conclusion. It can best be described as the redesign of entire industrial plants and entire manufacturing processes so that they are in effect completely "computerized" or "electronicized," so to speak. That is CAD, or computer-aided design, American-style. It will be the end product of the "information society."

This phase of the electronic revolution is also under way. As Peter F. Drucker has already pointed out: "This development is proceeding so fast and furiously that some observers speak of it as 'the third industrial revolution.' Its impact is fully comparable to the fractional horsepower motor 100 years ago."[5] And as we already know, the fractional horsepower motor changed the face of industrial America. It was the father of modern technology; of mechanized agriculture, of today's household appliances, etc. The electronic revolution is at hand.

[5]*Wall Street Journal*, June 13, 1980.

If the United States is to survive as competitive producer and exporter of manufactured goods and services on the world market, it must go on a labor-slimming regimen. It must restructure its industry so as to reduce the labor-intensive stages of manufacturing and also labor-intensive industries themselves. It will be a painful and unpleasant exercise, like going on a diet to lose weight. American labor is too expensive by world standards. The American economy has to find a way out of this dilemma. Otherwise virtually all the labor-intensive manufacturing in America today can and will be performed just as well and a great deal cheaper in the developing countries of the Third World. Here are some signs of these changing times.

General Motors began manufacturing its new compact J-car line in Brazil in April 1982. GM also announced at the start of 1982 that its plans to produce its new S-car line in its American plants have been cancelled; instead the S-car will be produced in Japan in conjunction with Isuzu Motors of Tokyo. These developments confirm the growing belief that the world's largest automotive producer is convinced that in the future *about 40% of the U.S. car market will be supplied by foreign manufacturers.* So General Motors is expanding its overseas production facilities. It will then export these foreign-made cars for sale in the United States. It is another step in the economic imperatives of the times: Go where the labor is cheaper! The Americans and their German, French, and Japanese competitors are now producing car motors and other automotive parts in Mexico, for example. GM has to pay only $2.15 an hour to a skilled Mexican worker, compared to $19 an hour to his assembly-line counterpart in Flint, Michigan. Over fifteen hundred Brazilian firms are now manufacturing automotive parts and accessories for U.S. and European car manufacturers. Brazil is also increasing its exports of machine tools and heavy equipment to the United States, Europe, and Japan.

This trend has been called "production sharing," and obviously the American workers and the trade-union leadership will fight to preserve their jobs with all the political clout and economic pressure that they can muster. But another unobtrusive but very important trend has been developing for some time, which in the short range is negative for organized labor but has a positive, even a silver-lining, prospect for the U.S. worker as it progresses. The big corporations are no longer growing bigger in terms of workers and employees. Since the mid-1960s, the thousand biggest U.S. industrial corporations— regularly listed by *Fortune* magazine—have been steadily reducing the numbers on their payrolls. Of course, the pending Reagan recession with its increasing plant closures, bankruptcies, etc. has accelerated this trend. However, since the mid-1960s some 15 million jobs have been created in the private sector, and of these new work places, more than 10 million have been made in smaller business firms. Of course, a large number, perhaps as high as half, of these new firms never succeed in staying in business beyond a five-year period. But those who fail are quickly followed by others entering into the fields of industry or commerce, like bubbles constantly rising in a glass of champagne.

Big business is like big government—it operates by the same principles, though the public generally respects the former and constantly criticizes the latter. But the day of the industrial dinosaur is coming to an end. The bigger it gets, the more money it spends, the more it expands, the more its efficiency declines; its productivity stagnates and its profitability vanishes. There is a point reached when further growth ceases. The list of recent invalids is impressive: Lockheed, Chrysler, Penn Central, United States Steel, International Harvester, etc. Not so long ago IBM dominated the infant computer industry, at home and abroad. But the competition in the computer industry today is developing with the speed and persistency of crab grass. The development of "Silicon Valley" in California, the mushroomlike growth of independent long-distance phone companies in the shadow of A.T.&T.'s communications stranglehold—all signs are that no one corporation can sit astride a vital industry without continual attempts being made to break its monopoly, usually with success.

Even Exxon Corp., "the giant among giants in the most prosperous of industries . . . may have already seen its best days," reported *Business Week* (June 7, 1982). The oil company has spent $53 billion in the last ten years in new capital investments and exploration projects, yet in the same period its oil production has dropped from 4.8 million barrels per day in 1973 to 1.6 million in 1981. Exxon has also invested nearly "$6 billion to $7 billion in largely futile attempts to find a new base for its future earnings," the magazine reported, including nearly $2 billion trying to create an information-processing and office-systems business to compete with IBM and others in this field.

While the giants totter, weighed down by their industrial obesity, new small businesses are being started in the United States at a higher rate than ever before. The entrepreneur and his sidekick, the inventor, are returning to the marketplaces of the nation with their new products and innovations. In 1981 some 587,000 new companies were incorporated, which was 53,000 more than in 1980 and 80% more than in 1975.[6] Hard times stimulate the formation of new business ventures. For example, the entrepreneur finds ways and means to manufacture a new household appliance cheaper than firms long established in this field. The entrepreneur has the freedom to take risks that are denied a larger firm with its fixed business practices, cost controls, and tradition. Besides, starting a small business to market a new invention or some new commercial innovation does not require a large amount of capital; the principal asset required is a viable idea or invention. In 1980 and 1981 hundreds of entrepreneurs and inventors became millionaires and multimillionaires when shares of their new companies were sold to the public for the first time.[7] Steven Jobs, a twenty-six-year-old college drop-out, almost singlehandedly created the small personal desk computer industry. He formed his Apple Company, located in Silicon Valley, with one partner and an initial investment of $1,300. Within six years his firm had prospective sales for 1982 of $600 million. George Gilder, economist and author of the best-selling *Wealth and Poverty*, writes that "entrepreneurs are fighting America's only serious war against poverty. The potentialities of invention and enterprise are now greater than ever before in history."

The good news for the working class is that the formation of these new business ventures created 3 million new jobs in ten years, according to the magazine *Venture Capital Journal*. This development continues the trend first observed several years ago by the American sociologist John Naisbitt. He surveyed the operations of *Fortune* magazine's list of the thousand largest industrial corporations from 1969 to 1976. In that period 9.5 million new jobs were created in American industry—but not one new work place on the payrolls of the *Fortune* list of companies. However, he found that small business firms alone accounted for 6.5 million of the 9.5 million new work places.[8]

This trend in employment growth, starting at the bottom, is uniquely American.[9] There is little tradition or experience in Europe for one-man enterprises, either in obtaining the necessary financing or in making it a success. In Japan, emphasis is on corporate development at the expense of individual initiative. Kenjo Tamiya, president

---

[6]Figures from *Time*, Feb. 15, 1982.

[7]Ibid.

[8]*Economist*, Jan. 3, 1981.

[9]Further confirmation of this trend comes from California. A 1982 survey by the Center for Continuing Study of the California Economy reports that in 1970 high-technology enterprises employed 273,000 persons, and in 1980, 492,200; and by 1990 the total is expected to be 726,700 persons. This relates to total California employment: 1970, 8,023,900 jobs; 1980, 11,146,500; and a projected total state employment of 13,917,000 by 1990.

of the Sony Corporation of America, told *Time* magazine: "Japanese society is more highly organized and big organizations tend to avoid risk. . . . This gives the United States an advantage."

The creation of new small business enterprises, particularly in the field of high technology, has been given a shot in the arm by a more favorable tax situation. In 1969, in a sharp spasm of avarice to atone for its massive spending, the U.S. Congress raised the capital gains tax from 25% to 49%. This had a devastating effect, virtually drying up all risk capital, the life's blood for new business ventures. By 1975 only a piddling $10 million was available for this type of financing. Then in 1978 Congress lowered the capital gains tax to 29%. This produced a flood of pent-up risk capital investments totaling $1.3 billion, which is largely responsible for the proliferation of new small business ventures. In turn, this trend is begetting the Horatio Alger stories of the electronic era.

The true sign of the economic health of a nation is a progressive and changing industry. The industry that stagnates sounds the death knell of a country. In modern history, changes occur swiftly. Before World War I—about the time Ronald Reagan was born—nearly one-third of America's workers were farmers and farm laborers. In Great Britain at that time, ministers of religion outnumbered scientists by ten to one. Then came the postwar expansion of American industry, triggered by mass production of the motor car. Farm workers migrated to the cities to get better-paying jobs in the new factories. But they were replaced in part by harvesting machines and tractors. Today, only 4% of America's work force is engaged in farming, yet the output of meat, grains, vegetables, and fruit has been increasing with every passing year. The United States is truly the only nation in the world with a full cupboard.

And on the industrial side, two or three Japanese workers, plus robots, can produce as many cars per day as ten Americans in Detroit's semi-obsolescent automotive plants. The car industry in America is under heavy pressure from foreign competitors, and so are other industrial giants, such as textiles, steel, shipbuilding, etc.

However, there is a solution to this problem: large-scale automation where assembly lines are involved in manufacturing. One robot can replace three or four workers on their present jobs. At the 1981 price of $40,000, a U.S. Unimate robot can handle a double shift every day for a period of eight years. Including maintenance costs and depreciation, that works out to a labor cost per robot of less than $5 an hour, compared to the $15 per hour paid to the typical American assembly-line worker. Hence it is not surprising that the rush to produce robots is on.

And if Detroit should become the major world producer of robots for modern industry—as it is planning to be—it will be sweet revenge for Japan's invasion of the American car market with its armies of Toyotas, Hondas, Datsuns, and Subarus. This new industry will give employment to large numbers of technicians, as well as skilled workers—many of whom will be wearing white dust coats instead of dirt-stained denim jeans while on the job. They will have graduated to be "knowledge workers" in the new hierarchy of the electronics age.

The impact of high technology on today's labor market, not only in the United States but also in Europe and Japan, appears at first glance to be very damaging. Labor-intensive manufacturing either must substitute robots and other labor-saving devices for workers, or shift its production to a Third World country where labor is plentiful and cheap. In either case, a great number of the domestic workers lose their jobs. However, this fear about the damage that can be done by technological change, both to the working classes and to established business concerns, has been voiced ever since the industrial revolution began at the start of the nineteenth century. In 1811 thousands of British handicraftsmen known as Luddites began to destroy textile mills after weaving machines were installed. But once they were in operation, the British textile industry expanded by leaps and bounds, and provided more jobs than any one had expected. Similar industrial sabotage occurred in France later in the nineteenth century after labor-saving machinery was introduced. The American railroads first scorned and then began to fight back against the stiff competition offered by the growing trucking industry. Then U.S. technology introduced the all-purpose unit cargo van, which can be transported on railway flatcars, carried on ships, and moved by trucks around the world, even across Soviet Russia by the Trans-Siberian Railroad. A standard cargo van can be loaded on a boat in Hong Kong, cross the Pacific to San Francisco, be reloaded onto a railway flatcar or a truck and cross the American continent to the Port of New York, again be reloaded onto a ship and transported across the Atlantic to Rotterdam, be put on a Rhine River barge to Düsseldorf, and finally be trucked to a German warehouse—without its cargo ever being tampered with en route from the Hong Kong manufacturer to the West German importer. U.S. technology has created the cheapest form of freight transportation in the world. By so doing, it has stimulated international and domestic industry and commerce. Everybody benefits—the shipping companies, the railroads, the trucking industry—with more revenues for businessmen and more employment for the workers.

Other examples come to mind to illustrate how new jobs are created when high technology supplants labor-intensive industries. New England was America's first region to industrialize on a large scale. In recent years the hundreds of textile mills, once the industrial backbone of this area, have moved out; other labor-intensive industries also left the scene. But they have been replaced by America's fastest growth industries: computers, electronic engineering, and the manufacture of digital equipment and precision instruments. And this means new job opportunities for tens of thousands of New England's residents. Incidentally, almost overnight the production of electronic toys has become a multi-billion-dollar industry.

When computers first made their debut on the American business scene it was said they would cause mass unemployment. Instead electronic technology has created new jobs, increased productivity, and provided soaring salaries for those who can meet its work challenges.

The invention of the automobile put the horse out of business, except for racing purposes. Yet the passenger car made fortunes for the five Studebaker brothers of South Bend, Indiana, who before World War I were the largest manufacturers of horse-drawn vehicles in the world. At the turn of the century they began experimenting with the manufacturing of passenger cars, producing their first Studebaker automobile in 1904. After World War I, where before they had employed hundreds of workers to manufacture horse-drawn wagons, the Studebaker brothers now gave jobs to thousands to produce automobiles. Their medium-priced car held a firm place in the U.S. market for almost a half-century until it finally could no longer compete against the Big Three of Detroit—GM, Ford, and Chrysler—and went out of business in the 1960s. However, the Studebaker brothers demonstrated that technological change can spell opportunity and not economic disaster, if one has the imagination and managerial skills to bridge the gap between the old and new order of things. The Studebakers made South Bend famous long before Knute Rockne and his Notre Dame football teams captured the national spotlight.

Technology, which reduces labor costs, thereby increases the productivity of a manufacturing firm or an industry. Hence it is more competitive both in the home and international markets. The resulting savings, together with increased income, enable the industrial firm to expand and to diversify its operations, which means increasing the number of workers on its payroll. These economic benefits also serve as a brake on inflation. Hence it is a fallacy to assume that labor-saving, productivity-increasing technology *kills* jobs.

As the *Economist* has pointed out in its detailed survey of technology and its relationship to workers' jobs (Jan. 3, 1981): "The easiest trap to fall into is the 'lump of labour' fallacy—the idea that there is a fixed amount of work to do, to be shared amongst available workers. No country has ever satisfied all its wants and needs."

Industrial production in this time of constant change and innovation is a most flexible component of the national economy. It can contract or expand; it is affected by all the forces impinging on the economic development: social, educational, political, military, etc. Hence what disappears today from the marketplace will be replaced by a substitute for tomorrow's buyers.

Finally, there is another fallacy that needs to be exploded. That is the assumption that when a labor-intensive industrial firm transfers its manufacturing to a Third World country, the American economy suffers from a net *loss* of jobs. Such a transfer of an industrial operation to a Third World country helps its economy to grow. The extra income earned by its people creates a demand for consumer goods and capital equipment from the United States and other industrial nations. In the early postwar years when West Germany and Japan were rebuilding their war-shattered economies, the dollars they earned for their first exports were quickly spent to buy capital equipment and services from the United States to further quicken their industrial growth. For example, Armco of Middletown, Ohio, provided millions of dollars' worth of planning, expertise, and capital equipment for the complete modernization of West Germany's and Japan's war-shattered steel industries. This was repeated in virtually every industrial sector of the two ex-enemy nations. Today it is again being repeated in the Middle East oil-producing states, which are spending hundreds of billions in Europe and the United States to industrialize their economies. Also other developing states like Taiwan, South Korea, and Nigeria, which have close ties to America, are steady purchasers of U.S. goods and services to make themselves more competitive on the world markets.

A nation which has technology for export is indeed in the driver's seat, with considerable advantages over countries which are not equally advanced. Technology is an *ecopolitical* instrument of immeasurable value, if utilized with intelligence and imagination.

CHAPTER TEN

Ecopolitics Instead of Geopolitics

The supreme art of generalship is to break the enemy's resistance without actually fighting.

—SUN TZU, *The Art of War*
4th century B.C.

There is no fortress so strong that money cannot take it.
—MARCUS TULLIUS CICERO

The lack of money is the root of all evil.
—GEORGE BERNARD SHAW, *Man and Superman*

IN the preceding chapters, we have focused on postwar developments in certain areas and countries. Our selection has been based on economic events and trends, both positive and negative, which have substantial repercussions beyond the frontiers of these countries. For example, of the Third World countries we have concentrated on the People's Republic of China, on the "NICs"—the newly industrial countries, such as South Korea, Taiwan, Singapore, and Malaysia—and on the black African states. Red China, the most populous nation on earth, is slowly and inexorably changing from its hard-line doctrinaire Communism to a more flexible form of state capitalism. The NICs of the Far East, though small in population, are providing examples of vigorous and profitable technological advancement by the hitherto unschooled Asians. And the belt of black African states across the waist of the Dark Continent demonstrate the high cost of unbridled political struggle for the control of these former colonial domains in the resulting bankruptcy of their economies. We have bypassed India, Bangladesh, and other important members of the Third World bloc because they are by comparison with the NICs or the African countries virtually stagnant, from an economic and political standpoint. We have also omitted Western Europe, except for West Germany. The Federal Republic of Germany is the most important nation of Western Europe, on the political and economic front line of the Continent. If West Germany holds fast to her NATO alliance, then Western Europe can defend itself against the rising tide of Russian pressure tactics and nuclear blackmail. If West Germany falters, then France, the Low Countries, and Great Britain can do little to halt the westward spread of Russian power and influence. Central and South America are also not included in this study, because Latin America lies outside the areas of serious confrontation between the superpowers.

What are the lessons of this global survey just concluded? There are several:

1. Only economic growth can provide prosperity and political stability for a nation seeking to survive in a turbulent and fearful world. When the chips are down, money speaks with as much assurance as a gun. A gun can conquer a country, but it can't plow a field, dig a well, or fuel a power plant. In the final analysis, economic strength is the true source of a nation's power and influence on the world scene.

2. Economic strength can be gained only if there is a free market system at work. A government can neither dictate nor plan how the law of supply and demand—the vital ingredient of a free market economy—will function. The free market system can also work efficiently and profitably, even in a society that is basically undemocratic, as it does in Singapore, South Korea, and Hong Kong. The essential element must be a political climate that is favorable and supportive of business operations.

3. The twin plagues that afflict a majority of the Third World countries are chronic food shortages and inept, corrupt, and rapacious native-ruled governments. And each plague lives off the other. Control of a government is a supreme prize, for it is just about the only immediate source of power and wealth for those strong enough to gain public office. There are few other channels to personal advancement in a Third World country. But corrupt and inept government results in economic disruption and serious damage to the local agriculture. In general, shortages of food are caused by widespread poverty and mismanagement. In recent years the myth has been perpetuated by the Club of Rome and leading demographists such as Paul Ehrlich that the world's population is increasing faster than food production. This is a quick and seemingly plausible explanation for the "hunger belts" which now disfigure the global landscape. Yet this simply is not true, as is clearly set forth in a new study by Prof. Julian L. Simon of the University of Illinois.[1]

Prof. Simon, using the official statistics of both the U.S. Department of Agriculture and the United Nations Food and Agriculture Organization, points out that there has been a *steady per capita increase* in world food production for the last three decades. For example, the

[1]Julian L. Simon, *The Ultimate Resource* (Princeton, N.J.: Princeton University Press, 1982).

FAO data shows a 28% increase in food production by 1972 compared to the 1948–52 period. The U.S. Department of Agriculture shows an even bigger per capita gain in available food for the same period. Yet food shortages continue. Two examples: years ago Indonesia grew enough rice to feed its population, with a surplus for export. Now it has to import rice for its 160 million people. The African Republic of Gabon was blessed with a robust and money-making agricultural economy a decade ago, producing more than enough food to feed itself and export its surplus to neighboring countries. Then oil was discovered and the farm boys rushed off to the cities to get high-paying jobs created by the new petroleum prosperity. Today Gabon must import over 95% of the food consumed by its population of 600,000.

The insecure governments in most Third World nations try to keep down the prices of food for the benefit of their growing and restless urban populations, which are the base of their political support. Since the remaining farmers can no longer eke out a living in the depressed market, they are harvesting only enough to feed themselves and their families. Once this fact of life is clearly understood, practical measures can be undertaken to alleviate the situation, and to cease squandering immeasurable billions of dollars in foreign aid loans and grants to the Third World. Then, and only then, can mutually beneficial collaboration between the industrial nations and the Third World bloc develop. Once a Third World country can "get off welfare" and get involved in productive work, it can become self-supporting. It then can become an expanding market for the goods and services of the industrial nations.

4. Marxian socialism and its errant sibling, Communism, have lost their credibility. They are the "paper tigers" of the political world. The Marxian formula of a "planned economy" to assure adequate food and other necessities for the poor and the oppressed just doesn't work according to plan or promise. The prime fault is not hard to find. It lies in a denial of one of the most basic instincts of mankind: It seeks to outlaw or immobilize man's appetite for material gain by identifying it as antisocial. But men and nations become rich and powerful largely because of their sharpened acquisitive talents.

5. Nationalism is the dominating political force in the world today. It overshadows the unceasing rivalry for the attention of the masses between political parties and ideologies from the right to the left. In 1945 when the United Nations was formed there were fifty charter members. Today there are over 150 states on the UN roll call. Nationalism is, after all, an advanced form of tribalism, which by itself develops the cohesive quality of any society. Nationalism gives

people a sense of identification in the family of nations. By evoking it, the rulers of these new nations can consolidate their political power in their own countries. And nationalism can also mobilize the strength and resources of a country faster and to a greater degree than any political ideology. For example, in the bitter cold winter of 1941–42 when Hitler's armies reached the outskirts of Moscow, the call went out from the ramparts of the Kremlin to the Russian people "to defend *Motherland Russia* against the Nazi invader"—not to defend the "Union of Soviet Socialist Republics." Also contrast the fervent and angry patriotism displayed by the American public after the bombing of Pearl Harbor and throughout World War II with its skeptical and critical attitude toward the involvement of U.S. forces in an ideological war against Communism in the jungles of Vietnam some twenty years later. Thus the new postwar nations are learning that nationalism serves them better in the pursuit of their own self-interests than any political ideology.

6. Finally, there is definite and perceptible shifting in the balance of power away from the Communist bloc toward the industrial nations of the free world. It has been set in motion by economic forces at work. Just as a vat of fermenting grapes, if properly handled, can be transformed into wine, so too can the economic processes of change and evolution alter the shape and character of international affairs so that political stability and prosperity become achievable objectives. They are goals within our reach, but we have to work for them. They can be snatched from our grasp by an outbreak of war in Europe or the Middle East involving the superpowers. But the prize is supremely worth our best efforts: the possibility of ending the cold war between the superpowers; the lessening of the threat of a nuclear holocaust. The following pages consider how the global transformation can be attained through the application of ecopolitics.

In its troubled and mutually hostile relationship with the Soviet Union, the United States has been influenced by old concepts and beliefs which are so rooted in the national thinking that they have acquired the patina of revealed truth. They are serious obstacles in the search for an acceptable solution to the seemingly endless cold war with the Kremlin in Moscow. Also the government in Washington has become unthinking in its almost Pavlovian responses to Russia's provocative words and deeds. In their fear of being cast in an aggressive role, the Americans always let the Russians keep the initiative in their global contest for supremacy. For example, in the long history of the United Nations, the United States has exercised its right of veto over the Security Council's decisions only sparingly because it did not want to appear to be abusing its special great-power status and its unchallengeable ability to block UN action inimical to its self-interests. The Russians have used their veto power without any hesitancy to serve their own self-interests, racking up hundreds of "No" votes. It is ironic that for all its forbearance, today the United States finds itself constantly under attack in the halls of the United Nations by almost all of its members. The Americans seem to be always on the defensive, ignoring the time-tested maxim that in politics and in war, as in sport, the best defense is to go on the offense. That is a ploy constantly used by the strategists in the Kremlin.

The U.S. government is always strong on rhetoric—constantly "viewing with alarm," "deploring," and so forth—in reacting to events and situations that are politically favorable to the Russians. The U.S. State Department seems to regard the spoken word as a weapon which can decisively influence international affairs; the Russians instead put their trust in the Kalashnikov automatic rifle or the S-20 nuclear missile to communicate their foreign policy. If a government is truly competent as well as confident of its power to influence world affairs, it does not require its secretary of state to be constantly issuing statements every time somebody in the Politburo slams a door or makes a rude remark.

Another misconception that afflicts Washington's policymakers is the assumption that the "Russian problem" will be close to solution on the day when America enjoys full military parity, if not superiority, with Russia on the land, on the sea, and in the air. For military strength is mistakenly viewed as the most accurate yardstick to measure America's power and influence on the world stage. Military parity, however, won't end the cold war or lower international tension; it can only produce a stalemate for an indefinite period of time. What is required is a new instrument to finish off the cold war; some new form of leverage other than brute military strength that can force or persuade the Russian leaders to revise their present aggressive and imperialistic policies. Then, and only then, can a big step be taken by the two superpowers to reduce their nuclear arsenals, with some degree of mutual trust prevailing between Moscow and Washington.

Finally there is the myth that the Soviet Union is an ideologically motivated country. If that were really so, the world would not be such a perilous place for mankind today. In theory, Communism is a secular religion, whose widely proclaimed objective is economic improvement in the daily lives of the masses of workers and farmers. Communism is to liberate mankind from the economic bondage allegedly imposed by the capitalist system on the poor and powerless of this world. However, if the Soviet Union truly practiced Communism as preached by its founding father, Karl Marx, Russia and its satellites would be much happier and more prosperous nations than they are today. Instead, under the "dictatorship of the proletariat," the Russian people have exchanged their "capitalist chains" for the real-life bondage of the KGB, the Gulag Archipelago, and the conformity of the totalitarian state. Considering that Russia is the second-ranking industrial power in the world—though Japan probably has surpassed Russia in this category—it has not accomplished very much in improving the living standards of its peoples in almost seven decades of Communist rule. Russia's millions of citizens still have to spend long hours each day in queuing up for scarce supplies of food and consumer goods. As an ideology claiming to be solely concerned with the building of a better and more equitable way of life for the great unwashed Russian *Lumpenproletariat*, the Soviet system falls far short of fulfilling its social contract with the people it governs. And if Communism were a living and working ideology, relevant to the spiritual and physical needs of mankind—if, for example, it were comparable in its operations to the Catholic Church with its global network of followers—then Communism would be a much more formidable political force around the world. It would have established a grip on the masses, not only in Europe but throughout the Third World, that would be extremely difficult for anti-Communist governments to combat successfully in peace or in war.

Stripped of its political camouflage, the Union of Soviet Socialist Republics is an *imperium*, ruled by a self-perpetuating oligarchy, the Politburo. This body politic, which has its headquarters in the Kremlin—the Russian word for "fortress"—maintains unbending totalitarian control of Russia and its satellites, socially, politically, economically, and militarily. When the 1917 revolution toppled Nicholas II, the last of the Romanov czars, from his throne, a small band of resolute Bolsheviks led by Lenin seized control of Russia. Through terror, intimidation, and military force, they established their "dictatorship of the proletariat" as the opening phase of Communism. But the "withering away of [state] government" originally promised by Karl Marx and Friedrich Engels, and echoed by Lenin, that was to occur once Communism was established was never to take place. Instead the mindless and cruel autocracy of the Romanov dynasty was replaced by the more inhumane and ruthless autocracy of the Kremlin in the persons of Lenin, Trotsky, Stalin, Khrushchev, Brezhnev, and their Politburo colleagues.

The most effective way to checkmate the Soviet Union is to exploit its glaring weaknesses, notably in the field of economics. What will bring to a halt Russia's geopolitical expansion can be summed up in one word: *ecopolitics*—that is, the intelligent mobilization of the superior economic strength of the United States and its resources, and applying this force to achieve certain political objectives at the expense of the Soviet Union. Whenever possible this program should be undertaken in concert with the other industrial nations. Hence, instead of concentrating on trying to correct the present military imbalance now favoring the Soviet Union—though it is questionable whether the Russian armed forces actually are militarily superior to those of the United States—Washington would do well to recast its long-range strategy in line with economic realities rather than military imponderables.

At this point it is important to keep in mind that any ecopolitical program of action should not close out the possibility, if time and circumstances are ripe, of arriving at some new pragmatic relationship with the post-Brezhnev leaders of the Soviet Union. As the members of a new and younger Politburo finally reach the seats of power, they will obviously have their own ideas and objectives concerning the future of the Soviet Union. They may be more hard-line and politically adventurous than Brezhnev & Co., willing to risk an all-out military confrontation with the United States for control of the Middle East or Western Europe. On the other hand, the members of the new Politburo may seek to avert a collapse of the Soviet Union by pushing through a crash program of economic reforms. This alternative, which would involve a 180-degree turnabout in foreign policy, also has its attractive possibilities. As the London *Economist* reported (Dec. 27, 1980):

> The Soviet Union's Europeans (West-oriented) are almost as educated as the West Germans were in 1948. A dash for freedom on the West German 1948 pattern could bring a Russian economic miracle. Western strategy should be directed towards giving Russia's quite intelligent *apparatchiks* every incentive to start this dash for economic freedom without losing face. . . .

So U.S. ecopolitical policy should have both the carrot and the stick, but in the opening phases, the stick has to be applied rather vigorously, so as to make the Kremlin fully aware of the price it must pay for continuing on its present neo-imperialist course.

The biggest and most readily available stick is money power. A second stick is technology, and a third measure to shock the Kremlin into a new awareness of Western ecopolitical power is to create an entirely new and pragmatic economic relationship with the Third

World countries, home of three-quarters of the globe's population. It would be based on "trade, not aid," giving commercial and industrial incentives to the less-developed countries to align their economic future with international trends and high technology.

The cold war between Moscow and Washington is entering into a new and unforeseen arena of conflict and contention. As Felix Rohatyn, senior partner of Lazard Frères, stated recently: "World events make it increasingly clear that trade and credits will be a major element in our international posture towards the Soviet Union for the rest of the century."[2]

In the field of international trade and finance, the United States appears to hold most of the trump cards; it has resources, background, and experience that overshadow the Russians. In this new relationship, money speaks with more authority than weaponry. The United States possesses an instrument with which it can exert great leverage on the Kremlin. It could be the decisive factor in the cold war; it could force the Russians to reform their own economy and the economies of their satellite countries, or it could also goad the hardline militarists in the Politburo to stake all on preemptive strikes at the Middle East or Europe. However, until now the United States has been on the point of throwing away this advantage through the short-sighted policies of leading Wall Street banks and the State Department in Washington.

The long cold war between the Soviet Union and the United States has had its periods of armistice and détente, alternating with high tension and confrontation, such as the Cuban missile crisis. The period of détente, which has now waned, was originally introduced by the late Premier Alexei Kosygin. He was one of the few members of the Politburo who had an understanding of economic realities. Kosygin saw the opportunity for the Soviet Union to obtain the technology of the industrial nations by opening up Russia to increased trade with the West. Russia's credit with the West was good; the Soviet Union had plentiful oil, gold, and vital minerals to pay for its purchases. And western industrialists were happy to oblige with generous credit terms. London and New York bankers established offices in Moscow to facilitate East-West trade. The satellite countries also opened their doors to western businessmen. Détente was not only politically but economically popular on both sides of the Iron Curtain.

But Russia could not increase its exports to pay for the capital

---

[2]Quoted in the *Wall Street Journal*, April 19, 1982.

goods and technology imported from the West. This was largely due to the fact that Kosygin's program of economic reforms was dropped. These reforms threatened to disrupt the totalitarian control of the Soviet Union imposed by the Communist Party apparatus. Lacking stimulus, the economic growth rate began its slow but steady decline from a high point of almost 11% annually for the 1951–55 period to 4% in 1977. It is now impossible to obtain reliable reports on the current state of economic health of the Soviet Union, except that it is getting worse.

However, Russia and the satellite nations of Eastern Europe continued their buying of western technology as well as consumer goods, despite the fact that their own exports were falling behind their imports. In the last seven years, according to reliable estimates (*Wall Street Journal, Business Week, New York Times*, etc.), the cumulative trade deficit of the six satellites for the period 1975–81 inclusive has totaled about $80 billion. The Russian trade deficit alone for that period was $19 billion. These are the Communist bloc's debts now owed to western bankers, who financed this trade. (Incidentally, the financial assistance given by the western bankers to the Warsaw Pact countries is about four times the amount of Marshall Plan assistance given to Western Europe by the United States after World War II.)

In other words, Russia and the six East European satellites—East Germany, Czechoslovakia, Romania, Bulgaria, Poland, and Hungary—have about exhausted their reserves of hard currency to pay their import bills and to meet the scheduled payments of principal and interest on their multibillion-dollar foreign bank loans. For Russia this situation has been further aggravated by the third consecutive bad harvest in 1981. This requires increased outlay of scarce hard currency of an estimated $7.5 billion in 1982 to pay for foreign wheat, corn, and soya beans to feed Ivan Ivanovich and his family, as well as the pigs, cows, and chickens down on the collective farm. Hence, the Soviet Union has been dipping into its gold reserves—90 tons in 1980, 235 tons in 1981, and an estimated 400 tons in 1982 to satisfy its hard-currency needs of upward of $30 billion in 1982. According to knowledgeable bullion dealers in Zurich and London, the Soviet Union has an annual gold production of about 300 tons. Professor Philip Hanson of England's Birmingham University was quoted in the *Wall Street Journal* (March 18, 1982) as estimating that Russia's gold reserves are about equal to one-half the cost of its yearly imports at the 1982 rate. And they are steadily being reduced in tonnage and in value to about $22 billion.

So the economic scene is inexorably changing. The glaring weakness of the Communist bloc is becoming more exposed every day. Poland, which owes western bankers some $27 billion, and Romania, which owes over $12 billion, are in serious financial difficulties. Their economies are so disrupted that they cannot possibly earn enough hard currency to keep up payments on the western loans. For all practical purposes they are bankrupt. Governments cannot admit to bankruptcy. However, failure to pay their bills means risking a complete cut-off from western credit sources, which could lead to the collapse of their individual economies.

The cost of operating its new *imperium* is becoming prohibitively expensive for the Kremlin. The six satellites were scheduled to pay the western banks $14.8 billion in 1981, while Russia itself had to lay out another $3 billion for its own principal and interest payments. These debt charges amounted to almost 60% of the export earnings of the satellites, and obviously they cannot continue this payment schedule on their own. The Soviet Union has to come to their rescue. Until now (the spring of 1982) the Russians have been doling out hard currency to the nearly bankrupt satellites, totaling over $6 billion in 1981. This is a drain which the Soviet Union can ill afford as its oil income declines—$3 billion drop in 1981—because of the world petroleum glut. The western bankers, now far out on a limb with loans to the Communist bloc, are in no mood to extend fresh credits, unless there are drastic changes in fiscal policies and practices on the other side of the Iron Curtain. As the London *Economist* pungently editorialized (Feb. 13, 1982):

> The whip of withheld credit is now shifting into Western bankers' hands, not into Russia's. Russia and Eastern Europe are going to need at least a minimum trickle of credit from the West's bankers; either that or the Communist empire in Eastern Europe is going to be forced into so complete an economic isolation over the next ten years that every Russian rifle will end up turned on its own peoples, every Russian tank will cost 1,000 unfertilized acres of grainland to manufacture, and any Russian adventure abroad will eventually stretch its resources beyond what is possible. . . . The whiphand is there because Eastern Europe has come to depend far more heavily on imports from the main credit-suppliers of the West than either Western bankers or Western exporters depend on East Europe's market. People forget this. . . .

There is an old adage in business circles: If you owe your banker $1,000, you have a problem; if you owe him $1 million, it becomes *his* problem. Hence it would appear at first glance that the Warsaw Pact nations are in a relatively good bargaining position to pressure the western bankers into restructuring the terms of their loans on a more favorable basis. The mountain of debt owed the West is piled high, up to $80 billion, and may reach $140 billion by 1985, that is if the bankers involved will renegotiate these loans and extend fresh credits. However, Wall Street, London, and Düsseldorf are reacting negatively to Moscow's siren song. High interest rates in Europe and the United States make it more attractive to keep money at home. Hence the unthinkable looms up on the horizon—the possibility of declaring Poland and other satellites in default on their bank loans. But any stoppage of East-West trade brought about by default action would be catastrophic for the Warsaw Pact bloc, collectively and individually. Their import programs are tightly organized to cover the most essential capital equipment and spare parts to keep local factories in operation and also to include those consumer goods necessary to hold public discontent under control. In short, the Communist regimes are down virtually to a bare-bones subsistence level; they have no room for maneuver, no time to play for new and more favorable trade and credit arrangements with the western industrial nations.

As Felix Rohatyn pointed out: "We should recognize that the availability of large-scale credit facilities is a strategic weapon, the one major item the U.S. can withhold which the Soviet Union cannot obtain elsewhere. In a world increasingly short of capital, credit is harder and harder to obtain."[3]

Financial and political circles in the United States are somewhat divided over whether or not to invoke default on debts of the Warsaw Pact countries that will never be fully repaid. The same reluctance is voiced in Europe about taking this step. However, that is more a question of tactics than of grand strategy. In the final analysis, the important factor is that America has an *ecopolitical* weapon which can decisively affect the fortunes of the Soviet Union and its satellites, adversely or favorably. In essence, the unchallengeable financial strength and assets of the United States can be either a carrot or a stick in our relationship with the Soviet Union and its *imperium.*

It is an amazing development in the cold war. Now it can be seen quite clearly that we have reached a point *where western financial aid is vital to sustain the economies of the Communist bloc.* It is a surprising discovery that the Communist monolith on the other side of the Iron Curtain requires blood transfusions of cold capitalist cash to stave off bankruptcy and economic collapse. This in itself is a new indictment of the Communist system, as fathered by Marx and developed by Lenin, Stalin, Khrushchev, and Brezhnev.

[3]Ibid.

This new phase of the cold war arises out of the faulty judgments of western banks. Financing a new surge of exports of western capital and consumer goods to the Communist bloc seemed like an opportunity to profit, one not to be neglected. For the Russians and the satellite governments it was a heaven-sent chance to get into business on somebody else's money. Loaning hundreds of millions of dollars without any collateral, solely on the untested credit-worthiness of the Communist regimes, did not appear risky to the banks. For example, West Germany's banks, which made the biggest loans to Poland, had the support and encouragement of the Bonn government. Like Adam and Eve in the garden of Paradise, the Communists "ate the forbidden fruit"—they borrowed to the hilt to shop in the western markets for technology, capital equipment, and consumer goods. Soon they too were "hooked" by their new dependence on western financing and goods.

Let us consider this development further so as to understand its potentials for the superpowers. Considered by itself, the Soviet Union is not in any serious financial crunch. In a less turbulent world, it is a good credit risk. The Soviet Union is rich in natural assets: oil, gas, gold, diamonds, strategic minerals, etc., all of which have a ready world market to bring in hard currency. The trouble is that its fabulous reserves of energy and other assets are for the most part buried under the frozen tundra in remote Siberia. To extract and process these assets for the world markets, Russia needs western technology—and that in turn requires hard currency. And the world's bankers are becoming more reluctant to extend fresh credits over the Iron Curtain.

In addition, the satellite countries, led by Poland and Romania, have gotten into deep financial waters, well over their heads, for a total of $80 billion. To keep its *imperium* intact the Russians cannot permit any of these nations, particularly Poland, to be declared in default of its debts to the West. For this would precipitate "a tidal wave of uncreditworthiness across Eastern Europe. . . . After any stoppage of east-west trade, the wind blowing through Russia's east European empire would be extreme indeed."[4] In other words, it would shake the foundations of the Russian *imperium*. Russia's No. 1 priority is to prevent this "tidal wave" from getting started, because if it does start, the Kremlin lacks the hard-currency reserves or a central banking mechanism to get any control over it, once it is set in motion.

The only way to stave off the economic collapse of the Soviet *imperium* is for Moscow to underwrite the extra costs of the declining

---

[4]*Economist*, Feb. 13, 1982.

industrial and agricultural production brought on by the continuance of the iron-clad Communist Party rule of the satellites. The first sign of rebellion against the Communist straitjacket must be snuffed out quickly, as we have seen in the imposition of martial law in Poland and the outlawing of the Solidarity free trade union movement. The Kremlin cannot permit the satellites to enjoy any real freedom to run their own economies as they see fit. For that inevitably leads to the dissolution of Communist control. Now faced with the results of their totalitarian system's inflexibility, the members of the Politburo must get queasy feelings in their guts when reviewing the latest trade figures. For 1982 the Soviet Union will have a $9 billion deficit on its own foreign trade balance of payments. It will pay over $25 billion in hard currency for its imports, of which $7.5 billion will be for grain and other food stocks, because of successive bad harvests. On top of these expenditures will be another $6–8 billion to western banks to pay installments on the foreign loans of the satellites. This financial burden comes at a time when the long-term deterioration of Russian economic performance is reaching a crisis level.

Bernard Dettweiler, chief economist for the West German Bank für Gemeinwirtschaft, has summed up the growing pessimism in western financial circles about the Soviet Union crisis: "If they can't modify the economic system within three to five years, it will break down."[5] Herr Dettweiler should know; his bank is the biggest single creditor of the U.S.S.R. with $265 million in outstanding loans to the Russians.

If the United States seeks to punish the Soviet Union through trade sanctions and embargos, it must be very careful. For example, it would be a serious mistake to impose another embargo on grain shipments to the Soviet Union. On the contrary, Washington should pray that Russia has a succession of bad harvests in the coming years, forcing it to spend its reserves of gold and hard currency to buy American wheat, soya beans, etc. Depriving the Soviet Union of hard currency is a more damaging economic measure than a grain embargo. Besides, a grain embargo also reduces the income of American farmers.

Invoking trade sanctions and other economic disciplines is always a chancy operation. There are always other countries which stand ready to supply the embargoed goods and services. When President Carter cut off grain shipments to the Soviet Union, Argentina and other wheat-producing countries were quick to supplant the United

---

[5]Quoted in *Business Week*, March 1, 1982.

States as a prime supplier to the U.S.S.R. Years ago the U.N. trade embargo placed on Rhodesia (now Zimbabwe) leaked like a sieve. The former British colony managed to survive despite sanctions, because it was a market for western-made goods, and its products—copper and chrome—were needed in the industrial countries. It is likely that if the United States unilaterally seeks to cut off Russia from importing high-technology products and systems from the West, this blockade might also develop serious leaks. However, there is one important new factor in this field of economic warfare: The number of countries involved in high technology, including electronics, is small.

The Russians and the Czechs, Poles, Romanians, and other Eastern Europeans need western technology to modernize their industries and their armed forces, and machinery and equipment to produce a minimum of consumer goods to placate their restive populations, which are hungry for improvements in their drab and skimpy daily existence. Sanctions on technology as well as western credits can be made to work if Washington can clearly convince the other industrial nations that it is the most practical and cheapest way to reduce the threat of a war between the superpowers.

If, for example, the United States could organize an OTEC—an Organization of Technology Exporting Countries—similar to OPEC, the Middle East oil cartel, a greater measure of control could be exercised on exports of technology to the Warsaw Pact bloc. OPEC has lost much of its effectiveness because it could control only about 44% of the world's daily production of crude oil. It also concentrated on keeping the prices as high as possible. Thus, when conservation measures created an oil glut OPEC was subject to the laws of supply and demand and the oil cartel could no longer control world prices. By contrast, an OTEC could be a much more effective cartel, because it could control virtually *all* western technology. But it must involve the active cooperation of the United States, Japan, West Germany, Great Britain, France, and perhaps one or two other industrial nations as a nucleus. Working together such a group could cut off up to 90% of Russia's imports of western technology, including electronics. Simultaneously it could also control the flow of credit and loans. In the final analysis, Russia and the satellites need western financing to purchase western technology. And in this connection, the big commercial banks in Britain, Western Europe, and the United States always look over their shoulders at their respective governments for guidance in the field of international financing. If, for example, the French or West German government refuses export guarantees for goods and services to certain foreign countries, the banks involved will usually hesitate to participate in such projects.

High technology can also be a carrot instead of a stick in its application to international affairs. In the previous chapter we have examined the changing shape and character of the economies of the United States and other industrial nations in the foreseeable future. In these developments, which are highly ecopolitical in their nature, new political and economic equations are being formed, new fields of industrial, commercial, and financial developments are opening up. In the international field of ever-changing situations and developments, the United States must employ its high technology and financial powers as instruments of foreign policy to hold its friends in line and to deter its opponents from hostile action. In foreign affairs, technology and financial power are relatively new ecopolitical weapons. Americans must learn how to utilize them effectively. Mistakes will be made. But few other nations—certainly not the Communist bloc— have the freedom to experiment with them to the same degree that America now enjoys.

In late 1981, Ivan Arkhipov, first deputy premier of the Soviet Union, told *Time* magazine that his government had no obligation to promote economic development of the Third World countries. Unlike the western nations, he claimed, the U.S.S.R. had never been guilty of exploiting the natural resources of the less-developed nations, as did the "capitalist-imperialist" powers. However, as postwar history clearly shows, the Russians provided these ex-colonial domains with weapons and an ideology to enable their new rulers to stay in power, with or without a mandate from the people. Alain Besançon, the French historian and sociologist, concisely summed up the relationship between the Soviet Union and the Third World: "Everyone in the world knows that Communism produces neither social justice, nor economic development. But it is still seductive because of another promise: to bestow power. That is why many Third World leaders readily identify themselves with socialism in the Bolshevik sense. It seems to afford them a possible guarantee of power."[6]

However, the Third World countries, particularly in black Africa, are becoming more aware that only economic growth, coupled with modern technology, can produce prosperity and a stable society. After a quarter century of tribal conflicts, of one military coup following on

[6]Quoted in *Time*, Jan. 4, 1982.

the heels of another, of graft and corruption, of looted public treasuries, of Marxist-oriented governments which lowered instead of increased the standard of living, the Third World's "reeducation" has begun. The men in government—a minority but a growing minority—are grasping the realities of modern society, learning that true and sustained power develops out of a smoking factory chimney, not out of the smoking gun barrel. A viable economy and a productive agriculture can raise the living standards, while governments whose mandate rests on guns and a Russian ideology impoverish people and provide the political stability of the prison or the grave.

For almost the last two decades the United States and the industrial nations of the West have dealt at arm's length with the Third World nations, individually and en masse. The language of communications has been mainly concerned with how much foreign aid was necessary from year to year to modulate or to temporarily quiet the incessant demands of the less-developed and backward countries for a share of the wealth of the rich and prosperous nations. The relatively short era of colonization of vast areas of Africa, the Middle East, Asia, and the Far East cast its long shadows over the postwar relations between the First and Third Worlds. A "guilt complex" arising out of this colonial past was a powerful factor in the uneasy relationship between the haves and the have-nots. And the Russians, together with the power-hungry and politically amoral rulers of the former colonies, exploited this psychological advantage to the hilt. They extracted all the concessions, political and economic, that the traffic would bear.

As the "world cop and banker" of the postwar era, the United States adopted an avuncular, moralistic approach, taking great pains to avoid giving any offense or arousing suspicions that it was a lineal descendant of "Uncle Shylock" of post–World War I days.[7] The new nations could do no wrong. The growing appetites of their rulers for money and power were viewed as the normal hunger of the adolescent, of a new young and active generation of nations.

However, the time has come to ring down the curtain on this comic opera. The situation is ripe for the United States as the leader of

---

[7]In the mid-1920s, the U.S. government sought repayment of loans granted to the French and British governments during World War I. The European allies claimed that such funds should be considered part of America's contribution to the war effort, inasmuch as the French and British had done most of the fighting and dying. President Calvin Coolidge acerbically responded, "They hired the money, didn't they?"—adding fuel to the controversy. The French newspapers angrily described the U.S. government as "Uncle Shylock, determined to have his pound of flesh." And the slander passed into history.

the industrial nations to go on the offensive with two major objectives in view:

1. To *ecopolitically* outflank the Soviet Union and to sabotage its long-range objectives involving the Third World, which are to deny the capitalist nations easy access to its raw materials and to create as much hostility as possible between the Third World and the United States.

2. To formulate a new and mutually profitable economic relationship with the Third World, or at least with those less-developed countries which have real potential for economic growth. Such a relationship would open up new export markets for the industrial nations as well as provide them with cheaper imports of raw materials and light industrial products from their Third World collaborators. This will take years to fructify, but at least a start can be made in transforming these new nations from being welfare clients of the affluent industrial countries into becoming self-supporting, economically viable states. Countries which enjoy economic growth become the customers of the industrial nations, especially of those nations which assist them in this transition from dependency. West Germany has shown that to be true.

The theme of this new ecopolitical relationship between the "haves" and the "have-nots" should be "trade, not aid." Two basic principles should be laid down as the basis for new economic arrangements between the industrial nations, led by the United States, and the Third World countries. They are:

1. Foreign aid should be given only for development projects which strengthen the economy of the recipient country and also benefit the donor nation.

2. Foreign aid should be conditional on the willingness of the government of the recipient country to give the private business sector the direction and management of the nation's economy.

These new ground rules will no doubt be rejected out of hand by some of the angry and insecure governments of Third World countries. These conditions will be viewed as a distinct invasion of their sovereign rights. Such conditions would contravene or nullify the "New International Economic Order" (NIEO) approved by the United Nations in 1974. This resolution barred "discrimination of any kind" against a Third World country. Placing conditions on foreign aid, taking control of foreign aid out of the hands of local governments, etc., would be regarded as violating the letter and the spirit of NIEO. However, the need to impose new conditions on any foreign aid to the Third World nations is an integral phase of the reeducation of the industrial nations to modern-day realities. This reeducation has cost the industrial nations approximately $500 billion in loans and grants to the less-developed nations; most of it is lost money which can never be retrieved, while the conditions which required this foreign aid have remained the same. That was the lesson to be learned by the affluent industrial countries.

The United States must be prepared to take a hard line in dealing with the Third World countries. If they want foreign aid or financial assistance in one form or another, they must accept certain conditions and abide by them. These conditions will be essentially economic, not political. The prime qualifications are:

1. To let a free market economy function in place of state-imposed controls of prices, exports and imports, agriculture, industrial production, etc.; to have a tax policy with incentives that encourage private business to develop, industrially or commercially.

2. To create a business climate favorable to private enterprise. The more freedom of action a businessman enjoys, the more he increases his own wealth, and in so doing, the more he contributes to the economic health of his own country. Adam Smith, father of capitalism, is the prime reference on this point.

3. To give assistance to agriculture so that the farmer can earn a decent living by local standards, and to make it attractive for him to continue to produce food and keep his workers down on the farm. This reduces the need for foreign aid.

4. To require any industrial development program to be realistic and cost-effective. Building a steel mill or starting a national airline solely to gratify the ego of the ruling shish-kebab is wasteful and counterproductive. Money would be better spent on schools and teachers, or plows and fertilizers.

The state of Pakistan is a prime example of a Third World country engaged in a costly and unrealistic industrialization program. The government is building a $2.5 billion steel mill with a production capacity of 2 million tons a year. However, Pakistan is almost entirely dependent on imports of iron ore and coking coal. Electrical power and water are in short supply. The new steel mill is located in the desert and will consume one-quarter as much electricity as all of Pakistan now uses. In addition, the steel mill lacks a trained cadre of workers. Pakistan Steel is now producing pig iron for delivery to neighboring India for $150 a ton, but its costs per ton are twice that amount. Meanwhile Pakistan's farm output is rising at 8% a year, and its exports of cotton and rice find ready markets throughout the Middle East. Pakistan's industrial potential is questionable, as it has few minerals and fossil fuels, and a primitive transportation system. But as a governmental promotional film about this industrial white elephant proclaims: "A steel industry reflects the economic independence of a country." Maybe there is a future for Pakistan Steel, but it is a long way down the road, according to observers in the country.

5. To survey industrial and commercial capabilities very carefully. Any industrial development program, or the exploitation of its resources such as oil, minerals, food, etc., should be aligned with global economic and technological developments and trends. Japan owes its amazing postwar growth largely to its early recognition of the wide-open global markets for electronic consumer goods and fuel-saving cars.

The general purpose of the economic reforms listed above is simple and basic: to create conditions which enable the private business sector to take root, grow, and flourish in the Third World countries. Perhaps the only reason to feel optimistic about such a program is that it is aligned to a basic instinct of mankind—man's unsatiated desire to acquire wealth and material possessions, which blossoms when freedom and opportunity come together. We are not proposing a utopian formula or a way of life based on ideals rather than the ugly realities of everyday existence. The economic formula herein proposed has been put to the test and it has succeeded beyond all expectation, producing prosperity and stability. Postwar Japan and the Federal Republic of (West) Germany are living proofs of what a free market system can accomplish. These two ex-enemy nations, broken and bankrupt in defeat and severely damaged by the war, were transformed into the major economic powers in the Pacific and European communities of nations. In 1948, Prof. Ludwig Erhard, the architect of postwar Germany's *Wirtschaftswunder* ("economic miracle"), proclaimed: "Turn the people and the money loose and they will make the nation strong." A quarter of a century later West Germany, a nation of only 60 million people, had piled up the largest gold and dollar reserves ($55 billion) of any nation in the world.

Germany and Japan did receive help from the United States in the early postwar years, which enabled these two nations to start their economic revivals. West Germany was granted more than $3.5 billion of Marshall Plan assistance, which acted like a blood transfusion for a man on the point of death. Japan received about $4 billion in procurement orders from the U.S. Army during the Korean war, which provided a foundation for the rebirth of its industry. However, there is absolutely nothing comparable in the way of economic development by the Third World countries to show for the $500 billion in loans and grants they have thus far received. For example, Tanzania, the black African state which has been granted more foreign aid, on a per capita basis, than any other country in the whole world except Israel, has been in a steady economic decline and now requires more handouts. ("Tanzania is still as poor today as it was when it first received its independence in 1961," the *New York Times* reported, Dec. 6, 1982, in a survey of world economic problems.) Julius K. Nyerere, its president, has recently proposed the creation of a technical secretariat by the world's developing nations, the purpose of which is to extract further economic concessions from the industrialized nations and thereby make foreign aid a permanent factor in international affairs.

However, in the future Julius Nyerere and his fellow welfare statesmen are going to find it more difficult to pick the pockets of the industrial nations than it was in the past. Robert McNamara, the president of the World Bank for the period 1968–81, has been replaced by A. W. (Tom) Clausen, former chairman of the Bank of America. In his first speech in his new role as banker to the world, Mr. Clausen warned that no longer will the World Bank be considered the "Robin Hood of the international financial set," which takes from the rich and gives to the poor countries. Mr. Clausen has also made it clear to the developing countries, particularly the black African states, that they will have to put through some basic and painful economic reforms if they wish to obtain further financial assistance. These reforms will involve denationalizing industries and business firms in favor of private ownership, lifting restrictions on foreign imports, ending price controls, etc. The industrial nations will also be asked to increase their foreign aid, which could boost financial assistance for black African nations from $5 billion to over $17 billion a year by 1990. The whole thrust of the Clausen program is to encourage and to strengthen the role of the private business sector in the economic development of the Third World countries; in short, "trade, not aid."

Europe's first ecopolitical state, West Germany, was the first of the industrial nations to see the money-making possibilities of a foreign aid program for its own economy. After much study in the 1950s, the West Germans evolved a loose program based on the unspoken premise that foreign aid should produce trade. A special Federal Ministry for Economic Cooperation was formed, headed by banker Walter Scheel, who later became president of the Federal Republic. Bonn's foreign aid had two basic purposes: to harvest some international goodwill for Germany, still suffering from being the postwar pariah in the family of nations; and to establish business bridgeheads in the Third World countries as future markets for West Germany's goods and services. Water Scheel put it frankly in an interview in the magazine *German International* (March, 1965):

> From an economic standpoint, the development policy is of vital importance to us because the country's economic growth will in the future be even more dependent on development of foreign trade . . . and because our overseas partners can become better and more stable partners only if they themselves achieve economic growth. I should emphasize that in the future *we should be even more courageous in our economic exploitation of development aid.* [Italics added.]

The West German contribution to the foreign aid program was largely in the form of government guarantees of repayment for exports of goods and services to Third World countries which are not reimbursed, or for commercial loans and credits to these developing nations. However, there was a minimum risk involved, for the ground rules were clearly defined. To be eligible for West German government support, a foreign aid project must increase German exports of goods and services or help to secure a continuous flow of vital raw materials from the developing countries. Second, a foreign aid loan or a credit guarantee was evaluated on the same basis as any private investment: Could it be repaid or pay a dividend? If not, the funds were allocated to some other project with better prospects of earning a return to the German economy.

And as the West German foreign aid program expanded in scope and money volume, further guidelines were laid down to make it even more businesslike and orthodox. The prime objective was to utilize foreign aid to expand West Germany's markets in the Third World by assisting in the economic growth of the recipient country, while at the same time assuring the German industrialists and exporters a profitable return on their investments or loans. The main guidelines were as follows:

1. The developing nations in possession of vital raw materials that German industry needs (except for oil) would have to become "active partners" with German firms in the extraction and processing of these commodities as a condition for receiving foreign aid.

2. West Germany's participation in industrial development projects would be concentrated in those Third World nations with "good future prospects" as markets for German goods and services. (West Germany's trade with the developing countries has burgeoned. For example, in 1981 these Third World countries, excluding the OPEC states, took 17.8% of the Federal Republic's exports and provided 19.4% of its total imports. In that year, the combined value of West

German world trade was $340 billion, compared to $507 billion for the United States and $295 billion for third-place Japan.[8])

3. The Bonn government would make financial commitments only where there was "mutual trust" and "long-term legal protection" for the German partner.

4. Transfers of West German capital funds would be made only to those countries with demonstrably good prospects for economic growth.

Finally the Bonn government disclosed its psychological master-stroke. The government and private industry were in full agreement about the long-term value of developing strong and lasting ties with the present and future generations in the new nations of Africa and Asia. The most effective way to impress on their awakening populations the intrinsic merits and superiority of West German goods and services was to initiate and maintain physical contact with their younger people. To this end the Ministry of Economic Cooperation spent millions to bring thousands of young Africans and Asians to West Germany to attend vocational schools and technical universities. By 1970 more than twenty thousand scholarships had been provided young Africans and Asians. They came to study engineering, chemistry, electronics, machinery, auto production, and related heavy and light industries. In addition over two thousand vocational training teachers from the Third World were given an education in the latest of West Germany's industrial production and techniques. These cadres of vocational teachers, as well as the students, would return to their native lands to seed their knowledge and experience of German technology to new generations of students who might never have the opportunity to study in a modern industrial state.

Equally important, out of this large-scale educational program would come the future overseas sales representatives and technical personnel to staff the offices of German subsidiaries in the Third World. The ultimate value of this program would lie in the fact that thousands of Africans and Asians would henceforth "think German" when faced with economic and industrial development in their home countries. And that would help to hold and to expand these market areas for German exports.

Quite surprisingly the Japanese have never followed the West Germans in this field of economic promotion. The xenophobic Japanese do not welcome foreigners in their closed society. About half-a-

[8]Figures from German Information Office, New York City, May 1982.

million Koreans are resident in Japan, the largest group of foreigners in the country. But their presence is mutually vexatious, perhaps more so because the Japanese have always regarded the Koreans as a subject people rather than equals.

The Russians, while welcoming African and Asian students to the Soviet Union and also offering them political indoctrination disguised as education, could not duplicate the high level of technological training that West Germany offered the young men and teachers from the Third World. The United States has opened its doors to some 1.5 million Asians and Africans and other Third World nationals, but Washington aimed at attracting students to the halls of academe and not to the assembly lines of Ford or Chevrolet for on-the-spot vocational schooling.

In the final analysis and stripped of its political euphemisms, West Germany's "foreign aid" program was based on a simple *quid pro quo:* no foreign aid unless it could pay a dividend to the Bundesrepublik. And to make them work on a businesslike basis, the foreign aid projects were handled from the beginning by individual companies or by consortiums of German industrial firms and banks. The Bonn government provided export and financing guarantees against loss if the projects strictly followed the guidelines set forth by the Ministry for Economic Cooperation. The philosophy behind it was simple: Foreign aid should be viewed as an investment in a development project that produced benefits for the recipient and donor alike.

This uncomplicated theory and practice of foreign aid enabled West Germany to steer clear of the burdensome social, moral, political, and economic considerations, attitudes, and controversies that have roiled the relations between the affluent industrial countries of the world and the Third World. This pragmatic approach to foreign aid did wonders to expand West Germany's exports of its goods and services to the global markets. Economic orthodoxy again scored another major if unpublicized victory in world affairs; it made a substantial contribution to Germany's economic rebirth and to its unexpected rise to become the second trading nation in the world after the United States. It was also a prime example of ecopolitics in action.

The United States would do well to incorporate a large measure of West Germany's foreign aid policies and practices in its own approach to the Third World countries. The original purpose of U.S. foreign aid was to assist "the undeveloped countries"—as they were originally labeled—to become economically self-sufficient as far as circumstances permitted. In theory this would give them a stake in a capitalist world economy and effectively immunize them against the viruses of socialism and Communism. Unfortunately theory clashed with reality—and lost.

Billions of dollars in grants and loans, as well as shipments of foods, medical supplies, and other necessities, were handed over to the local governments. They used this largesse in many cases to consolidate their own political constituencies and to open up new financial connections with Swiss banks, as repositories of their skim-off of foreign aid pelf. The net political return to the United States for its multibillion-dollar foreign aid has been virtually zero. If there is any doubt about that, check the latest voting breakdown in the United Nations General Assembly on any issue which involves the United States. There is, as former Ambassador Daniel P. Moynihan once described it, a "tyranny of the majority," a bloc of almost a hundred countries which votes as a unit against any position taken by the United States in the deliberations of the UN. And they are all Third World nations.

Incentive is the key which opens up the Third World. If applied intelligently, an ecopolitical program based on incentives can accomplish for the United States what billions of dollars in "foreign aid" have thus far failed to attain—political stability and economic growth in the turbulent Third World. If a significant number of African and Asiatic nations can be involved in this new form of foreign aid, the United States will have successfully outflanked the Soviet *imperium*, economically and politically. The ebb tide will have set in against Soviet expansion, as the Third World—covering three-quarters of the global population—will begin to become aware that capitalism and not Marxist socialism can better their bare-bones existence. And as the economic growth flourishes in these countries, the Third World can become the new business frontier for American multinational corporations, both large and small.

An incentive program has to provide economic rewards for the participating parties—for the U.S. multinational firms as well as for the industrially backward countries which collaborate in any joint development program, at least for those nations which are important in Washington's foreign policy. An incentive system replaces the traditional foreign aid of loans and grants. It is virtually all carrot and no stick, but most important it does not involve large cash outlays from the U.S. government to a Third World country to buy its political friendship and support. And what is proposed here is not a theory, untested in the political marketplace. West Germany has effectively demonstrated how a so-called foreign aid program can be an instrument to increase its exports of goods and services, as well as to obtain favorable business arrangements for the imports of vital raw materials from Third World countries. The West German program is based on incentives both for the German firms and for the recipient states. The basic German premise is: *Foreign aid develops trade.*

A practical example of the incentive system at work to promote U.S. overseas industrial operations is given by Peter F. Drucker in his latest book. He reports how a "well-known electronics company and a pioneer in semi-conductor technology" has twelve thousand people—more than half of its work force—in West Africa and does two-thirds of its manufacturing there, thousands of miles from Silicon Valley. The project is handled by a West African subcontractor and the whole operation is financed by local banks. The security for this financing is the firm commitment of the parent company to purchase the entire output of the West African workers. When asked how much U.S. capital is invested in the production-sharing venture, a company official replied: "Two Pan American round-trip tickets a month."[9]

This is almost a textbook case of how the private business sector can accomplish the goals that governmental foreign aid policy sets for itself but cannot achieve, and at a minimum of risk and expense. The incentive system is the only effective way to promote economic growth and political stability, because only through incentives can the talents and energies of a society be fully mobilized and made productive. In this instance, the production-sharing project provides jobs for local natives who would otherwise be unemployed. The country's economy is benefited by the export of the made-in-Africa electronic components. As its economic growth increases through this and other industrial development ventures, the Third World country will be able to increase its purchases of capital and consumer goods from the United States and other western nations. Thereby it boosts its potential industrial capacity to manufacture and export more products. In this progressive fashion a market is built up for western goods and services, the developing country's standard of living increases dramatically, and incentive to continue along this road to prosperity and political stability is strengthened. The Soviet *imperium* has nothing comparable to offer the Third World—where it will eventually lose whatever gains it has thus far achieved in three decades of mischievous troublemaking.

---

[9]Peter F. Drucker, *Managing in Turbulent Times* (New York: Harper & Row, 1980). Asked to name the electronics company involved in this production-sharing venture, Mr. Drucker replied: "Sorry, this is confidential information."

On the American side, such a production-sharing venture does not involve a major monetary investment, yet the parent company is better able to compete on the domestic and international markets with its cheaper electronic components made in Africa. And a start has been made to establish an American business bridgehead in this West African nation. This encourages other U.S. corporations to initiate similar production-sharing projects. This trend could be further stimulated if the U.S. government also provided incentives for multinationals to expand their overseas operations, such as special tax deductions, export guarantee insurance, etc. In any event, the amount of money involved would be far less than the billions of regular foreign aid which Washington hands out annually. These incentives would ultimately generate a far higher rate of economic growth per dollar previously spent trying to keep the Third World out of Russian hands. This is assured because control of the industrial development of a Third World country would be taken out of the hands of the corrupt and inept local government officials and given over to entrepreneurs who have to survive and profit by the inexorable laws of supply and demand.

The United States leads the world in the dollar volume of its exports, but its share of the international trade pie has dropped from 22% to 10% in the last three decades. Only America's agricultural exports have doubled in recent years, largely because of Russia's faltering harvests and global food shortages. And that gain owes nothing to U.S. commercial initiative. Fortunately until now America's national economy has been more evenly balanced than those of other countries. Except for some strategic minerals and oil from the Middle East, it has been almost self-sufficient. Hence its exports account for only 9.9% of its gross national product. In other industrial countries, exports are vital for their economic survival. By comparison, West Germany's total exports are 28.9% of its GNP, Great Britain's 28%, France's 21%, and Japan's 13%. Japan is the Third World trader, because, for example, it must import about 90% of its fuel and energy (oil and coal) and about the same percentage of its food. It must export or go hungry and see its industry decline for lack of sufficient fuel and energy.

However, technology is changing the form and character of the modern industrial state, at least for its three leaders: the United States, Japan, and West Germany. High technology is able to reduce their production costs, principally by reducing the numbers of workers involved in manufacturing operations. Those labor-intensive industries which cannot drastically cut their labor costs must shift their operations to countries where cheap labor is available. For example, South Korean steel can be sold on the world markets today at half the cost per ton that U.S. Steel must charge. U.S. Steel can stay in business only if it is protected by a high tariff. However, as the old-line industrial giants gradually transfer some of their operations to new overseas bases, they help the Third World countries to develop their own industrial potentials. In turn, these countries become expanding markets for the capital and consumer goods and services of the high-technology countries.

Hence it is imperative for the whole U.S. business community to become more internationally minded and knowledgeable about overseas developments than ever before. America's two principal trading competitors, Japan and West Germany, have a long lead on the United States in overseas business operations, particularly in the Third World sphere. For the Americans to lag behind, in the face of the new technological revolution that is taking place, is to court economic disaster in the long run.

The threatening character of the 1980s requires some new strategies and tactics to break the long deadlock between the two superpowers. For three decades the cold war has persisted, its intensity rising and falling from one international crisis to another. Washington and Moscow are bending their minds and their muscles to strengthen their respective armed forces, as if these factors alone contained the answers to questions that plague their every waking hour: Who will be victorious? What will be the price of survival, win or lose? Even if a fragile peace can be maintained, poised on a razor-thin margin, the fundamental conflict between the two superpowers and their differing philosophies of life will not be resolved until some startlingly new and decisive element is introduced in the struggle.

Just as Adolf Hitler's *Blitzkrieg* conquest of Poland and France and Admiral Yamamoto's successful aircraft carrier attack on "battleship row" in Pearl Harbor changed the character and tempo of modern warfare, so too can a new and unexpected development in the cold war decisively tilt the balance of power between the United States and the Soviet Union.

The time has come for the United States to open up a new phase in the political cold war that has been hampering global stability and economic development ever since the end of World War II. It is a situation that truly calls for an "agonizing reappraisal," but *not in the terms of military brinkmanship*—of going to the edge of the precipice—as the late hard-lining John Foster Dulles so often threatened.[10]

The time has come to go on the offensive in an area of confrontation of America's own choice, with weapons that surpass anything that the Russians can bring into play. This is the moment to mobilize America's vast reservoir of economic capabilities and experience, of financial resources and monetary expertise, of industrial and technological capacities. The long-range objective of this new ecopolitical campaign is to halt the outward spread of the Soviet *imperium*, but not in a military struggle. The objective is to disrupt the whole body politic of the Communist world and instill a new philosophy, which will replace the failed ideological beliefs and hopes of some 1.5 billion people in Europe, Asia, Africa, the Middle East, and the Caribbean, who for too long have pursued the myth that only Marxian socialism can bring security and stability to their troubled and precarious lives.

In the mid-nineteenth century when he wrote *Das Kapital*, Karl Marx predicted that the Industrial Revolution in England and other countries would inevitably lead to a workers' revolution. It would be instigated by the widening gaps in living and working conditions between the rich and the poor, between the capitalist bosses and the powerless working classes. However, the industrial nations have grown richer and stronger with the passage of time and their workers are enjoying the living standards of the lower middle classes of society. *Instead of taking root in the industrially developed countries, Marxist-Leninist doctrine and rule have thrived in the countries which are economically backward and industrially undeveloped, with a decaying social pattern, and often involved in wars or existing on the fringes of military conflict.* That was the true state of affairs in Czarist Russia when Lenin and his handful of Bolsheviks staged their revolution in October 1917. And that also described the situation in large segments of the Communist-ruled world today.

A Communist government cannot permit a free market system to function inside its frontiers. The forces of the marketplace and the incentives of profits in normal industry and commerce would loosen

[10]In his most remembered pronouncement as President Eisenhower's secretary of state, Mr. Dulles epitomized the cold war rhetoric of U.S. foreign policy with his statement that "the ability to go to the verge without getting into war is a necessary art . . . if . . . you are scared to go to the brink you are lost." (*Foreign Affairs*, January 1956). In retrospect, this evokes the image of Sherlock Holmes battling valiantly in hand-to-hand combat with the malevolent Professor Moriarty on a mountain ledge overlooking the treacherous Reichenbach Falls. If memory serves, both survived to continue their feud in the pages of Victorian England's *Strand* magazine and later for Warner Brothers' line of B movies. It is worth noting that the cold war is also still with us, brinkmanship notwithstanding.

the controls the Communist regime has imposed on its citizens and their activities. A veteran Kremlinologist has commented on this recently: "The market mechanism is the re-introduction of something that Lenin hated—spontaneity. He hated it because it runs counter to managed history, an idea crucial to Leninist dogma."[11]

In Poland, the sudden explosion of the Solidarity movement has shaken the Russian *imperium* to its foundations. The Poles may have been pushed back into their cages temporarily by the imposition of martial law, but the Communist and non-Communist worlds will not soon forget the political, economic, and social bankruptcy of the Communist regime in Warsaw that was exposed when Lech Walesa and his freedom fighters challenged its right to govern the country.

It may take years, and the unfolding of events will not be so starkly dramatic as the Solidarity uprising, for the Third World countries to face up to the question of their ultimate survival. Will they align themselves with the Communist bloc or with the United States and the industrial nations? Will they follow the precepts of Karl Marx or Adam Smith—the "planned economy" of Marxian socialism or the free market system?

The United States is the only country in the world today with sufficient concentration of economic power and resources to mount an ecopolitical campaign to weaken and then halt the geopolitical expansion of the Russians on the Third World front. With or without the Europeans, America is in a position to get the Third World nations to pay attention to the economic consequences of their own national policies. But it is action and not diplomatic rhetoric that is required in this ecopolitical offensive for the minds of the African, Middle Eastern, and Asian governments and their leaders. While the United States may lack background and experience in foreign affairs, largely because the Atlantic and Pacific oceans separate it from Europe, Asia, and Africa, it comes to this struggle well equipped. Its "secret weapon" is human nature—man's instinctive hunger to make a better life for himself, to acquire some economic security for himself in an uncertain daily existence—which cannot be curbed or extinguished by any government or ideology. It is manifest through a man's life, from the newborn baby suckling at its mother's breast to the old man worried about his pension, or lack of it.

The supreme task of America and the western world is to liberate this elementary life-force and put it to work in a constructive fashion. The basic objective is simple: to give as much economic freedom of

---

[11]Leopold Labedz, editor of *Survey*, a British journal concerned with Communist affairs.

action as possible to the entrepreneurs of the Third World in its industrial or commercial development. Only by working examples will the free market system prove itself in the Third World. The initiative, however, has to come from the United States, with or without the collaboration of the other industrial nations. What is called for is a new form of foreign aid: active participation of American and European companies in projects which the local governments cannot handle by themselves for lack of know-how, managerial resources, technology, or money. But if there are sufficient profit and/or tax incentives for the participants, these development projects will be launched and western managerial experience and skills should assure a measure of success. The cost will be measured in two ways: the cost of the incentives to the U.S. and allied governments in the form of tax deductions, etc.; and the cost to the government of the Third World country in the surrender of power by allowing the free market system to operate within its frontiers without interference or controls. These concessions will not be granted without much opposition and controversy. But the ultimate benefits of this new form of foreign aid will far outweigh the political and economic costs involved for all the participants.

This ecopolitical approach to the Third World seeks to achieve political gains through economic measures; to extend political stability and economic growth to as much of the Third World as can be influenced, thereby weakening and bringing to a halt the geopolitical expansion of the Soviet *imperium*. Yet this does not involve a political crusade like Woodrow Wilson's "Make the World Safe for Democracy!" It has been the major fallacy in American foreign policy in the post–World War II years to think, plan, and act only within the restrictive framework of a political philosophy. Trying to convert the rest of the world to "democracy" in order to attain and to expand international power and influence is like trying to win the Indianapolis 500 on a bicycle. Now is the time to measure foreign governments and their leaders by other standards than their aptitude for or their adherence to democratic principles. International stability and prosperity are not won and maintained by abstract political concepts such as democracy. They are the rewards of economic growth. They are the result of the smoking factory chimney and not the smoking gun.

However, at this juncture one important factor in America's international relations should be brought into our focus. For too many years America has been afflicted with a massive guilt complex. It is not of our own making or responsibility. Rather it has developed because the United States, alone among the great and small powers, emerged from World War II rich and powerful. The United States also suffered fewer casualties and physical war damage than the other countries involved. As a result of this phenomenon, a worldwide cottage industry has developed to perpetuate the myth that America has fallen far short of its obligations to share its wealth and power with those countries less fortunate when the shooting stopped.

This guilt complex—this feeling of a moral obligation to alleviate the burdens of the rest of the world—must be erased from the American frame of mind. The United States must formulate a foreign policy designed to serve its own legitimate self-interests, first and foremost, at home and abroad. It is much more important and rewarding to hold the respect of foreign countries than their friendship. Nations never become friends—only allies, and temporary allies at that.

However, that is just the beginning of America's education to the *Realpolitik* of the world we have to live in. Unless it wants to abdicate its position as the foremost economic power in the world, the United States must divest itself of some misconceptions and come to grips with some of the uncomfortable truths: that peace and prosperity are no longer cheap and readily attainable; that the life in a risk-free society that seemed to be the birthright of every American is now a piece of history. Today and for the foreseeable future, the world is in a period of transition. New economic and political forces, as well as social developments, are at work. Americans must know them and understand them, adjust to them and attempt to control them, if the United States is to achieve political stability and economic security for the non-Communist world.

The second part of America's reeducation to international affairs is also fundamentally simple. Today the basic issue between the two superpowers and their satellites and allies is essentially economic: Which system provides a better way of life for mankind? Despite all the emphasis on national security and nuclear warfare, for all practical purposes there is a military stand-off between the Soviet Union and the United States. Each superpower has enough weaponry to destroy the other and much of the habitable world as well. This stalemate brings us back to square one: How do we end the cold war? How do we persuade or force the Russians to curb their aggressive imperialism? And the answers are right before our eyes. Take the initiative in a sector of international competition which will come as a distinct surprise and shock to the leaders in the Kremlin. Outflank the Russians by creating a commotion in their own backyard, so to speak. Mobilize and deploy America's economic power and resources on a selective industrial development program in the Third World—an area which the Russians have long regarded as their own political sphere of influence. For example, a U.S.-sponsored production-sharing project in India or Pakistan would have a greater and more lasting impact on the peoples of these Third World nations than a fleet of Mig planes from Russia. It would contribute to the economic growth of the recipient country, create thousands of new jobs for its unemployed, be good business for the United States, and enable Uncle Sam to get a big foot in the door of a key sector of the turbulent Third World. In short, it would be good politics and economics for all parties concerned. That is *ecopolitics* in action!

In closing this study of contemporary world developments, the thought-provoking lines from Shakespeare's *Julius Caesar* come to mind:

"There is a tide in the affairs of men, which, taken in flood, leads onto fortune."

Wake up, America—the tide is coming in for you!

Index

301